SEE A***a 2002 WITH

Chicken Soup for the TRAVELER'S Soul

Exercise Your Freedom To Travel

CO-SPONSORED BY
Couchmen RV

CREDO OF THE PEACEFUL TRAVELER

Grateful for the opportunity to travel and experience the world and because peace begins with the individual, I affirm my personal responsibility and commitment to:

Journey with an open mind and gentle heart.

Accept with grace and gratitude the diversity I encounter.

Revere and protect the natural environment which sustains all life.

Appreciate all cultures I discover.

Respect and thank my hosts for their welcome.

Offer my hand in friendship to everyone I meet.

Support travel services that share these views and act upon them and, By my spirit, words and actions, encourage others to travel the world in peace.

—THE INTERNATIONAL INSTITUTE FOR PEACE THROUGH TOURISM

For up-to-date tour information, please go to:
www.chickensoup.com

What People Are Saying About
Chicken Soup for the Traveler's Soul . . .

"Here's an eclectic collection of true stories that will make seasoned travelers smile in recognition and infrequent travelers want to head out and discover their own path."

Rudy Maxa
original host of public radio's "Savvy Traveler" and host of
the public television series, "Smart Travels in Europe and Asia"

"As this book wonderfully demonstrates, once we embrace the concept of travel as a form of release, we are then open to embrace one of the most essential components of travel—that it is the most powerful force to tear down walls, circumvent arbitrary borders and destroy stereotypes—all the necessary ingredients we need to build bridges to peace."

Peter Greenberg
travel editor, NBC's *Today Show*
chief correspondent, the Travel Channel

"The perfect prescription for the frequent flyer. *Chicken Soup for the Traveler's Soul* reminded me that as a business traveler I'm not out here alone and despite the trials of travel, there is so much to be thankful for. Don't leave home without it!"

Randy Peterson
editor and publisher, *InsideFlyer* magazine

"I love a good story, and when the stories happen to revolve around one of my passions in life—the freedom of hitting the open road in anticipation of discovery, what's around the next bend—so much the better. *Chicken Soup for the Traveler's Soul* will both inspire and enlighten those who travel the highways and byways, as well as those who travel without leaving their favorite armchair."

D. H. (Jeff) Jefcoat
president, Family Motor Coach Association

"This book is much-needed comfort food for all travelers, and especially the frequent flier. It's an inspiring reminder of the opportunities travel affords us to find life-changing experiences, even in the most unlikely places."

Wendy Perrin
Conde Nast Traveler magazine
author, *Wendy Perrin's Secrets*
Every Smart Traveler Should Know

"Like travel itself, this book gives us the opportunity to share experiences of other cultures and helps to promote international peace and understanding."

Jean-Claude Baumagarten
president, World Travel and Tourism Council

"*Chicken Soup for the Traveler's Soul* will inspire you to hit the road and create your own family adventures brimming with special memories!"

Deb Cornick
publisher, *Have Children Will Travel*

"*Chicken Soup for the Traveler's Soul* reveals the very essence of travel's countless wonders, inspiring readers to come aboard and explore the job of cruising the open sea."

Jim Godsman
Cruise Lines International Association

"If you thought that travel must necessarily be a difficult experience, *Chicken Soup for the Traveler's Soul* will set you straight. Read the stories—then 'Go thou and do likewise'."

Ed Perkins
nationally syndicated travel columnist
former editor, *Consumer Reports Travel Letter*

CHICKEN SOUP
FOR THE
TRAVELER'S SOUL

Stories of Adventure, Inspiration and Insight to Celebrate the Spirit of Travel

Jack Canfield
Mark Victor Hansen
Steve Zikman

Health Communications, Inc.
Deerfield Beach, Florida

www.hci-online.com
www.chickensoup.com

We would like to acknowledge the following publishers and individuals for permission to reprint the following material. (Note: The stories that were in the public domain or that were written by Jack Canfield, Mark Victor Hansen or Steve Zikman are not included in this listing.)

We Almost Did That. Reprinted by permission of Steve Gardiner. ©1998 Steve Gardiner.

A Boy's Bike. Reprinted by permission of Caryl Bergeron. ©1999 Caryl Bergeron.

Polar Wish. Reprinted by permission of April Riggs. ©2000 April Riggs.

To See a Volcano. Reprinted by permission of April MacNeil. ©1998 April MacNeil.

The Sand Dollar Theory. Reprinted by permission of Pat Hanna Kuehl. ©1997 Pat Hanna Kuehl.

Hitchhiking. Excerpted from *The World Is My Home: A Memoir* by James Michener. ©1992 Random House.

(Continued on page 377)

Library of Congress Cataloging-in-Publication Data

Chicken Soup for the traveler's soul : stories of adventure, inspiration and insight to celebrate the spirit of travel / [compiled by] Jack Canfield, Mark Victor Hansen, Steve Zikman.
    p.   cm.
  ISBN 1-55874-971-3 (hardcover) — ISBN 1-55874-970-5 (trade paper)
  Travel—Anecdotes. 2. Travelers—Anecdotes. 3. Travelers' writings.
 I. Canfield, Jack, 1944- II. Hansen, Mark Victor. III. Zikman, Steve.

G465 .C4364 2002
910—dc21

2001051462

©2002 Jack Canfield and Mark Victor Hansen
ISBN 1-55874-970-5 (trade paper) — ISBN 1-55874-971-3 (hardcover)

Publisher: Health Communications, Inc.
           3201 S.W. 15th Street
           Deerfield Beach, FL 33442-8190

Cover design by Michele Wetherbee with illustrations by Nicky Ovitt
Cover collage photos by Steve Zikman
Inside formatting by Dawn Grove

We dedicate this book
to those who are living their travel dreams
and those who have yet to set out.

Contents

5. THE HEALING PATH

6. ON LOVE

7. A MATTER OF PERSPECTIVE

8. THE KINDNESS OF STRANGERS

9. WISDOM ALONG THE WAY

Acknowledgments

Chicken Soup for the Traveler's Soul has been a wondrous three-year journey made all the more beautiful by the many "companions" who have been there with us along the way. Our heartfelt gratitude to:

Our families, who have been Chicken Soup for our souls!

Inga, Travis, Riley, Christopher, Oran and Kyle for all their love and support.

Patty, Elisabeth and Melanie Hansen, for once again sharing and lovingly supporting us in creating yet another book.

Rob, for his sweet loving on each step of the path. To Steve's parents, Thelma and Joel Zikman, for being there at every twist and turn with open hearts. To Steve's sisters Janice Gritti and Susan Zikman, Revo Gritti and Steven Wise, and nephews and nieces—Josh, Justin, Michael, Karissa, Meredith and Rebecca Baylee—for all the joy and laughter.

Sandra and Desmond Fung, for their gentle support and generous supply of mangoes. To Lisa Carnio, for always being there, even when far away. And a special hug of loving thanks to Barbara Freeman and Lea Freeman, for their constant inspiration and wisdom.

Kim Kirberger, from your very first meeting with Steve at the traveling school, for your encouragement to "go for it."

Our publisher Peter Vegso, for his vision and commitment to bringing *Chicken Soup for the Soul* to the world.

Patty Aubery, for being there on every step of the journey, with laughter, creativity and endless enthusiasm—the perfect traveler's companion!

Heather McNamara and D'ette Corona, for producing our final manuscript with magnificent ease, finesse and care. Thanks for making the final stages of production such a breeze!

Leslie Riskin, for her care and loving determination to secure our permissions and get everything just right.

Nancy Autio, for nourishing us with truly wonderful stories and cartoons.

Deborah Hatchell, Dana Drobny and Kathy Brennan-Thompson for listening and being there throughout with humor and grace. You have made this one great road trip!

Our tag team of associate-editor interns: Liana Allday, Thuy Banh, Sheri Barlia, Dena Bess, Cheryl Cheng, Tabby Davoodi, Rebecca Elliott, Trina Enriquez, Corina Garona, Emmy Gilliam, Michele Fitts, Eugene Lee, Helen Mardirosian, Marisha McGaffee, Jung Park, Jennifer Prakash, Krithana Ramisetti, Yolanda Sanchez, Cindy Teruya, Chaniga Vorasarun, Carrey Wong and Yeun Ju Yim, for learning and for teaching.

Mark and Chrissy Donnelly, our friends and colleagues, for their exceptional marketing skills and for representing *Chicken Soup* in such great style.

Maria Nickless, for her enthusiastic marketing and public relations support and her brilliant sense of direction.

Patty Hansen, for her thorough and competent handling of the legal and licensing aspects of the *Chicken Soup for the Soul* books. You are magnificent at the challenge!

Laurie Hartman, for being a precious guardian of the *Chicken Soup* brand.

Veronica Romero, Teresa Esparza, Robin Yerian, Cindy Holland, Vince Wong, Geneva Lee, Jody Emme, Trudy Marschall, Michelle Adams, Dee Dee Romanello, Shanna Vieyra, Dawn Henshall, Lisa Williams and David Coleman, who support Jack's and Mark's businesses with skill and love.

Christine Belleris, Lisa Drucker and Susan Tobias, our editors at Health Communications, Inc., and especially Allison Janse, our managing editor, for their devotion to excellence.

Terry Burke, Tom Sand, Irena Xanthos, Lori Golden, Kelly Johnson Maragni, Karen Bailiff Ornstein, Randee Feldman, Patricia McConnell, Kim Weiss, Maria Dinoia, Paola Rana-Fernandez, Claude Choquette and Terry Peluso, the marketing, sales, administration and PR departments at Health Communications, Inc., for doing such an incredible job supporting our books.

The art department at Health Communications, Inc., for their talent, creativity and unrelenting patience in producing book covers and inside designs that capture the essence of Chicken Soup: Larissa Hise Henoch, Lawna Patterson Oldfield, Andrea Perrine Brower, Lisa Camp, Anthony Clausi and Dawn Grove.

All the *Chicken Soup for the Soul* coauthors, who make it so much of a joy to be part of this *Chicken Soup* family: Raymond Aaron, Patty and Jeff Aubrey, Nancy Mitchell Autio, Marty Becker, Cynthia Brian, Cindy Buck, Ron Camacho, Barbara Russell Chesser, Dan Clark, Tim Clauss, Barbara De Angelis, Mark and Chrissy Donnelly, Irene Dunlap, Rabbi Dov. Elkins, Bud Gardner, Patty Hansen, Jennifer Read Hawthorne, Kimberly Kirberger, Carol Kline, Tom Lagana, Hanoch and Meladee McCarty, Heather McNamara, Paul J. Meyer, Marion Owen, Maida

Rogerson, Martin Rutte, Amy Seeger, Marci Shimoff, Sid Slagter, Barry Spilchuk, Pat Stone, Carol Sturgulewski, LeAnn Thieman, Jim Tunney, and Diana Von Welanetz Wentworth.

Our glorious panel of readers who helped us make the final selections and provided invaluable suggestions on how to improve the book: Fred Angelis, Linda Beckwith, Barry Belford, Mara Bennett, Stephanie Carter, D'ette Corona, Lorraine Drown, Julie Easton, Cory Fisher, Shirlee Fitleberg, Mary Flynn-Guglietti, Robert Fung, Melanie Halpern, Denene Van Hecker, Larissa Heyman, Alison Ivan, Allison Janse, Janet Jensen, Danny Kamen, Josh Kamen, Laurie Kinerk, Sandy Krauss, Barbara Lomonaco, Marisha McGaffee, Heather McNamara, Linda Mitchell, Ron Nielsen, Deborah Porte, Ward Prystay, Susan Renshaw, Randi Reneud, Sue Rogers, Diana Schnapp, Shari Shields, Brad Smith, Simone Thompson, Carla Thurber, Fran Walker, Robin Worman, Robin Yerian and Susan Zikman. Your feedback was a gift! John LoMonaco, for his kind assistance and Gerri Rose, for typing all those stories with a smile.

Gila Shapiro, for sharing her thoughts at the very start.

Beverly Merson, Carol Kline, Marci Shimoff, Jennifer Hawthorne, Sid and Ilene Slagter and Marty Becker, for their guidance and thoughtful suggestions.

Aaron Saxton, Joel Roberts and Nancy Greystone for all of their magnificent media guidance.

Rich Allen at Coachmen RV, for all of his efforts in making our "See America 2002" RV tour a reality.

Sherry King and everyone at Southwest Airlines, for helping us take to the sky and celebrate the spirit of travel on our "Fly America 2002" tour.

Marcus Brewster and Antonia Ashton of Marcus Brewster Publicity for helping us reach places afar.

The folks at U.S. Post Office 90069 and at Staples in

Glendale, California, who worked so hard to get what needed to be done, done.

All those who have preceded us in the making of travel anthologies, especially Larry Habeggar, James O'Reilly and Sean O'Reilly at Traveler's Tales (*www.travelerstales.com*). We highly recommend this wonderful series!

The many extraordinary organizations who helped spread the good word including: John Coyne and Shanta Swezy at the Peace Corps, Ryan Mucatel at Alan Taylor for World T.E.A.M. Sports, Christine Vogel at the American Field Service, Lorrie-Lee Ragan at the International Association of Convention and Visitors Bureaus (IACVB), Kristina Kreamer at the American Foreign Service Association (AFSA), Gilles Lebreton at CUSO, Jean Deschenes at the Canadian International Development Agency (CIDA), Kelly Brock at the United States Tour Operators Association (USTOA), Blue Magruder at Earthwatch, Catherine Kehrig at Global Nomads, Sarah Barker at Global Volunteers, Karen Lienau at Habitat for Humanity, Toby Pyle at Hostelling International, Jerry Mallett at the Adventure Travel Society, Clayton Hubbs at Transitions Abroad, Kevin Iwamoto of the National Business Travel Association, and Mike Pina, Dee Minic, Susan Green and their many colleagues at the Travel Industry Association of America (TIA).

Cathy Kerr at the Society of American Travel Writers, Brett Harvey at the American Society of Journalists and Authors, Debbie Ridpath-Ohi and Sal Towse at Inklings, Eileen King at Outdoor Writers Association of America, Beverly Hurley at Midwest Travel Writers Association, Clive Tully at the British Guild of Travel Writers, John Bell at the European Federation of Associations of Tourism Journalists (FEDAJT), Ron Hodges at the International Food, Wine and Travel Writers Association, Robert Milne at the *Travel Market Newsletter*, Joyce Banaszak at

Minneapolis Writers Workshop, Bradley Kirkland at the Writers Club, Amber Vogel at the Journal of African Travel Writing, Ishbel Moore at the Canadian Authors Association, James Plouf at *Travelwriters.com*, Meera Lester and Kim McKinney.

Beth Ballew at Continental Airlines, Jim Feldman at *Doctor-Travel.com*, Joan Tapper at *Islands Magazine*, Julia Brookes and Lori Lincoln at *Business Traveler*, Beth Superfin and Jan Woods at *The Student Traveller*, Christine Tatum at the College Press Exchange, Elizabeth Smith at *Student Travels Magazine*, Wendy Ballard at *Doggone*, Douglas O'Neil at *Leisure World*, Randy Peterson at *InsideFlyer*, Byron Lutz at *The Shoestring Traveler*, Mitchell Smyth and Bill Taylor at *The Toronto Star*, Ron Epstein at *Highways*, Brian Nichols at *Home & Away*, Lynn Hughes and Paul Morrison at *Wanderlust*, Peter Jensen at *Footprints*, Janice Lasko at *Escapees* (especially for all of her enthusiastic RV guidance and wisdom), Lesley Abravanel at *Porthole Cruise Magazine*, *The Weekend Argus*, *The Cape Review*, *ExpateExchange.com*, Allen Klein at *AllenKlein.com*, Catherine Kaloutsky at VIA Rail, Monica Campbell-Hoppe and all of her colleagues and participants at Canada Media Marketplace, Lucy Izon at *Izon.com* and Evelyn Hannon at *Journeywoman.com*.

And, most of all, everyone who submitted their heartfelt stories, poems, quotes and cartoons for possible inclusion in this book. While we were not able to use everything you sent in, we know that each word came from a magical place flourishing deep within your traveler's soul. May the wind continue to carry you toward all of your travel dreams in love and peace!

Because of the size of this project, we may have left out the names of some people who contributed along the way. If so, we are sorry, but please know that we really do appreciate you very much.

We are truly grateful and love you all!

Introduction

Stories, if they become alive in the mind of the listener, wrap themselves around the journey like arms and legs, holding the traveler within their embrace, carrying her along.

Irene Guilford

Travel is one of our most precious freedoms. From a young age, we are drawn to captivating and faraway places. The impetus to stretch our horizons, to go around the next bend, to meet new people and search out uncharted lands, is powerful and inviting. Today, travel is faster than ever before; in the space of one or two days, we can be almost anywhere in the world. And yet, regardless of our destination, it is ultimately the journey that is the source of our most treasured tales and the wellspring of *Chicken Soup for the Traveler's Soul.*

Be it a romantic weekend getaway, a hurried business trip, or an extended overseas adventure, travel provides us with immeasurable opportunities to enhance, enrich and expand our lives. Our senses are bombarded by the new and the unfamiliar. We encounter a myriad of novel customs, fresh faces and magical moments that transform the

way we think and how we feel. We face an array of challenges that test our deepest-held beliefs, and in the process, we learn more about who we are and who we can be.

We learn not to fear the unknown but to savor its many
surprises. We learn to live less in our heads and more in
our hearts. We form friendships, fall in love, cherish the
hospitality of people we've only just met, and find ways to
make a real difference in our world.

We learn to trust the untraveled path, to revel in our
wanderlust and to nurture our intrepid soul.

We begin to view our electronic tickets as opportunities
for greater understanding and personal growth, precious
passports to a richer and deeper connection with our fellow human beings—a path to peace.

Over the course of the last three years, we have heard
from thousands of travelers wishing to share their own
unique perspective of travel's boundless possibilities. We
hope that the selections found in *Chicken Soup for the
Traveler's Soul* will take you on an unforgettable and heartwarming voyage of adventure, inspiration and insight.

Whether you're just contemplating some time off or
already on your way, *Chicken Soup for the Traveler's Soul* will
inspire you to exercise your freedom to travel, to appreciate the very best the road has to offer and to view life in
a bold and refreshing light.

In the words of St. Augustine, "The world is a book, and
those who do not travel, read only a page."

Share with Us

We would love to hear your reactions to the stories in this book. Please let us know what your favorite stories were and how they affected you.

We also invite you to send us stories you would like to see published in future editions of *Chicken Soup for the Traveler's Soul.* You can send us stories you have written or stories written by others you like.

Send submissions to:

Chicken Soup for the Traveler's Soul
Web site: *www.chickensoup.com*
P.O. Box 30880
Santa Barbara, CA 93130
Fax: 805-563-2945

You can also access our e-mail or find a current list of planned books at *www.chickensoup.com* or *www.clubchickensoup.com.*

We hope you enjoy reading this book as much as we enjoyed compiling, editing and writing it.

1

LIVING
YOUR DREAM

*Whatever you can do, or dream you can,
begin it. Boldness has genius, power and
magic in it.*

Johann Wolfgang von Goethe

We Almost Did That

*Most of us have dreamed, if just for a moment,
of chucking life's encumbrances and wandering
free through exotic ports of mystery and magic.*

Theodorea Nelson and Andrea Gross

When my wife Peggy and I quit our jobs to go teach in Lima, Peru, we heard many comments and questions about our plans. One phrase, repeated often, haunted me.

Most of our colleagues and friends simply thought we were crazy. "But you have a perfectly good job right here," they said. "Maybe you lost something down there and need to go get it, but I don't." "Do you know how to speak Peruvian?"

Yet, after the surprise settled in and the jokes about our mental stability ceased, we heard the other comment. It came in several variations, and it wasn't so much the wording, but the frequency of the remark and its emotion that troubled us. It went something like, "We almost applied to teach overseas a few years ago." "We almost took a trip to South America once." "We almost quit our jobs and traveled."

When we heard this and sensed the lingering regret hidden behind the words, Peggy and I knew what we were doing was right.

We spent hours studying maps of Peru, Ecuador, Bolivia and other South American nations. Books about Bolivar, Sucre and Von Humboldt introduced us to the personalities who had left their mark on the land of the Incas. Descriptions in travel guides launched us on dreams of traveling to the Atacama Desert, Amazon River and Andes Mountains.

In Lima, we got off the plane and rode in a school bus through the Pueblos Jovenes. These "Young Villages"—a euphemism for the miles of cardboard-shack slums housing some of the poorest people on Earth—were our first impression of how tough life was going to be.

For over a year, we boiled every drop of water we drank. We were regularly troubled with upset stomachs and were constantly aware of what we were eating. We struggled to learn Spanish and to find our way around in a city of 7 million, where half the population lives without electricity or running water. Beggars grabbed our arms, and once, four robbers jumped us in the town square in Huancayo.

We dodged rats in the streets during early morning jogs and squared off against a pack of dogs that trapped us at the edge of the cliffs overlooking the Pacific Ocean. When members of the terrorist group *Sendero Luminoso,* "The Shining Path," bombed the power lines to the city every month or so, we spent candlelit nights writing letters to friends and family. When nauseating earthquakes racked our apartment, we huddled in the doorway, listening to the prayers screamed in Spanish outside.

But we also slept in ancient ruins while hiking the Inca Trail, finishing the eight-day trek by looking down on the lost city of Machu Picchu. We climbed mountains and jumbled glaciers in the Cordillera Blanca near the 22,205-foot Huascaran massif. We soaked in natural hot springs in the Ecuadorean village of Banos, where the hostel owner treated us like her own children, bringing us a pitcher of hot chocolate every evening and recounting the history of her country.

Waving white handkerchiefs, we cheered the matadors and banderilleros at bullfights at the Plaza de Acho, the oldest bullring in the Americas. We went deep into the Amazon jungle, where we swung on vines, gazed at giant spiders and ants, hiked trails through the dense undergrowth of the rain forest, and paddled a dugout canoe on tributaries of the Amazon River.

We decided against a second year in Lima when we realized that if we traveled around South America from Christmas to March and then headed north of the equator, we could have two consecutive summers.

With our savings account converted into traveler's checks, we journeyed on trains and buses for three months, staying in dollar-a-night hotels or with friends we met along the way. Crossing the sands of the driest desert in the world, we bounced along inside an old school bus, chatting for hours in both Spanish and English to a Chilean businessman about the joy of learning to speak, read and think in a new language. As we sipped *platano con leche* (bananas with milk) at a sidewalk cafe in Montevideo, Uruguay, a young boy approached asking for help with his English homework. I'm sure his teacher was quite impressed with his paper the next day. On the border between Argentina and Brazil, we spent two days admiring the cascades at Iguacu Falls before reaching Rio de Janeiro in March.

A cheap charter flight sent us across the ocean from Rio to Geneva, Switzerland, where a German climbing friend picked us up and helped us buy a car, a used French

Peugeot, for eight hundred dollars. We drove for five months throughout Europe, camping out in the Black Forest, Lake District and Alps and walking miles in Paris, Amsterdam, Brussels, Berlin, Munich, Salzburg, Rome and Venice.

After eighteen months overseas, we arrived home with no money. In fact, we were in debt.

But our riches include a shelf of ragged guidebooks, a trunk of well-worn maps, two minds filled with memories and no urge to say, "We almost did that."

Steve Gardiner

A Boy's Bike

Travel has been my comrade, adventure my inspiration, accomplishment my recompense.

Charlotte Cameron

I grew up in the small town of Cazenovia located smack in the middle of New York state. At thirteen, I met Ruth, a girl with a personality like an unbroken mare, wild and unpredictable. We became fast friends.

Ruth had a way of convincing me to do things I normally would not do. For example, when my parents were going to buy me a new bicycle, I had planned to get a regular girl's bike, the one without the top crossbar. Ruth suggested a boy's bike instead. I was scared of that horribly high top bar. I just knew I'd fall flat on my face trying to get my leg over it. Ruth convinced me I could do it, and soon a blue ten-speed boy's bike became my pride and joy.

Ruth and I rode our ten-speeds everywhere—around town, around the lake, into the hills, and over to Syracuse and back. We even bought saddlebags and racks so we could carry gear for overnight trips. For us, there was no greater pleasure than climbing on our bikes and heading off for a twenty-mile jaunt.

One day I heard a story about a group who had ridden from Buffalo to Albany, along the old Erie Canal tow path. The idea of a long-distance bicycle trip captured my imagination. So it was I who talked Ruth into doing something—a five-day tour to Buffalo and back, halfway across the state. We could stay with my grandparents in Rochester and Buffalo.

Plans were made. We got maps, put together gear and set the date. We were all ready for our trip when, suddenly, Ruth's parents told her she couldn't go. So ended our bike tour before it began.

Grudgingly, I accepted that we were not going on our long-distance bike tour, but in the back of my mind I knew that someday I would.

Years later I got married, moved to San Diego, and had a successful career, a nice car and a wonderful house—everything the yuppie could ever desire. I convinced Brian, my husband, to buy a ten-speed bike, and most Saturday mornings we would go riding somewhere out in the country.

It wasn't too long before memories of that aborted bike trip returned, and my yearning to do it grew. But this time, my ambitions were much higher, a coast-to-coast ride. So one day I said to Brian, "Somehow all this riding doesn't seem worthwhile unless we're going somewhere. What would you think about riding cross-country?"

I couldn't believe it when Brian said, without hesitation, "Sure."

Soon we were selecting routes, buying new bikes, borrowing equipment, arranging time off from work, and training, training, training. We were excited, yet at the same time, we were somewhat apprehensive.

How would we do? Could we handle sitting on the seat

of a bicycle day after day, mile after mile? Would we get injured or sick? Could we tolerate whatever Mother Nature could throw at us? What about those infamous headwinds of the plains? Would they force us to quit? Is two months long enough? And would we still be talking to each other at the end?

On August 5, 1988, after months of preparation, we turned our first pedal and our journey of four thousand miles began with just one push.

Two months later, on October 2, we arrived in Bar Harbor, Maine—safe, pooped and still very much in love. In fact, on that first day out of Bellingham, while riding on a quiet road along the Skagit River, Brian had made a prediction: "This could be addictive." And it was.

By the time we reached Bar Harbor, we were hooked. As we pushed our bikes down to the water's edge to dip the wheels in the Atlantic Ocean, I kept repeating, "I wish we could take a week rest and then keep on going." Jobs, a new house, car payments and one cat awaited us in San Diego. We had to go back. But a new dream had begun to form for both of us—a worldwide bike journey.

For the next eight years, we continued taking short bicycle trips, a few weeks each year. Yet our dream of a worldwide bike tour persisted. We knew that riding around the world at a pace that would allow us to explore would take many years.

Could we gather the money to allow us this amount of time? How much would it take? While bicycling can be cheap—basic food and camping is about all that's required—it does take some capital. So we started saving.

We sold our house, all our furniture and our cars— almost everything we owned. It was heart-wrenching. We gave away or sold everything that had defined our lives for nearly fifteen years. But we had our goal: We knew what we wanted to do and that kept us going.

I often felt frustrated, angry and depressed, questioning if we would ever be able to do it. I had heard that if you have a goal, you need to place some item that represents that goal, in a place where you see it each and every day. Otherwise it can easily get lost in the shuffle of day-to-day life. So, in my office, right in front of me, I hung a poster of a bike tourist riding up the Going-to-the-Sun Highway in Glacier National Park. This poster was my reminder. I'd look at it, say to myself, *Soon. It's not far off,* regain my composure and get back to the job at hand.

On August 3, 1995, in sweltering heat just outside Denver, Colorado, we climbed aboard our loaded bicycles and took off on a journey around the world.

Two years later, on October 9, 1997, after riding through Mexico, Belize and Guatemala, and up the east coast, we rode into the small town of Cazenovia, New York.

There, after so many years, I pulled up at Ruth's house, on my "boy's bike."

As I walked up to the door, I recounted all the miles I had clocked since that bike trip she and I never took. I could feel tears welling up inside me as I rang the bell and awaited the familiar face of my childhood friend and the opportunity to thank her for pointing me in the right direction.

Caryl Bergeron

"Which direction is around the world?"

Polar Wish

Begin doing what you want to do now. We are not living in eternity. We have only this moment, sparkling like a star in our hand—and melting like a snowflake.

Marie Beyon Ray

I came around the corner just in time to see that my seven-year-old son, Nick, was upset. "I'll never get to see where polar bears live," he cried.

Nick's dream of seeing these magnificent animals with his own two eyes started years before, when he was just a toddler. We had gone to a neighborhood garage sale with his four-year-old sister, Jessie. Nick had found a sweet-but-old stuffed polar bear in a box of old junk selling for a quarter, and he instantly latched on to the bear. Seeing this, Jessie took out her money and proudly bought "Spot" for her little brother.

Soon, Nick had created a whole life of adventure for his newfound friend. Together, they would raid the kitchen, cover the floor with oil to slide on and play pranks on everybody in sight. But mostly, Spot's adventures consisted of traveling with Nick along to the tundra to find his parents to take care of the polar bears.

Now things were different. Nick was in the middle of chemotherapy to treat a tumor around his optic nerve. The chemo and drugs caused mood swings and depression. Because of his illness, he missed a lot of school and no longer had time with his friends. Now Spot was his constant companion as he went for his weekly treatments. My little boy had been a model patient, but that day he hit a low point and had given up on his dream.

Then, just a few days later, we attended a Children's Miracle Network fundraising reception and Nick's nurse told us that he qualified for a wish. We couldn't believe it. A representative came to our home and asked Nick what his wish would be. We all knew what he would say.

The possibility of seeing polar bears helped the months of treatment go by. The stories of Spot's adventures grew, and we all started sharing Nick's dream. By the day our trip began, Nick was healthy and he had the most important item in his bag—Spot.

From the moment we headed out, it seemed that everyone we met knew how important this trip was for Nick. People went out of their way to ensure his wish was perfect.

The kids were even allowed into the cockpit and got to wear the captain's hat. In Winnipeg, the driver gave Nick and Jessie stuffed animals. The hotel manager gave us a complete tour including a ghost story. Even the hotel cook left the children with hugs. It was already the best adventure they had ever had.

The train was going to take us to Churchill, a small town on Hudson Bay. The first morning, the chef came out to greet Nick and to invite us to meet his family who happened to be riding along. We spent the day playing Monopoly with his children and were treated to special snacks that he himself prepared. The train's engineers spent hours explaining the engine and the unusual aspects of traveling on the frozen ground. The train attendants became our best friends and explained the sights and local traditions of the towns we passed.

When we arrived, we headed out to the tundra. We saw polar bears everywhere. At one point, Nick was nose to nose with a beautiful bear who was as curious about him as he was about her. She stood on her back paws to look through the tundra buggy window, her black nose hitting the spot where Nick's face peered out. The driver quickly named her "Suzy Doorbanger," and she became our favorite polar bear.

The days were filled with activities. The driver and his family gave us a tour that included the history of Churchill. A local scientist spent part of his day telling Nick his polar bear adventures and shared with him what it would take to be a scientist. We met other travelers and together we found igloos, sleigh dogs and more bears. In town, we would run from one heated building to another. Each breath felt like our lungs were freezing, but Nick wanted to be outside all the time.

When we finally boarded the rail to come home, we thought our adventure was over. However, we were completely surprised when the train stopped at a small town late one night and an attendant named Sandy asked if we would mind a visitor. We were introduced to the mayor of Pas, Manitoba. He had gone out in the cold weather to present Nick with a special pin representing their town.

As we headed back to Winnipeg, Sandy even got off the train and started a snowball fight with Nick and Jessie. She told us that often, when returning home from trips, she would look out of the train to see her grandmother watching for her from her apartment balcony. That night as we pulled into town, all four of us were at the window looking for her grandmother.

Nick is eleven, and next year he'll be considered a cancer survivor. His room is filled with posters and school reports of polar bears, and Spot still sits on his bed. He's a bit worn and fragile now, but we'll never forget our precious garage sale gift from God—the spark for a child's dream that helped heal our family.

April Riggs

To See a Volcano

To shut our eyes is to travel.

Emily Dickinson

My son sits across the aisle from me, his whole body beaming with anticipation. Playfully he puts on the headphones handed to him by the stewardess. He turns to me and signs, "I didn't know there were movies on planes."

I just smile, wanting to laugh—and cry.

Kevin is a handsome, blond, blue-eyed fourteen-year-old who has been deaf since birth. But throughout his life, I have tried to teach him not to give up. And he hasn't, excelling in both academics and sports.

In the fall of 1997, I received a phone call from his teacher. She suspected that Kevin was having problems with his vision. We took him to the doctor and they told us that he had Usher's syndrome. His peripheral vision will get narrower and narrower until, eventually, he will be completely blind.

"How? This can't be true," I cried. How could my dear, sweet son be both deaf and blind? It was incomprehensible to me.

When I was finally able to muster up enough courage, the counseling staff at his school helped me break the news to Kevin. He sat quietly, paying close attention to this diagnosis—a deaf person's worst fear.

He is a brave young man, but from his body language, I knew that he wanted to cry. However, he made sure the tears waited. With all of his strength and smile he simply asked, "Can I please go back to class now?"

Kevin's world was closing in on him, and I struggled against the rage and injustice of it all. A short time later, after putting some of my anger and fears of the future aside, I asked Kevin, "Before things really change, what one thing do you want to see more than anything else?"

He thought for quite a while and then said, "A volcano . . . I want to see a volcano in Hawaii."

I choked back my tears and responded simply, "I'll see what I can do," all the while knowing that short of a miracle, there was no way I could take him to Hawaii.

I spoke to everyone and asked everywhere, and just when I was about to give up on Kevin's dream, I heard about an organization that works to fulfill the wishes of chronically and critically ill children. So with great hope, I crossed my fingers and phoned them.

In a couple of weeks, we were interviewed, and three months later we were sitting on the plane bound for Honolulu.

On the morning of the big day, we climbed into a helicopter and headed toward the volcano. We were all excited. While hovering over the cinder cone, we could see the vibrant red, yellow and orange colors sluggishly moving around. We could feel the immense heat on our faces. We could smell the pungent stench of sulfur seeping in. As we hovered, I was struck not only by the volcano's raw beauty but also by its strength, and I thought of Kevin's strength.

Looking over at my son, there was a peaceful glow about him. I tapped him on his shoulder. I wanted him to look back so I could sign and ask him what he was feeling. He signed back, "Not now . . . if I look away, I'll miss it." He was right. He needed to see all he could see—now.

Kevin had an offering for Pele, the fire goddess. It was made of tea leaves, her favorite, and a symbol of good luck. He stuck out his hand and dropped his gift. Then he bowed his head and signed, "I wish she can be strong for an eruption."

As we watched the leaves fall into the lava, the most amazing thing happened. The sluggish mixture began swirling around and started popping—a tiny eruption began before our very eyes—Pele's gift to Kevin.

With permission from the gods, we brought some lava rock home. Every now and then, I catch Kevin sitting with the same peaceful glow he exuded in the helicopter that day. When I look a little closer, I notice the small piece of lava rock in his hand.

I pray that our journey will last forever in his mind's eye, especially when the disease finally consumes Kevin's eyesight. Then I'll know that my son still sees the swirling hues of red, yellow and orange, and not just blackness.

April MacNeil

The Sand Dollar Theory

Travel not only stirs the blood—it also gives birth to the spirit.

Alexandra David-Neel

My German husband, Max, claimed he was born under a wandering star.

He moved to Denver as chief engineer for a firm that built dams in the Far East. Max was off to the Philippines, Hong Kong, Indonesia or wherever at the ring of the telephone. Herr Kuehl was the ultimate frequent traveler.

I met him in St. Croix on a Denver travel-club trip. He called me the next time he was in town, and we clicked. At first it seemed terribly romantic—phone calls from Manila, letters from Seoul, gifts from Istanbul. Meeting his plane when he finally got home was a joyous occasion to be toasted with champagne and a late candlelight dinner.

A few weeks later, when it was time to take him back to the airport for another long separation, I felt like Bergman saying good-bye to Bogart in *Casablanca*.

Still early in the relationship, we flew to Mexico for a week's vacation. It was glorious! I loved Mazatlan.

I loved walking the beach for miles and watching schools of dolphins cavorting in the surf. We made a big thing about gathering sand dollars. I'd spot one, and then lose it when an incoming wave would wash it away before I could pick it up. But Max rarely missed. His long arm would sweep down to the sand and pluck the treasure just before the water carried it off.

"Let that be a lesson to you," he would say. "Grab happiness when you see it, before something washes it away."

When we came upon the site of some new beachside condominiums, we stopped to investigate. From my first glimpse of the model plans, I knew it was time to put the Sand Dollar Theory into practice. I would own one of those beach condos in Mazatlan.

Max thought I was crazy. I didn't care. I was going to give them my down payment. He could do as he liked— he'd be off somewhere exotic anyhow. And I would have my own piece of paradise on the Pacific.

Two weeks later, he called from Honolulu en route to Manila to say that he'd be my partner in the condo.

It was a wild year, but finally our unit was ready for us to move in. Soon, we were sitting on our own patio, sipping margaritas and watching the sun sink into the Pacific while the sky turned magnificent hues of peach and blue.

A short while later, we got married. We loved our life together in Mazatlan, mostly on restful visits after Max's returns from his assignments "in der chungel"—only Max thought he had lost his German accent.

After he returned from almost two months in the Philippines followed by a brief stint in Lebanon, we made another trip to Mazatlan. He was exhausted and badly needed time to bask in the sun and take our long strolls on the beach.

It was just before Thanksgiving. We joked about the snow back in Denver as we stretched our *serapes* on the sun-bleached sand. I sat down and opened my paperback thriller while my Max trotted down to the water's edge, then waded out to where the whitecaps started to break.

I looked up from my book from time to time to watch him body surfing like a teenager. Sometimes he seemed to disappear, the waves claiming him like those sand dollars. I was relieved when he finally came back to shore and walked toward me, beaming as he dried off with his towel.

"The water's wonderful!" he said. And then, in an instant, he collapsed on the sand like a fallen redwood.

His heart had stopped.

Our last drive through the streets of Mazatlan was in a rickety ambulance wailing its way to a tiny emergency aid station where Max was pronounced dead. He had left me again, this time for good.

But Max's days of traveling weren't over.

We had agreed long before that we both preferred cremation. Max had specified that he wanted his ashes to go into water, completing the cycle of his lifelong fascination with hydraulics. "Just flush me down the toilet and I'll make my own way," he had quipped.

My first thought was to have the service in Mazatlan and leave his ashes there, where we'd been the happiest. But arranging a cremation is extremely difficult in Mexico. Instead, I arranged for his body to return with me on the plane to Denver where cremation wouldn't be a problem.

We arrived back in Denver, but I wasn't sure what I should do with his ashes. Still deep in grief and not thinking too clearly, I asked one of Max's business associates to take the ashes to the Philippines and put them in the water at the Upper Luzon Dam, which Max had designed and built—he considered it his major achievement.

The engineer took Max to Manila but then, instead of quietly dispersing the ashes into the dam, he asked Filipino government officials for permission. After much discussion and miles of red tape, they declined his request. The engineer returned to Denver, and I received a telephone call saying my husband was back in his office six months after he'd died.

Finally, some close friends and I took Max's remains up to a Colorado mountain lake. This time, we didn't ask for permission.

The sunset was blazing peach and blue, not unlike those in Mazatlan. When we emptied the urn over the water, the ashes seemed to pour out like an Olympic diver plunging into the depths.

After a few tears, we found ourselves starting to laugh. My husband had finally gotten his wish—and who else could have racked up thousands of frequent flyer miles six months after his death?

I figured Max was up there somewhere, riding his wandering star. And it was time for me to get back to collecting sand dollars.

Pat Hanna Kuehl

Hitchhiking

Afoot and light-hearted I take to the open road, healthy, free, the world before me, the long brown path before me leading wherever I choose.

Walt Whitman

When one hitchhikes, one spends long hours either waiting at a likely intersection or trudging down the road, and when I was so engaged, I found comfort in singing Caruso's arias or in reciting the many poems I had memorized, or recalling the latest postcards I had added to my art collection.

I was in many ways the poorest boy on the road, in others the richest, and I was always happy to be on the road meeting new people, hearing new stories and seeing new landscapes.

Was it some psychic maladjustment that drove me then and later to this incessant traveling? Was it some sickness of the spirit, some malaise of the kind that follows if the body is deprived of some essential vitamin, or the mere perversity of a restless, young male?

I have never been clever enough to analyze the impetus, but I doubt that it was related to any deep-seated psychic deficiency. I've said that home was not exciting enough to keep me tied to it, and I had no physical possessions of any kind to hold my interest for long periods of time. Yet I was not unhappy with my family, my school or my friends.

When I was fifteen, hiking westward from Detroit with thirty-five cents in my pockets and a thousand miles from home, I was convinced that I would complete my journey safely, for I was as optimistic then with untested life before me as I was at sixty with so many challenges behind me. It seems that I was born to smile at the world, and such men do not write tragedies.

The simple fact seems to have been that once I saw that mysterious road outside my house, the eastern part leading to a dead end, the western to worlds unknown, I was determined to explore the latter.

James A. Michener

The Jennys and the Aprils

People travel because it teaches them things they could learn no other way.

Lance Morrow

When my college friend Steve first asked me whether I'd be interested in putting my music career on ice to join him on a five-year expedition to attempt the first circumnavigation of the planet using only human power, my head was instantly filled with wildly romantic images: riding bicycles across the steppes of central Asia, trekking through the frozen wilderness of the Himalayas, staring into the flames of a roaring campfire after a hard day hacking our way through the Amazon jungle.

Before I signed on the dotted line, one question sprang to mind: How would we get across the big watery bits, the Atlantic and Pacific Oceans, without the assistance of the wind or a motor?

"Easy," Steve replied, "we'll use kayaks. All you have to do is go like this until you get to the other side."

And with those reassuring words, he waved his arms

around his head in energetic circles, mimicking the strokes of a paddling kayaker.

Clearly, neither of us had the *faintest* clue as to what we were getting ourselves into at that point. But, as we found ourselves reminding each other on numerous occasions from then on, not being an expert is never a good enough reason not to try.

Two years along the learning curve found us bobbing about a thousand miles from land in the equivalent of a floating broom closet. The kayak idea was given short shrift in the early planning stage, and we built a twenty-six foot wooden pedal boat named *Moksha* instead.

Armed with a global positioning system, some charts, a hundred days of dehydrated food, a desalinator pump to make fresh from seawater, and a total of about ten days of sea experience between us, we surrendered ourselves to the mercy of the waves.

Despite storms that drove us backwards for days at a time, narrowly missing container ships and encountering large beasts that used the underside of the boat as a scratching post, we washed up in Miami, Florida, 111 days later. Emaciated and sore, we surrendered ourselves to the mercy of the American people. Between us, we had fifty dollars, three items of clothing (the rest had washed overboard during the crossing) and one passport.

After making our way across the country, Steve and I found ourselves in San Francisco and in desperate need of funds. We gave talks to Rotary and Kiwanis clubs, bicycle club meetings and yacht clubs, signing up people for twenty dollars to have their name inscribed on *Moksha's* hull.

It was at one such meeting that I met Jenny. She introduced herself after hearing my invitation for people to join us for portions of the journey, regardless of how much experience they had. The next leg was to cycle five thousand miles overland from Monterey, California, through Central America to Peru, and Jenny wanted to be a part of it.

The following day she bid farewell to Mack, her husband, bought a new bike with all the gear and turned up on the morning of our big departure.

I have two pictures of Jenny in my head—before and after.

The before picture has her standing behind her bicycle, just minutes before we set off. Her body looks stiff, face tense—eyes fixed rigidly at the camera—smile clips attached. Her clothes are spotlessly clean, the bike brand-new. She looks terrified.

The after shot is of her in a similar pose two and one-half months later, just prior to leaving the group to travel on her own for a while.

We had just biked over one thousand miles down the California coast and kayaked one hundred miles across the Sea of Cortez in northern Mexico. In this picture, she looks filthy, her bike is trashed and most of the accompanying equipment either lost or stolen. But she is also suntanned, fifty pounds lighter and has an enormous grin on her face stretching from ear to ear. Her poise is relaxed and confident. She's outgrown the nest and is ready to strike out on her own expedition.

Looking back on the last five years with another four to go before completing our circumnavigation, I find myself casting back to that image of Jenny—now back at school in Minnesota studying aviation mechanics—standing on that beach in Mexico.

I look again and see April, a fifth-grade teacher in her early forties, living with her family in a small, rural town in southern Colorado.

I first met April while giving a slide presentation about the trip to her class. I was in a wheelchair at the time, just weeks after having been run down by a car on a highway leading into Pueblo, Colorado, while Rollerblading across the United States. Both of my legs were smashed.

April was even more enthusiastic than her students, and seven months later, when I was looking for someone to accompany me on a bicycle for the remaining seventeen hundred miles of my trip to San Francisco, she volunteered.

"I'd really like to give it a go," she said. "I've never ridden more than a mile before, and I don't know what my family will make of it. But what kind of a mother am I if I can't show by example to those I love how important it is to live one's dreams?"

I jumped at the chance. I was tired of people telling Steve and I how lucky we were to do something they themselves could never do for whatever reason. But here was a person willing to risk being labeled an outcast from her local community for embracing something her soul ached to do.

Our road took us twelve thousand feet over the Rocky Mountains, mile after sweaty mile through 100-plus degree heat in Arizona and finally rising up over the Sierra Nevada mountains to come to rest on the cool shores of the mighty Pacific.

April's return to her hometown wasn't easy. A number of people in the predominantly ranching community, including some of the parents of the kids she taught, labeled her adventure as irresponsible: "The mother of a seventeen-year-old daughter just doesn't do that sort of thing."

But there were those she inspired, especially her students, and in time, her daughter, to trust and follow one's deepest desires, changing the world by example from the inside out. She proved that you don't need to be an expert. You just need to begin.

And it really was only the beginning. For April joined me again, this time for the final leg of my Pacific crossing, from the Solomon Islands to Australia—a torturous voyage, with strong southeast winds and rough sea conditions that threw us severely off course and made pedaling conditions barely survivable.

"Seeing Australia rising above the Coral Sea, I immediately sensed its sand between my toes," said April. "At that moment, I thought this has to be one of the most glorious feelings in all the world."

And then there's Eilbhe, who traveled with Steve across the United States. And Carole, and Ollie, and Theresa and Travis, and Edie, and Scott—and all the people who have been a part of the making of this expedition, and who in return have used it to get where they're going next.

And, of course, Steve, who recently left the expedition to follow his dream of setting up a center in New Zealand for people to learn traditional skills and sustainable ways of living. The expedition served a purpose for him also: a stepping stone to get where he needs to be now.

Every journey has an end, and I certainly haven't reached mine yet. However, my reasons for traveling now are different from those with which I started out.

Back then, I needed to escape England and I traveled to explore my soul. To identify what was most important to me and to use that as a reason to live my life.

Now, I use the expedition as an educational tool for teachers to use in the classroom and a vehicle for children all around the world to connect with each other across barriers like language, race and religion. And along the way I hope to still meet the Jennys and the Aprils, inspiring them to search for their own path, push their limits and discover where they need to go.

There's a saying by Ursula Le Guin that helps me to keep going when the road ahead gets foggy and I lose heart: "It's good to have an end to journey toward, but it's the journey that matters in the end."

Jason Lewis

Loose Chickens

It all started with a few loose chickens. . . .

I was a real estate agent and had gone to check out one of our listed properties. It was an egg-laying operation, a commercial facility involving thousands of caged chickens. The warehouse-like building held hundreds and hundreds of small cages, each containing two hens. The cages were so small that the chickens were unable to turn around. In front of the chickens, one conveyor belt brought feed and behind them was another belt that carried their eggs away. While the plant manager was briefing us, I noticed a dozen loose chickens and an employee following them and scattering grain.

"Do you need help catching them?" I asked.

"I'm not trying to catch these birds," he replied. "Oh no, we let these wander around. If the caged ones can't see a few chickens living a free life, they'll lose hope and stop laying their eggs. Without these loose chickens, the rest will just give up and die."

Instantly, it struck me how similar our lifestyle was to these caged birds. How many of us live our lives in cages, looking out and seeing others having the adventures, living their dreams, being free? I realized that there are two kinds of chickens: those who live in cages and those who roam freely. I wanted to be one of those loose chickens!

Within a couple of months, we wangled a year's unpaid leave of absence from my husband Tom's university employers, closed my small business, found someone to house sit our home, took $10,000 out of our retirement savings, bought an old VW camper-van and set off to explore Mexico and Central America.

That year stretched into two, and we decided not to return to our old jobs.

It's been nine years now of full-time RVing, full-time exploring, full-time living. The house-sitter became a tenant who became the guy who bought our house. The camper-van turned into a twenty-five-foot trailer, which turned into a thirty-seven-foot motor home. And, a few years ago, our son Bill also became a full-time RVer—a family of loose chickens, roaming free.

Nancy Vineski

Reprinted by permission of Robert Fung.

2

GETTING THERE

The journey not the arrival matters.

T. S. Eliot

Banner

Life is already too short to waste on speed.

Edward Abbey

The poet William Stafford once said that we are defined more by the detours and distractions in life than by the narrow road toward goals.

I like this image. But then I am a highly distractible person. Oh, I get things done and have goals like everybody else. But it is the crazy asides in a day that lead me to fruitful territory.

Like a good road trip. Ah, road trips! For this family of mine, a good road trip is one long and lazy detour after another—a saunter down back roads that eventually lead to the final destination. The lid is off time. Beyond every curve are possibilities.

A stop in the desert turns up a rattlesnake skin. The hot glimpse of a slow-moving river leads to a swimming hole. We stop at barn sales and buy the world's juiciest peaches at local fruit stands. On tape, we listen to Greek myths that make the miles fly by. And because we are in the climate of unhurriedness, we talk.

We talk about our dreams and the best meal we ever ate. We talk about our hopes for making the majors baseball team and winning blue ribbons in the horse show. We talk about the best kind of pet to have, and the importance of kindness—"Remember the ice cream certificates from the lady we helped out of the ditch?"

But it wasn't always this way for us. We discovered the lush side of road trips quite by accident—by detour, you could say.

My family lives in Idaho, and for years I made the nine-hour Seattle to Boise drive, and, like most people, used the fastest, shortest and easiest route possible. Especially if Greg, my husband, couldn't join us and it was just me. Me and four noisy, restless, lively kids who hate confinement and have strong opinions about everything.

Road trips felt risky. I drove fast. Stopped only when I had to. I was disciplined, with my eyes on the road and my arm stretched and waving into the reaches of the car like some kind of crazy conductor. We ate at fast food restaurants. We stuck to the freeways. We counted the hours and miles. Road trips made us wish that we were anywhere but here. We arrived tired and cranky.

But then Banner was born.

Banner is our sheep. Our baby really—we raised him from birth. He was born and rejected by his mama only days before a planned road trip to Boise. I had two choices: Leave the lamb with Greg, who could take him to the office, feed him every two hours and remember to change the diapers; or I could take Banner to Boise. Greg made the decision for us.

And that's how I found myself on the road with four kids, a baby lamb, five bikes, a tote full of formula and diapers, and nothing but my eternal optimism. We took the back roads to Boise out of sheer necessity. I had to stop every hour and let Banner skitter and shake out his long wobbly legs. The kids chased him and then one another, before climbing back into the car smelling fresh and breathless with the cold air.

We began to think ourselves weird in a wonderful sort of way. While the world was whizzing by, we were not. Family legends were born—"What kinda dog is that?" an elderly woman in Umatilla asked us—to be retold for years ever after. We stopped to eat in local cafés because McDonald's are few and far between on the back roads. Instead of pushing through to Boise in one shot like always, we stayed in a small motel in Baker. This led to a long walk in the morning where we discovered a local diner that served up the best, most tender and fragrant cinnamon rolls we ever ate.

Surrendering to a less-than-speedy trip, we explored side roads off of side roads. Even if we simply looked out the car windows at clothes flapping on a line, or baby pigs waddling after their mother or the rise of a trout on an elbow of creek, it was better than the best ride down the freeway. Here was life. And fresh horizons.

We eventually arrived at my parents' doorstep astonishingly invigorated and full of stories. I figured it had taken us an extra five hours in the car. Heck, in the past we usually spent five hours just recovering from the ride.

I grew brave with this venture. I grew a little giddy. On the way home, I looped us through Idaho's panhandle to visit my grandmother. We paused at a hot spring I had raced past heedlessly for years—Zim's, just outside of McCall—a remarkable, utterly restorative stop that required all future road trips to include any hot spring remotely close to our wayward path.

And I grew creative with my discipline. On an empty stretch of road in eastern Washington, everyone started to bicker. I stopped the car, ordered all kids and lambs out and told them to meet me up ahead. I drove about a mile, parked on the side and read my book in sweet silence.

Road trips changed forever after that one journey. It opened our eyes to a world available to anyone reckless enough to idle and wander. Wild enough to race through a wheat field at dusk. Or eat at a diner instead of a drive-through.

Can you stop at a river just because your toes are hot and the water is cold? Can the world wait while you pull over and read the historical markers with your children and imagine for one brief moment the courage and grit it took to survive a hundred years ago? Are you willing to trade time for a detour that may uncover the best part of a journey, the best part of yourself?

It took a tiny black lamb to make me realize the answer is yes, yes, yes.

Nancy Blakey

Airport Dining

There are no days in life so memorable as those which vibrated to some stroke of the imagination.

Ralph Waldo Emerson

Several years ago, as I was looking over my travel itinerary for a business trip from San Francisco to New Orleans, I noticed that I would have some time at the airport in Dallas before catching my connecting flight.

So I called my friend Luke who lives in Dallas, and said, "Luke, I've got an hour-and-a-half layover at the airport. If you'll come out and meet my plane, I'll treat you to dinner."

Luke enthusiastically agreed, and I was excited by the prospect of getting to spend a little time with him.

When the pilot announced that our flight would be delayed on the ground an extra few minutes in San Francisco because of air traffic control I paid no attention, but as those few minutes dragged on, I became more agitated and upset. Every minute that passed was one minute less that I would be able to spend with my friend.

The pilot promised to make up the lost time en route,

but he wasn't able to do so. The plane arrived in Dallas an hour late. That left me only half an hour to visit with Luke, and I still needed time to catch my connecting flight. At this point, I knew that our having dinner together was totally out of the question. The Dallas-Fort Worth airport is too big; thirty minutes is barely enough time to dash from one plane to the next.

When I stepped off the plane, Luke was there, waiting for me.

"Hey, Luke," I said apologetically, "thanks for coming out to meet me. I hope you didn't have to wait here too long."

"Oh, no problem," he replied easily. "I called ahead and found out your plane was going to be late."

"Oh, good," I replied, distracted by the time pressure. "Look, I'm really sorry about dinner, but I'll owe you one next time. Come on, we'll find out what gate my next plane is leaving from. We can head over there together and talk a bit."

I started walking but Luke didn't budge.

"I am very invested in having dinner with you," he said to me.

I looked back at him incredulously. "What are you talking about?" I laughed. "The only way you're going to have dinner with me tonight is if you buy a plane ticket to New Orleans!"

"We're having dinner," replied Luke with determination. "Believe me, I have this whole thing scoped out. Just follow me."

He picked up one of my bags and carried it out through the security check. I followed him closely, silently protesting and growing more anxious with every passing moment. He started running, down into the parking garage, and I ran along behind him, thinking to myself, *There is no way we are going to get into his car, drive to a restaurant, have dinner, and still get back in time for me to make my plane!*

The two of us hustled down a short flight of stairs in the parking garage and walked rapidly along several rows of cars until we came to the place where Luke's car was parked. I immediately noticed that in the parking space next to his car, he had set up a folding table.

Luke pulled out his car keys and opened the trunk of his car. He reached in and pulled out a checkered picnic tablecloth, which he spread with a grand flourish over the table. Then he grabbed two folding chairs and set them up next to the table. Then a bottle of champagne and a large container of hors d'oeuvres. He set a candle in the center of the table and lit it. We popped the champagne and broke out the hors d'oeuvres.

There we were, sitting across the table from each other in the middle of a parking lot, toasting each other with champagne and grinning from ear to ear. Carbon monoxide fumes may have been swirling all around us, but we didn't care. Drivers in search of a parking place were annoyed at us for taking up the space, but once they took a closer look, many of them broke into astonished smiles.

With seven and one-half minutes to go, we put everything back in the trunk and ran for my plane. We readily got through the security check and arrived back at Gate 23 with five minutes to spare. What Luke and I had not remembered, however, was that my next flight was leaving from Gate 31, which was in the other terminal! There was no way I was going to get from Terminal 2 to Terminal 3 in time to make my plane.

I was starting to get hysterical. But Luke was ready for anything—he flagged down an airport employee who was driving an electric cart, and we jumped on the back.

"Our plane is leaving from Gate 31 in three minutes!" Luke implored.

The driver was up to the challenge. He drove the cart like a Grand Prix racer, dodging and weaving around the pedestrians. We loudly applauded his every move. We were laughing. We were screaming. We were cheering him on.

We arrived at the gate with only seconds to spare. The entire area was deserted except for one last flight attendant. She had spotted us in the distance, as our vehicle careened madly toward her gate. I leapt off, yelling, "Can I still make this plane? I need to get on this plane!"

The flight attendant scolded me, in mock anger. "Where have you been? You think we can wait all day for you? Get on this plane right now!"

She grabbed my ticket, rushed me on board and slammed the door behind me. I collapsed into my seat, relieved and energized by the whole bizarre experience.

Throughout the entire flight, images of my dinner with Luke popped into my head. But then I realized the whole thing had happened so quickly that I hadn't really had a chance to thank him properly.

So as soon as the plane landed I called him at home and said, "Luke, that was such a wonderful thing you did for me. I really want to thank you."

"You don't have to thank me," Luke replied evenly. "Somebody already beat you to it."

"What are you talking about?" I asked.

"When I got back to my car," he explained, "there was a flower on the windshield, with a little note that said: *Anybody who would do something like that for another person must be a beautiful human being.*"

Matt Weinstein

In Better Hands

All journeys have secret destinations of which the traveler is unaware.

Martin Buber

On the way home from the small Himalayan kingdom of Bhutan, I met with Mother Teresa. Not once but twice.

My friend Laurie and I had flown into Calcutta from Paro in the early afternoon. We had one day in the City of Joy before she would fly on to Bangkok and I would return to Canada via New Delhi, Bombay and a brief stay with my father in London.

Over lunch, we toyed with the notion of visiting Mother Teresa's orphanage. A taxi ride and a couple of hours later, we were touched by the sight of forty to fifty little kids playing in a small courtyard, half of them running around completely undressed, the others in blue and white striped outfits. As we were leaving, a sister informed us that Mother Teresa's residence was in a building called Mother House, only a few blocks away.

Within minutes we were standing in front of a rather inconspicuous wooden door with a large cross on it. On a

small wooden sign to the left of the door, in white letter-
ing, were the modest words, MOTHER TERESA. When
asked who we wished to see, we answered simply and in
unison, "Mother Teresa." The sister showed us in and, in a
short while, informed us that Mother Teresa would meet
with us.

We found ourselves waiting nervously on an old bench,
trying to figure out what we were going to say. Suddenly,
from behind two swinging doors, we saw a white-and-
blue sari and two bare feet in open sandals. We gazed in
awe as Mother Teresa moved briskly toward us. She sat
next to Laurie, took her hand, and got right down to
business.

She asked us where we were from and whether we were
volunteers. She described the trip she had just taken to
Montreal. She told us that she was in a hurry as she was
leaving again the next day. With that, she got up, disappeared behind a screen partition and quickly returned
with two cards bearing her picture and a small prayer. She
signed both: "God bless you. Teresa M.C." and left. Though
neither of us was particularly religious, we just sat there,
frozen in a state of reverence.

The next day Laurie left for Bangkok and I left for
London. Checking in at the Air India counter in Delhi, I
couldn't help but hear a woman with jet black hair draped
in flowing Indian fabrics shouting at the next counter. In
her distinctly Greek accent, she was raging about not getting a particular bulkhead seat. Within seconds, boarding
pass in hand, she brazenly marched away from the scene
and through the terminal.

A few hours later, when it came time to board, I started
towards the gate. As I approached security control, out of
the corner of my eye I noticed a pair of sandals and a blue-
and-white sari. I looked over and saw a sister of the
Missionaries of Charity. And then another. And another—

a gaggle of sisters scurrying straight through security. At the very end raced Mother Teresa, carrying nothing but a single book—her Bible. In a glance, she was out of sight.

At the gate, I looked around for a place to sit and spotted the Greek woman, anxiously staring at the departure board. I sat down, and sure enough, she sat right next to me.

We started talking and, when I mentioned meeting Mother Teresa, her mouth dropped. She reached for a cross around her neck and told me how much she had always wanted to meet Mother Teresa. I recounted how I had seen Mother Teresa again only minutes before. My Greek gate-mate struck my arm in disbelief. Oh, how she wanted the chance to meet this living saint!

When we arrived in the Bombay terminal, they told us that our connecting plane was going to be delayed for a "few hours."

Thirty or forty very irate Italian tourists were grabbing their heads, motioning madly with their hands, and screaming at the poor airline attendants and each other. I wandered away from the chaos in search of a place to sleep.

I finally found one of those horrible plastic airport chairs on the other side of the airport, and using my daypack as a pillow, I fell fast asleep.

A couple of hours later, I felt a hand nudge me. Startled, I looked up. It was the Greek woman.

She wanted me to go with her, to follow her. She was very forceful and determined. She explained that Mother Teresa wanted to see me. Of course, I had no idea what this woman was talking about but, after more pleading, I went along. After all, what else did I have to do at four o'clock in the morning?

We got to the door of the business and first-class lounge. She mumbled to the guard that I was with her, and I followed behind.

The room was small and dark. All ten people were

sprawled about on couches, fast asleep. The Greek woman motioned to the far corner near a dim light. Sitting there in a hard chair, hunched over, was Mother Teresa, reading. While every other much younger, mortal soul was sleeping, she was wide awake, praying in the middle of the night.

Whispering, the Greek woman prodded me, "You must go and talk to her."

"I can't, she's praying," I replied.

"Just go now!"

"I can't, not until she's finished," I insisted.

We sat down, gazing as she prayed, noting her every movement.

My Hellenic messenger introduced herself as Jenny and related in a soft voice how she and Mother Teresa had talked for a short while earlier on. This was not the same crazy woman whom I had first encountered at the check-in counter in Delhi. She carefully and proudly showed me the necklace of the Virgin Mary that Mother Teresa had given her. She rubbed it and continued.

"She's been praying the whole time," she said, shaking her head in reverent disbelief.

Suddenly, Mother Teresa placed the prayer book down on her lap.

"Go over now!" the Greek woman beseeched.

I got up and inched my way towards the light.

"Mother Teresa, I'm sorry to disturb you but we met yesterday in Calcutta at Mother House."

Her wrinkled face strained upwards to meet my puzzled eyes. "God works in mysterious ways," she quipped. She invited me to sit next to her.

As I sat down, I couldn't wait to ask her about the serendipitous nature of our two meetings. "What does this mean, meeting you again? Is there something I should be doing?"

"What *are* you doing?" she asked.

"Traveling," I replied impulsively.

She took my hand. "You must look for the truth, and guide others to look for the truth. Time is short. There is so much to do and so little time. You will know what to do."

We talked for an hour, mostly about her missions around the world, before she excused herself to return to her prayers. I withdrew and sat next to Jenny. Together, we studied this winner of the Nobel Prize in the peace of her prayers.

Just after seven o'clock, we heard our flight being called for boarding. As we got up, so did Mother Teresa. She was on our flight.

As soon as the plane took off, I fell asleep. A few hours later, I awoke and went to freshen up.

Leaving the toilet cabin, I heard commotion from the section ahead. I turned the corner, looked up the aisle toward the front of the plane, and glimpsed Mother Teresa's blue-and-white sari just as she was returning to the first-class section. In the brief time that I was in the restroom, she had gone through the whole plane and blessed all of its passengers.

In her wake, the large group of Italians, who only hours before were wound up in a frenzied state of frustration and anger, were now crying and praying, and very, very grateful. Many were down on their knees making the sign of the cross, while others couldn't stop hugging and kissing one another.

Men and women queued from the left side of the plane into a makeshift first-class confessional, emerging moments later on the other side into the embrace of their fellow countrymen and passengers.

The plane stopped in Rome, where the Italians and Mother Teresa deplaned. I read the next day that she had an audience with the Pope.

On my arrival at Heathrow, my father met me, his face

ashen. He recounted the morning's news: A plane had crashed in Bombay, around the same time that mine had taken off. He was terrified that somehow I was on that ill-fated flight.

"Well, Dad," I began my story, "if I were, I couldn't have been in better hands."

Steve Zikman

A Dog's Life

Today I live in the quiet, joyous expectation of good.

Ernest Holmes

Last summer, I traveled to Rockville, Maryland, to visit with my parents. The trip was special because I had brought along my ten-year-old dog Dakota, who had been part of my family since he was a puppy. My parents had not seen him since I moved to San Jose, California, two years ago, and they were excited about seeing him again.

On the way back, my brother dropped Dakota and me at the airport. After checking in, I stayed with Dakota until an airline baggage handler came to get him. Seeing him off, I headed to the gate. When the agent announced that boarding had started, I happened to look at Dakota's ticket and noticed that it was marked for Salt Lake City instead of San Jose.

In a panic, I went to the agent and advised her of the mistake. I wanted to know if Dakota was on my flight or on a different flight bound for Salt Lake City. The agent didn't have an answer and asked a supervisor to look into it. Ten minutes later, I looked out the window and saw that a baggage handler had pulled up to the aircraft with Dakota in his crate. After seeing Dakota being placed in the aircraft, I boarded the plane.

As I walked onto the plane, I spotted the same baggage handler at the entrance to the plane. Because I was still a little worried about Dakota being on the right plane, I asked him if he had loaded my dog on the aircraft. He said yes and assured me that I shouldn't worry, that everything was okay. His words were welcome relief.

I started to relax. Dakota had been loaded on the correct plane and the flight crew knew I had a dog on board. Because the flight was half full, I switched to a seat in an empty row located in the back of the plane and pulled out my laptop to get some work done. One of the flight attendants noticed Dakota's picture on my computer screen and struck up a conversation about dogs, as she also owned a dog.

About two hours into the flight, I felt a tap on my shoulder. It was that same flight attendant. The pilot wanted to speak to me about my dog, so I followed her up to the front of the plane. I wondered what he wanted to talk to me about, and as I approached the cockpit, the captain came out to meet me.

He told me that he had received a call from the dispatcher who said that Dakota had been inadvertently loaded in the wrong cargo hold. He went on to explain that the aircraft was divided into two cargo holds—forward and rear. The rear cargo hold was designated for animal cargo, as it was lighted, pressurized and heated, while the forward cargo is not designed or used for animal cargo. He said Dakota had been misplaced in the forward cargo hold, and since it was not properly heated, he could not be sure that Dakota was okay, especially in the freezing temperatures at thirty thousand feet.

I couldn't believe what he was telling me. I turned white as a ghost as my eyes watered with tears. The captain then told me that he was going to divert the plane in order to make an unscheduled landing in Denver. Again he cautioned that he did not know if Dakota was still alive. Even though I was very upset, I was grateful that the captain was going to stop in Denver. He went on to explain that once we landed, I could go with him to check if Dakota was alright.

As I sat down in my seat, the captain made an announcement about Dakota's situation and his plan to fly the plane to Denver in an attempt to save Dakota's life. After the announcement, I looked around to see the passengers' reactions, and to my amazement, there were no signs of disapproval.

Unfortunately for Dakota and me, we still had another hour to go before we could land in Denver. It was the longest hour in my life, and as I sat in my seat, I could no longer hold back the tears. I thought about Dakota in that cargo hold and what he might have been going through. I began to think of the worst: that he was already dead, that he must have froze to death in that cold and dark cargo hold.

I stared out the window and reminisced about my better days with Dakota, from the time he was a puppy through all that we had gone through together over the last years. I recalled the times when I was sad, when he was always there to cheer me up. I remembered the different places we had lived and the places we had visited together.

But then, the more I thought about Dakota, the more I started to wonder if, maybe, he was still alive. I thought about how stubborn and resourceful he was. If anyone could survive it would be him. By the time we approached Denver, I began to believe that Dakota might still be alive and that he would make it.

When we landed in Denver, I looked out the window and saw the ground crew waiting for us at the gate. As soon as the plane stopped, I could hear the ground crew opening the cargo hold door. Immediately, I unbuckled my seat belt and ran to the front of the plane. My heart was pounding in anticipation. As the captain exited the cockpit, we made eye contact, and I could tell that he had good news. With a smile, he told me that he had received a thumbs-up sign from the ground crew: I had not lost my best friend.

We both exited the plane and hurried down the stairs. When I reached the ground, what I saw amazed me: Dakota's crate had been unloaded from the plane and placed on the tarmac with the ground crew in a semi-circle around it. As I approached the crate, I could see Dakota sitting and looking out the wired door. Immediately I opened the door and took him out. He was very cold and shaking. While I was holding him, the ground crew was also excited that Dakota had survived, and they began to pet him. My Dakota was alive and back in my arms!

When it was time for me to put Dakota back into his crate, I couldn't do it. It was too cruel. How could I put him back into the aircraft's cargo hold after all he had been through?

I then asked the captain and the supervisor who had greeted us on the tarmac if I could bring Dakota on board. I reminded him that the plane was only half full and that I had three seats to myself. The supervisor said that it was against the rules and Dakota would have to go back into the cargo hold. The captain then interjected, indicating that since they make exceptions for Seeing Eye dogs, they could also make an exception in this case. The supervisor relented, and to my joy I was able to bring Dakota on the plane with me.

I picked up Dakota and carried him up the stairs and into the plane. As I entered the plane with Dakota in my arms, the passengers cheered and clapped. While I walked down the aisle to my seat, some of the passengers reached out in an effort to touch Dakota. I realized that they also cared and were excited that Dakota had made it.

When I got to my seat, I placed Dakota next to me, but he was still cold and shaking. The flight attendants provided several blankets, which I used to warm him up.

Soon, Dakota seemed more comfortable and was able to fall asleep. Throughout the flight, parents brought their children over to see Dakota, some even looking for him to keep their babies from crying.

And, for the passengers' troubles, the airline offered free drinks and a complimentary movie called *My Dog Skip*—a film about a boy and his dog.

Mike Bell

Well, Here We Are

Wherever man wanders, he still remains tethered by the chain that links him to his kind.

Alexander Kinglake

I come from a family that never planned summer vacations. As a child, I would just wake up one morning and find the curtains closed in every room of the house, the car loaded up with suitcases, and my father standing above my bed saying, "Let's go!"

At least that's the way I remember it: childhood vacations as spontaneous and full of surprises as life itself.

Usually there were five of us in the car: my parents, grandmother, older brother and me. Occasionally, out of pity, a stray cousin or an unmarried aunt got invited along and, after the inevitable fight about who got to sit next to the window, we would head to the back road and the so-called "scenic" route.

Early morning departures were the norm. Dawn would be breaking as we pulled out of the garage and headed up the alley behind our house. I was barely awake; often I slept for the first hundred miles or so, my head resting on my grandmother's shoulder.

We never knew exactly where we were headed, although usually, to escape the summer heat, it would be some place north like New England or upstate New York. My father was in charge of driving and destinations, and he didn't like to talk much about either.

He was a traveling man by profession, accustomed to the pressures of having to be in Brazil, for example, on a given date. Or India. What he needed from a vacation, he liked to say, was a sense of leisure, of unstructured time that did not require a calendar or a clock or being at such-and-such a place at such-and-such a time.

That was what the word "vacation" meant to him, he said; a vacation was not a place but a state of mind.

And although I could not have articulated it then, there was something else I recognized, even as a child, about my father's approach not only to vacations but to everything else as well—he was a man who was more interested in the journey than the destination, enjoying each mile of the trip for what it was and not where it ended.

It didn't seem to bother him that my brother, cousin and I bickered and fought with regularity during the trip. Or that my mother often threatened to stop the car right on the highway, put the three of us out, and make us walk back to Baltimore. Each morning my father emerged refreshed from whatever guest cottage we had stopped at, eager to resume the trip.

And so it was in the summer of my eighth year that we found ourselves in Massachusetts—car windows rolled down, hot, dusty breezes blowing in the left window and out the right—studying a white sign shaped like an arrow and neatly lettered: Mohawk Trail. It pointed to the left.

"Well, here we are," my father said, heading left. It's what he always said when some decision or another had been reached by him, "Well, here we are." And although I had no idea where we were, it didn't matter. The combination of an exotic sounding place like the Mohawk Trail, along with my father's familiar, "Well, here we are," was good enough for me.

That was our last trip together. The next year my father died suddenly and the only thing I could remember of that vacation was the white sign, the arrow pointing left, and the words Mohawk Trail.

Then, about five years ago, while driving from Williamstown, Massachusetts, to Boston with my college-bound son Andy, I saw the sign again—or one just like it—Mohawk Trail. Without hesitating, I turned left, as my father had so many years earlier.

As we drove along the winding, hilly roads, I felt disappointment. Nothing looked even vaguely familiar to me until we arrived at the combination souvenir shop and lookout tower at the top of the hairpin turn.

We stopped at the souvenir shop, my son and I, to stretch our legs and browse through the T-shirts, Indian tomahawks and beaded moccasins. The store smelled of cedar and maple syrup, and suddenly, I knew I had been here before—when I was eight years old.

It was the oddest feeling, standing in the middle of nowhere, a grown woman with a college-age son, remembering in ways deeper than ordinary memory, the child who stood in the same spot many summers before.

I turned and followed Andy up the steps of the lookout tower, where we silently viewed the valley spread out below us. Then, to my surprise, I heard a voice—my own—saying: "Well, here we are."

Alice Steinbach

Ticketless Travel

He who would travel happily must travel light.

Antoine de Saint-Exupéry

My friend's brother, Cliff, is a very serious, dignified man, so his actions at an airport's check-in counter were totally unexpected.

It seems that he and his wife were placing their baggage on the conveyor when her purse accidentally fell onto the moving belt. She scrambled after it but it eluded her, so she climbed onto the belt to try to reach it.

Just as she was about to disappear through the doorway with the baggage, Cliff began to wave frantically, "No, no dear!" he shouted. "It's okay! This time we bought tickets."

Jim Feldman

Just a Layover

The more I traveled the more I realized that fear makes strangers of people who should be friends.

Shirley MacLaine

When the man at the table asked me to join him, I scarcely gave it a thought. After all, I was just passing time on a layover, waiting for the real trip to begin. I wanted to get a good meal and a good night's rest, and that's about all I expected to happen.

I was en route to Namibia, a sparsely populated country in southwestern Africa. A dedicated outdoors enthusiast, I wanted to experience the wildlife and culture of Namibia's wild backcountry, far away from civilization. I had read of safaris since I was a kid, and I could scarcely contain my excitement that I finally had the chance to do it.

I decided to make the trip solo—no family, no friends, no tour group. I would meet my guide in Windhoek, the capital. To get there I had to spend a night in Johannesburg.

I love seeing new places, but my travel agent put me up

in a hotel right next to the airport so that I wouldn't have to go into the city itself. A lot of people were still concerned with the turmoil in South Africa. Apartheid had just ended three months before, and though the election process had gone peacefully, many still believed that dangerous conditions could develop.

So, as an unseasoned traveler, I took my agent's advice and treated the stop as just a place to get a rest before heading off to my real vacation. Nothing more.

When I arrived at my hotel room, I felt exhausted from the fourteen-hour plane trip, yet I was too hungry to sleep. So I figured I would go to the hotel lounge, have a drink, eat dinner and then prepare for the next day. I would be back in my room in an hour.

I was sitting at the lounge with some other travelers, no one saying much, when a man asked me to his table. Two other African men were seated there. I decided to join them. As I sat down, I noticed that all three smiled at me in amazement.

"I invited you on a whim. I don't know why," said the man, smiling. "We really didn't think you would sit with us."

They introduced themselves: David, Darius and Monte. They had come here—into this place that would have been off-limits just a short while before—and had not known what to expect. Yes, apartheid had ended, but old habits, old prejudices, don't just go away with a new government.

"It is time to celebrate. It is a good time in this country, and a good time for friends," proclaimed David. "Let us show you to dinner."

I wish I could say I had no apprehensions about heading off to dinner with three men who I had just met in a city seventy-five hundred miles from home. But I did. We walked into a large banquet hall serving a tremendous buffet of seafood and lamb dishes. We got our food and headed to a table.

I couldn't help but notice a dividing line, not marked but visible nonetheless. On one side of the line sat the white patrons, and on the other, the black. In the large hall, there wasn't one table where the two races shared a meal.

My newfound companions didn't seem to mind. I sat down and quickly felt comfortable with them: David, gregarious and loud; Darius, quieter but full of insight; and Monte, who appeared to think everything over before responding.

Our talk focused on our two countries and more basic misperceptions of each other. It was the kind of talk that fills every conversation when you meet someone from a fresh new place.

Sometimes you can know people your whole life and never get past this talk. You can work with them and attend the same parties and invite them to dinner, and it never progresses beyond sharing the basic facts—small talk.

But sometimes . . . sometimes you get past the talk of this government and that popular music and move to something deeper. It happens seamlessly, as if you had always known this person. As if you had always been friends. As if you were always *meant* to be friends.

And so it was with these three men who had invited me into their group. Quickly we found ourselves discussing wildlife, the cycles of life and death, and how we might best fit in on the Earth. These subjects are my passion, and these men shared that passion.

David described what it was like to dig in the soil for their vegetables, to take *kudu* and *springbok* from their land to feed their families, to live with the land and not apart from it. I smiled, knowing he was talking about beliefs I myself held dear.

He smiled back, reached across the table and grabbed my shoulder, so hard it hurt.

"You are our brother!" he exclaimed, loudly and unself-consciously.

When the waitress returned to see if everything was all right with our buffet, Darius said, "This man has come all the way from America, but he is our brother. We found each other at the hotel bar."

The waitress flashed a smile, as if she thought all of us were crazy, but by that point it hardly mattered. We talked and laughed for hours, about serious things and funny things, about our families and the future, about all that mattered.

At first, when I entered the restaurant, the racial division bothered me. *Apartheid is gone, but only officially*, I had thought.

Apartheid was over, my newfound friends told me, and that was reason enough to celebrate. But I realized that it went beyond that.

"People aren't going to change right away. They have lived this way a long, long time. They are full of these feelings; they know no other way," explained Darius. "But now we have *hope*. Things will change, maybe not right now, but they will. We can see a day when we can all be brothers and sisters, and that is reason to celebrate."

Soon, we had to go our separate ways, they to their families and I to my hotel room. When I attempted to help pay for the bill, David held up his hand and stopped me. As we departed, each of them hugged me, and David again grabbed me by the shoulder.

"No matter what, you will always be our brother. Thank you for sharing the evening and the conversation," he said.

And it was just supposed to be an uneventful layover, time to pass until my big trip.

I've since tried to eliminate this layover attitude, both in travel and in life. While on our way to the great destinations, and while planning for the big events, we can sometimes pass over the moments of joy and grace that are part of the journey.

These three men, friends who I will probably never see again but who will remain a part of me always, taught me the real way to travel—mindfully. For when you travel mindfully, you never know what jewels you may discover along the way. A warm meal. A trusted friend. A new-found brother.

Matthew Miller

One Stranded Bus and a Pond

The earth belongs to anyone who stops for a moment, gazes and goes on his way.

Colette

"I've been here a week, and I haven't seen anything."

I remember the look on the face of the man who told me this—the melancholy expression of someone who had worked, probably raised a family, doted on his grandchildren and now had come to Alaska on a two-week package tour, hoping for a change that still eluded him.

He had sailed on a cruise ship into the glacial fjords of the coast, then flown over the epic coastal mountains. He boarded a train and rode through wilderness, and now stood ready to step into a bus and enter Denali National Park.

Yet, he was dispirited.

Actually, he'd seen plenty. Fancy binoculars dangled around his neck to help him. What he meant to express, I think, was that he had encountered none of it. The landscape already was familiar to him from TV and the tourist videos. In case he forgot, a perky tour guide had explained everything again by loudspeaker. "Around the next bend, we'll be coming on . . ."

I soon learned that the man was not alone in sensing something missing from his travels.

A year later, I was writing a story about traveling. As it happened, I was driving north from Anchorage and came upon a tour bus along the shoulder of the highway with the engine cowling open. I stopped. Here was a stranded group of tourists. I would interview them.

I found maybe a dozen people on the bus. Some were absorbed in a card game. One read, and a couple snoozed. Another man seemed to be fuming. Where were the others? The driver pointed into the woods alongside the highway.

I walked into the spindly forest of black spruce that covers so much of the interior of Alaska. Less than a hundred feet from the road, I found the other passengers sitting at the edge of a pond. Just as I was about to speak, a woman held her finger to her lips. *Shush.*

I followed her eyes back to the pond.

A bird flickered through the limbs of a spruce. There was a boil in the water at the far edge of the pond and a beaver surfaced, leaving a dainty V-wake as it swam. Then it dived and disappeared again. Closer by, something moved, but I couldn't tell what. Maybe a squirrel.

By Alaska standards, there was nothing extraordinary in the scene. Countless amounts of little life-sustaining ponds dot these forests. This one had nothing to distinguish it.

Except . . .

These travelers had been held captive by a planned itinerary. They had been given pamphlets explaining where they would go and what they would see. They rose at a specified hour, ate at a designated time and boarded a transportation conveyance that advanced them onward according to schedule. This was the Alaska "adventure" they paid for. It was so safe and dependable that their eyes had gone glassy, their anticipation dulled by preprogramming.

Then a real adventure happened. The bus broke down and they wandered into the woods.

I kneeled down with the passengers. We waited for the beaver to surface again. I watched the flit of the busy black-winged bird. I felt the rising pleasure of quiet after the vigorous mechanical rumble of the highway. My nose filled with the sweet fragrance of spruce needles warmed by summer.

Together, these strangers and I drifted from the busy world at our backs to the calm of the pond. It was not just what we saw but how we felt as the canted sunlight of the far north threw yellow beams through the spruce and cast shadows onto the edge of the pond, where we could look into the water at the patterns of the stringy grass that grew from the bottom.

I noticed dimples made by nervous insects on the glassy surface tension of the pond. And paw prints in the mud nearby, probably belonging to an animal who made its way down in the moonlight for a drink.

The beaver materialized again, closer this time. Nostrils opened and wet, cinnamon eyes looked our way—perhaps astonished at the appearance of us people sitting like statues on the edge of its world. A cloud passed in front of the sun. The colors of the pond changed and so did its mood.

Time passed—how much, I cannot say. I was lost in the rhythms of pond life.

I backed away and returned to my car, leaving this place to its new discoverers. We never spoke. I didn't need to speak with them to know what had happened to these wanderers.

Seeing a place, any place, is not the same as experiencing it. The bulk of visitors are propelled down familiar, crowded corridors at a relentless pace. Many wear the same joyless expression of the man I first met: people detached from what they could see.

But these passengers stepped off the bus, and on their own they actually encountered the place they came to see.

I checked my map. The little pond was not even shown. Which made it all the sweeter.

John Balzar

A Full and Complete Stop

A little while ago, I was on a flight back home from a business trip.

After the aircraft landed and was taxiing toward the gate, the head steward got on the PA system and began the oft-repeated speech about destinations, gate locations and the service people waiting to help you.

Then, as the plane approached the gate, some passengers looked restless, and it appeared as if they were about to stand up.

Seeing this, the steward announced, "We have invested a lot of money to ensure that your flight has been safe and comfortable. We are also looking for ways to save money, and this aircraft is participating in a new experiment. To reduce costs, we are asking for volunteers to help clean the cabin upon our arrival. Those wishing to volunteer for cabin clean-up, please stand up before we come to a full and complete stop."

Not a single passenger left his or her seat until we were at the gate, and the seat belt sign was turned off.

Mary Hanson

3

OUR COMMON BOND

Be ye lamps unto yourself.

Guatama Buddha

Passports to Understanding

Only so much do I know as I have lived.

Ralph Waldo Emerson

Human beings are more alike than unalike, and what is true anywhere is true everywhere, yet I encourage travel to as many destinations as possible for the sake of education as well as pleasure.

It is necessary, especially for Americans, to see other lands and experience other cultures. The American, living in this vast country and able to traverse three thousand miles east to west using the same language, needs to hear languages as they collide in Europe, Africa and Asia.

A tourist, browsing in a Paris shop, eating in an Italian *ristorante,* or idling along a Hong Kong street, will encounter three or four languages as she negotiates the buying of a blouse, the paying of a check or the choosing of a trinket. I do not mean to suggest that simply overhearing a foreign tongue adds to one's understanding of that language. I do know, however, that being exposed to the existence of other languages increases the perception that the world is populated by people who not only speak differently from oneself but whose cultures and philosophies are other than one's own.

Perhaps travel cannot prevent bigotry, but by demonstrating that all peoples cry, laugh, eat, worry and die, it can introduce the idea that if we try to understand each other, we may even become friends.

Maya Angelou

A Waltz at the End of the Earth

Peculiar travel suggestions are dancing lessons from God.

Kurt Vonnegut

A friend and I were on our way to the "End of the Earth," the most remote beach on Hainan Island, the farthest south in a string of Chinese islands in the South China Sea. A ridiculous place to want to go. There's nothing there. But the ancient Chinese believed the Earth ended at the southern tip of this largest of China's islands. Thus, to journey there was to show great strength and courage, qualities of utmost importance to the Chinese. To journey to the End of the Earth was to bring good fortune to yourself.

The beach there is a peaceful, serene place with an aura of great continuity. Beyond, with quiet waves lapping at our feet, the sea did seem to stretch forever. Like the ancient Chinese, who could know what was out there?

In a tiny village nearby, we stopped for lunch at a small roadside house—a hovel actually—a one-room shack that served as home, restaurant and mini zoo, a combination so common in rural China.

This particular shack was poor even by Chinese standards. It held only a bare wooden table, some simple chairs and a rope bed. The dirt floor was swept clean, and an old bicycle hung on the wall. Nothing more adorned the place. Cooking, as is customary in the countryside, was done out back on an empty oil drum with a wood fire below.

The eighty-year-old owner immediately began to prepare lunch, and twenty minutes later, the food began arriving: the usual Chinese mystery soup, followed by several courses of vegetables, rice and endless pots of steaming tea.

In the oppressive one hundred-degree heat, even to sit still was to sit and drip. During lunch, the old woman kept smiling at me as if to say, "I forgive you for sweating in my house. There is no loss of face in this," and graciously fanning me with a marvelously ingenious fan made completely of feathers. I had never seen anything like it.

Since there was literally nothing else in the one-room house, not even a change of clothes, and, besides an old watch, the fan seemed to be her only possession, I was careful not to admire it openly. Chinese custom demands the giving to guests of whatever they admire. But despite my intentional disregard of the fan, I was immensely grateful for the momentary illusion of coolness each whoosh brought.

Perhaps because I was trying so hard to ignore the feather fan, what happened next caught me completely by surprise.

Suddenly, for no apparent reason, the old woman broke into a great grin, hugged me hard, handed me the fan and then hugged me again. I was stunned. It was obviously a gift, but her generosity under the circumstances was astonishing. What had prompted the act? What could I, a lanky, perspiring stranger with a sunburned nose—in her life for so short a time—have possibly done to deserve the gift of one of her few possessions? Nothing that I could conceive of, but something had changed dramatically in the little room. The old woman now sat smiling beatifically as though I had pleased her more than I could ever imagine. But I couldn't, for the life of me, figure out how.

Despite the baking heat inside the house, we lingered awhile after lunch and drank more tea just to stay and not seem to rush away. And then, to our amazement, the old woman began to speak in halting English, obviously a language she had not used for decades. Bit by bit, straining to understand the stumbling words, we learned her story.

Before the Cultural Revolution the woman had been a teacher, the daughter of educated diplomats. But in the years of hardship and turmoil that followed the historic upheavals in China, her life—like that of millions of others—was tossed like a leaf in the wind. Families were separated, never to find each other again. Fortunes were lost; material possessions and security were swept away.

She found herself at last at the End of the Earth, alone, able only to eke out a bare existence selling the snakes and rabbits she was able to trap. The only remembrance she had of her husband, whom she had not seen in three decades, was his old watch, which hadn't worked for years.

Her story, told with no rancor, captured our hearts, and despite the need to get on, we stayed. The long-forgotten English words seemed to get easier for her as we asked questions about her life and encouraged her to reminisce.

She told us of her childhood, of traveling and learning English at embassies as a youngster. Memories of another, so very different life. Yet, for all her losses, she truly seemed to have no bitterness. With one strange exception.

When I asked her if she had any regrets, there was only one, she said, smiling sweetly—that she had never learned to waltz.

One of her most vivid childhood memories was of being taken, as a young girl, to a grand ball in Hong Kong where there were many English guests in attendance. The music that night was international—the first time she had heard anything besides the harsh, sharp cacophony of China's music—and suddenly the ballroom was filled with swirling skirts and the sweetest sounds she had ever heard. Couples were waltzing and, to the young Chinese girl, it was the most beautiful sight in the world. Someday she would grow up to become one of those graceful waltzing women.

She grew up, but China changed. There were no more waltzes. And now there were no more illusions in her life.

In the silence that followed the story, I took her hand across the table. Then I quietly asked if she would still like to learn to waltz. Here. Now.

The slow smile that spread across her face was my answer. We stood and moved together toward our ballroom floor, an open space of five feet of hard-packed dirt between the rickety table and her narrow cot. "Please, God," I prayed, "let me remember a waltz. Any waltz. And let me remember how to lead."

We started shakily, me humming Strauss, stepping on her toes. But soon we got smoother, bolder, louder. The "Blue Danube" swelled and filled the room. Her baggy Mao pajama pants became a swirling skirt, she became young and beautiful again, and I became a handsome foreigner, tall, sure, strong . . . perhaps a prince who carried her away. Away from her destiny at the End of the Earth.

The time we spent together was brief. I never knew the woman's name, but the lesson I learned from her was profound.

Her life of privilege had been swept away. She was alone, at the end of her life, without even the comfort of the reverence Chinese families bestow so lavishly on their elderly. And yet she had no bitterness. She had moved beyond loss to acceptance. She was a happy woman.

Not long after I returned from China, a series of losses began to take their toll in my own life: a divorce, the death of my mother, a move to a different city. I was far from friends and familiar surroundings. I grieved for my past life. In moments of despair, I looked wherever I could for comfort, and I found it in the memory of the woman on Hainan Island.

Now, I live on a Pacific Coast beach, looking out toward China. And sometimes, when I listen very hard, I can almost hear the waltzes of Strauss.

The feather fan hangs on my office wall today, next to her picture. Next to our picture. The two of us, hands clasped, smiling strangers from such different worlds, waltzing around a steaming hut in a forsaken spot I visited by chance that one day—the day I met strength and courage at the End of the Earth.

Paula McDonald

CHICKEN SOUP TO GO

New York City, NY	Sioux Falls, SD
Philadelphia, PA	Omaha, NE
Baltimore, MD	Des Moines, IA
Washington, DC	Kansas City, MO
Niagara Falls	Topeka, KS
Cleveland, OH	Denver, CO
Ann Arbor, MI	Albuquerque, NM
Elkhart, IN	Flagstaff, AZ
Chicago, IL	Las Vegas, NV
Milwaukee, WI	Los Angeles, CA
Minneapolis/St. Paul, MN	and many others . . .

For up-to-date tour information, please go to:
www.chickensoup.com

CREDO OF THE PEACEFUL TRAVELER

Grateful for the opportunity to travel and experience the world and because peace begins with the individual, I affirm my personal responsibility and commitment to:

Journey with an open mind and gentle heart.

Accept with grace and gratitude the diversity I encounter.

Revere and protect the natural environment which sustains all life.

Appreciate all cultures I discover.

Respect and thank my hosts for their welcome.

Offer my hand in friendship to everyone I meet.

Support travel services that share these views and act upon them and, By my spirit, words and actions, encourage others to travel the world in peace.

—THE INTERNATIONAL INSTITUTE FOR PEACE THROUGH TOURISM

A Turkish Delight

Wherever you go becomes a part of you somehow.

Anita Desai

Her name is Pembe. Most people seeing the photograph remark that she looks like me—that there is a family resemblance. Even I see it—my face in her face, her face in mine.

She lives in my living room inside a simple oak frame that brings out the wisdom in her brown eyes. She is crouching, a dented metal pitcher in her left hand, pouring water over small fruits that look like large eggs but are actually from her apricot tree.

Eat, she is saying to me with every gesture. *You are my guest; this is my home; it is our way.*

The scarf that covers her head at all times is faded blue, trimmed with yellow stitching. Her wide-legged pants, sewn together from colorful fabric remnants, look chic within the comfort of my Northampton apartment. But in Turkey these pants are not a fashion statement. They are made for squatting in the fields, milking the goats, planting, carrying on daily life.

Her face appears ageless. We found each other in a hot dry field in the south of Turkey. I was walking, and she was watching her goats graze.

She approached, talking Turkish, and when I shrugged my shoulders and raised my palms up in an "I don't understand" gesture, she repeated the stream of strange sounds more loudly and slowly. She seemed irritated that I did not respond to her request, which I soon surmised was to cover my head. She removed the turquoise bandanna from around my neck and tied it kerchief-style, barely covering my profusion of curls.

"Better," she seemed to say, patting her chest with both hands.

She then removed my bifocal sunglasses, put them on and proceeded with a thorough hands-on investigation of my body, frisking and smelling me until she must have come to the conclusion that I qualified to visit her house.

Taking my hand in hers and maintaining a firm grip, Pembe escorted me across the field, pointing in the distance to a small gray shack, talking very loudly to me the whole way.

We left our shoes at the top of the third step of the entrance to her house, consisting of two small rooms. We entered through a crowded kitchen and living room with three windows. To the left was an even smaller, very dark room where her pallet lay on the floor next to the hay where her three prized goats slept.

Pembe pushed down on my shoulders, telling me to sit. I sat, not daring to disobey this person whose manner in any language could only be called "bossy."

When she resumed shouting her Turkish phrases at me, I realized that the only way I would make any headway in this one-way bilingual situation was to match her energy. I let the intensity of her voice into my body, allowing it to shape me the way pastry dough shapes the pastry bag.

Assuming a posture of strength, I repeated her Turkish back to her, matching the intensity, intonation and rhythm of the sounds the best I could. A small flicker of a smile cracked her face.

I held up an apricot and waited for her to say something. When she did, I repeated what she said—*"kayisi"*—and we went back and forth several times until she believed I knew what I was talking about. We shared a moment of satisfied silence.

Then, still holding the apricot, I said my new Turkish word, paused, and said "apricot," not too slowly or loudly, but with what I hoped was an attitude of stubborn strength.

"Ap-ri-cot," I repeated. Then I pointed to her.

And so we began, Pembe and I.

Two hours later, we walked together, arm in arm, out of her house and over to the fence that separated her land from the villa where my group was staying. There, Pembe gave me back my bifocals, smiled, said good-bye—*"guli guli"*—in a quiet voice, and waved. I sensed her beaming face watching me as I walked back to what seemed like another world.

The picture was snapped at the moment we began to feel truly comfortable with each other. I remember the exact instant when the small room grew very large, light streaming in, softening and releasing the beauty of her face and highlighting the huge kelly green pot behind her. All became clear. My hand reached down beside me, and I picked up my little camera from the worn wooden floor. Then, slowly, I took the picture.

I listen daily to the news of the deaths and disaster caused by the enormous earthquake that struck Turkey last month. Turkey is no longer a faraway, somewhat obscure place on a map. It is a country of apricots, goat cheese, dented metal pitchers, golden fields of grass, stories woven into colorful carpets, dancing children and wise women wearing the wide patched pants of everyday life.

Where are you now, Pembe? I ask myself. *If I shout and speak very slowly, can you hear me?*

Heidi Ehrenreich

Mohammed Ali

Serendipity was my tour guide, assisted by caprice.

Pico Iyer

My original plan was to spend my last afternoon in India daydreaming on the sprawling, green lawn of New Delhi's Connaught Circus.

But the instant I set foot on the lawn I felt scores of eyes lock onto me. I chose a spot and sat, and noticed a dozen bodies rise from the shade of the park's trees and begin moving toward me. Beggars, shoe-shine boys, massage men, fortune tellers. I was surrounded.

I let a boy named Jungi scrub my shoes. A man named Dasgupta massaged my neck and shoulders. Another read my palm: "You have been sick with stomach, but now you are well. You are missing a woman. You will soon be rich." The combined talents of these men cost me two dollars.

They drifted off until only a single man remained. I had spotted him earlier at the back of the mob, smiling patiently but saying nothing. Now he sat on the grass, two arm lengths' away, grinning shyly—as though he had some unbearably good secret.

"Hello, Baba," he said, using the familiar appellation denoting respect.

He had long eyelashes, teeth as bright and straight as piano ivories, and etched along his upper lip, the world's narrowest mustache. His smile was so sweet it might have graced India's tourist posters. His name, too, was a classic: Mohammed Ali. He was not young—he had three sons— but if playfulness was something barterable I'd have traded my money belt for a dose of his.

The Q-tip-like swabs tucked under the lip of his turban revealed his trade: ear cleaner. It's a common sight: an Indian man wielding cotton swabs and long forceps, and bent like a lab technician over the cocked head of a kneeling foreigner. I'd known travelers who had received this treatment and had later sworn that they could hear better for days afterwards, but I had remained doubtful. Imagine, in India of all places, letting a stranger—some man in a park, on a beach, in a train station—stick something in your ear!

When Mohammed Ali said, "Ears cleaning, Baba?" I only snorted.

"Oh, but it is nice, Baba," he said. "See my reference book?"

I looked to see what sort of idiots had risked their ear drums:

> *When Mohammed said he would make me hear better, I didn't believe a word of it. But now I'm sitting here, my ears vibrating with noises I haven't heard since I was a child. It was painless. Go ahead. Try it.*
> —Linda, Brooklyn

A year ago I went to an ear-nose-and-throat guy at home who charged me $95 to do what Mohammed Ali just did for twenty rupees, and he was nowhere near as personable.

—*J. T., Dallas, Texas*

Momma never told me ears could feel so good. I can hear birds singing that I didn't hear this morning. Mohammed has transformed my head into a symphony hall.

—*Paula, Santa Cruz, CA*

"Pretty happy customers," I said.

"Yes, Baba. Everyone happy. Have you ever—"

"No," I cut him short, "I clean my own ears." I pointed at the swabs sticking out from under his turban. "I have those, too."

He opened his pouch and pulled out a small vial. From the moment he sat down his smile had not left him. "I put some drops in your ear, wait some minutes, then I can clean."

"I can hear just fine," I said.

He folded his hands and sat there, smiling, as though content to wait for sunset and then dawn and then sunset again if necessary.

"What's the best thing that ever happened to you?" I asked him, changing the subject. It's a question I like to ask customers in my cab in San Francisco.

He considered for a moment. "People." He nodded at his book. "So many people. From all over the world. People from every country come here."

"What's the worst thing?"

As he mulled it over, his smile faded a notch. "I cannot read or write," he replied.

Mohammed Ali pulled an aerogram from his bag and

handed it to me. "Maybe you can help me, Baba. Maybe you can read to me?"

I took the letter and began reading.

It was from a Japanese woman named Kiyoko, written in English. Kiyoko had vacationed in New Delhi a month earlier, and Mohammed Ali had cleaned her ears. Now she was back in Tokyo, wishing that her trip had been longer and wishing health and happiness to Mohammed Ali, his wife and children.

He sighed when I was done reading, and put his hand to his chest. "Oh, I miss her so much. She was so kind person. Every day she sits here in the park with all of us. We would talk, oh, of so many things."

He took a fresh, blank aerogram from his pouch. "Baba, maybe you will write for me? To her."

I took the aerogram, wrote "Dear Kiyoko", and poised my pen. "What do you want me to tell her?"

He was still smiling. "You write."

"But I don't know her. You spent many days with her."

"You write many letters, yes?"

"Yes," I said.

"I never write, Baba. You write."

And so I wrote:

Dear Kiyoko,

It is a beautiful afternoon here. The only way it could be better would be if you were here. Since you left, the sun seems not so bright in New Delhi. We miss you very badly. There are cows wandering nearby. Most days they make a sound like "Mooo," but today it is different. Today they are saying, "We miss Kiyoko. We miss Kiyoko." Yes, even the cows miss you.

I was so excited today when I received your letter. The postman told me it was from Japan, and a man from America read it to me. You write so beautifully—your words are like Indian rubies. Thank you for your kind thoughts for my family. Yes, everyone is doing well, everyone except me and all your friends here in the park—we miss you so much. Me most of all. I look forward to your next visit. If you cannot come soon, I hope you will write again.

Your friend,
Mohammed Ali

Mohammed Ali pressed his palms together and bowed his head. "Oh, Baba! Thank you. That is beautiful."

"It's nothing," I said. But actually it was one of the most satisfying things I've ever done.

Mohammed Ali's first letter.

"Now you must let me do something for you," he said.

I had no choice. I sat up straight and tipped my head to the right. Mohammed Ali uncorked a small vial and eye-dropped a fizzing seltzer into my left ear. We sat and let it soak in.

"Please be careful," I said, when Mohammed Ali took out his forceps.

"Very careful, Baba."

For a moment I felt nothing, just a tickling in the ear canal. Then, with forceps and the softest of tugs, he fizzed and cleaned—and then toweled my neck dry.

I gave Mohammed Ali some money, wrote something nice in his book, and for a few moments we sat in silence—an intense, symphonic silence. And yet, I could hear everything: cows munching the lawn; airplane tires nicking down on the runway out at the airport; even trickles of snowmelt on the glaciers up in Kashmir.

There were whole days when this trip of mine seemed devoid of purpose. But moments like this revived its clarity and mission. I was a collector: Tony from the

Philippines, Shubash from Varanasi, Ram Ashray Prashad from Darjeeling, and now Mohammed Ali.

Time would airbrush away the filthy streets, foul water and overpopulation, but these beautiful souls would come home with me and stay there, somewhere deep in my heart.

Brad Newsham

Josef and Rebecca

A journey, one hopes, will become its own jus-
tification, will assume patterns, reveal its possi-
bilities—reveal, even, its layers of meaning—as
one goes along, trusting to chance, to instinct,
to hunch. When you start off you do not
necessarily know where you are going or why.

Shiva Naipual

In 1996, I decided to participate in the March of the
Living, an international program that brings six thousand
Jewish teenagers and a thousand adults from forty-five
countries to Poland to retrace the death march from the
concentration camp at Auschwitz to nearby Birkenau. The
group then tours Poland visiting the Treblinka and
Majdanek concentration camps and other sites of Jewish
interest. Finally, we travel to Israel for Holocaust
Remembrance Day and Independence Day.

Three months before the march, we were all given identification cards and told to take good care of them, that
they were important and that someday we would do
something with them.

I was given a copy of identification card #07175, issued 22 September 1941, by the Nazis, to Josef Bau, a Jew living in Krakow. It said that Bau was born in Krakow on June 18, 1920, exactly one year and five days after my father was born in Brooklyn. Josef went to Hebrew High School, was in the Boy Scouts and worked as a draftsman at the hard labor concentration camp in Plaszow.

I learned that Bau was at Plaszow when he fell in love with Rebecca Tannenbaum, also a prisoner. They met one gray morning when he stood outside, holding up a blueprint frame toward the low autumn cloud. His thin body seemed overburdened by the weight. She asked if she could help him.

"No," he said. "I'm just waiting for the sunshine." Then he said, "Why don't you be my magical sunshine?"

They were eventually separated when the Germans constructed an electrified fence between the men's and women's prisons.

Undeterred, Josef found a dead woman's dress in the clothing warehouse, and after roll call in the men's lines, he would go to the latrines, put on the long gown and place an Orthodox bonnet on his hair. Then he would come out and join the women's queues. With thirteen thousand women prisoners, he would pass into the women's compound and spend the night sitting up in Hut 57 keeping Rebecca company.

Josef married Rebecca on a fiercely cold night in February. As there was no rabbi, Josef's mother officiated. Their wedding bands were crafted in the prison workshop out of a silver spoon Mrs. Bau had hidden in the rafters.

Ten minutes after the wedding, Josef was discovered missing from his barracks. Unwilling to compromise the women in the barrack, he kissed his wife and ran from the hut.

In the fence between the men's and women's camps in Plaszow ran nine electrified strands. In spite of this, Josef launched himself high. He landed on the wires and hung there. He thought the coldness of the metal was the first message of the current. But there was no current. He vaulted into the men's camp.

As I traveled through Poland, I found it hard to connect with Josef Bau and his young bride, Rebecca. I couldn't relate to their lives in this horrible place. Instead, all I wondered about was where they had lost their lives, where they had been exterminated. Auschwitz, Birkenau, Majdanek, Treblinka—so many dead, so much unbelievable suffering.

On our first evening in Israel, we were asked to take out our identification cards. We were asked to think about our "Krakow connection" as real people: How old was Josef Bau when the war interrupted his life? What kind of life was he leading at the time? How would it have been similar to my own life? What kind of a life would he have had if he had survived?

Shortly after, we arrived at Atlit, the displaced person camp near Haifa that was run by the British after the war. We were welcomed in a small auditorium and the speaker introduced the guests that had joined us that night. They were the Krakow Jews whose identification cards we had carried all these months.

I stood there in utter disbelief—Josef and his bride Rebecca were standing there, right in front of me. I had not passed them in the ovens of Auschwitz or at the ash heap at Majdanek. Tears rolled down my face.

Slowly, I went over to meet Rebecca and Josef, sitting with their two daughters. Josef had survived Auschwitz and Rebecca had been a "Schindler Jew," on that fortunate list that spared her life. They reunited and made a life together in Israel.

They couldn't speak English, and I do not speak Hebrew, but that didn't matter. For me, nothing needed to be said.

Mark I. Farber

A Journey of Peace

If we have no peace, it is because we have for-gotten that we belong to each other.

Mother Teresa

When I remember Egypt, my mind is crowded with images—the towering pyramids of Giza, five-thousand-year-old temple drawings, the countless domes and spires of Cairo, the glittering treasures of King Tut's tomb—but perhaps the greatest wonder of all was the story told to me by a teary-eyed retired soldier as the two of us stood gazing across the Suez Canal.

Yosef was a *sabra,* a native of what is now Israel. At fifteen, he fudged his age on enlistment forms to join in Israel's 1948 War for Independence. He soon became an officer and went on to fight in the infamous Israeli-Egyptian battles, the Six-Day War of 1967 and the Yom Kippur War of 1973.

I knew Yosef as a master Israeli tour guide, a cherished friend, and one of the kindest and most selfless people I had ever met. As I was a tour leader to Egypt, Greece and Israel, I always looked forward to the time we spent together shepherding visitors through the Holy Land. Knowing his tender heart, it was difficult for me to imagine him engaged in war.

On this particular trip, Yosef accompanied my tour group as we jostled across the Sinai desert, crossing from Israel into Egypt, where he became a tourist himself.

Sitting beside me on the bus, Yosef eagerly took in the view from the window. "Look there!" he would exclaim, having caught sight of some almost invisible animal, camouflaged with desert hues, that none of the rest of us could pick out. He categorized every bush and boulder and explained how sand from Egypt blew all the way into Israel's interior.

At the Suez Canal, Yosef marveled at its workmanship. Suddenly solemn, he spoke of years of longing to see the splendors of Egypt.

"For many years after the wars," Yosef told me, "I could not travel through the Canal. Israelis were not allowed." In fact, he said, this was only his second visit to the country of his "cousins." The first time had been only a few years before our trip, and that journey was the fulfillment of a wartime vow. The memory of that promise was in his heart as he retraced his steps with me.

During one of the wars, Yosef and his company captured an Egyptian officer whose rank was identical to his own. Out of respect for his position, Yosef did not house the man with the handful of other Egyptian prisoners, but took him instead into his own quarters.

Through the evening, the two men conversed and found much to admire in each other. They talked about their mutual love for the desert terrain, their wives and children, their hopes for peace. Before they parted the following day, the Egyptian made a request of Yosef. If they both saw the end of the war, he wanted Yosef to come to his home to meet his family and celebrate a happier time.

He wrote his name and address on a scrap of paper and folded it into Yosef's hand.

Nearly two decades later, in spite of the lingering hostilities between their two countries, Yosef finally made that journey.

He traveled to Egypt, where the two men met as friends, embraced each other, and with the Egyptian's family, sat together for a meal much different from the one they had shared in Yosef's camp.

On that day, a "peace process" more effective than any ever wrought by governments—the opening of men's hearts to each other—brought together two soldiers of long-past wars in a joyful bond of reconciliation and brotherhood.

Kelly Mustian

The Little Black Book

Journeys, like artists, are born and not made. A thousand differing circumstances contribute to them. Few of them are willed or determined by the will, whatever we may think.

Lawrence Durrell

While my husband and I were packing for a trip to New York City, I found myself rummaging through an old drawer looking for a map of the city. It was then that I noticed a small, smooth object just the size to fit into a crack. Intrigued, I poked and prodded it, and with one final nudge the drawer released its treasure. There, in my hand, was my father's little black book, dated from 1929 to 1931, its soft, worn cover steeped in the years of my father's life.

I sat down slowly and opened it. Dad's words ran across the yellowed pages. Every line was tightly packed with dates, times and prices of places he had visited.

Right then I knew that I wanted to use this small journal

to map a journey he had taken long before he became a husband or a father.

Arriving in New York, we followed its trail. Battery Park, the Boardwalk, Broadway, Greenwich Village. Inspired by Dad's notes, we roamed the city's streets, captivated by its architecture and its people.

On our last night, however, the little book revealed one final gem of a memory.

Searching for a place to eat, we looked to Dad. My father had an insatiable appetite. He also had a nose for a good restaurant. So I hadn't been surprised to find two pages devoted to the small, intimate details of a dinner he had enjoyed one night in 1931. We hadn't expected to find Barbetta's still in business nearly seventy years later, but its listing in the telephone directory assured us it was.

Even though it was only three blocks from our hotel, it was hard to find. The sign was quite inconspicuous and the door merely one among a row of doors in a block-long brownstone building. Inside was a different story—suit-and-tie clientele, bowing waiters, chandeliers and a menu with no prices. We looked at each other in our rumpled shorts and T-shirts.

"Well, we can at least have a drink to toast your father, and then eat somewhere else," suggested my husband as he prepared to speak to the man in a tuxedo who was approaching us.

"I'm sorry, Sir, but our tables are full."

"Then we'll be quite content with your famous garden patio," I answered suddenly in my father's charming Irish lilt. It was the first indication that both my father and his little black book were with us and that this was his party.

"Of course then. Right this way." And we were led through the dining room of full tables to the garden patio beyond, empty except for the sculptures and fountains, fragrant flowering bushes and starry sky above.

As a waiter came in to greet us, he started to remove the extra place settings from the table.

"There will be three of us," I said quietly to him.

"Of course, Madam, and may I serve you something while you wait for the third party?"

"Oh, he's already here. He could hardly wait to get back here after sixty-eight years," I smiled.

When it appeared that he didn't quite understand, my husband told him the story of my father's two-page report of this restaurant in his diary in 1931. "That's actually why we're here, in fact. We'd like to toast him. Perhaps you have some champagne . . .?"

But the waiter had disappeared.

"So are we to have our champagne or not?" I wondered aloud. "Although it's a beautiful place to be, with or without it. Dad's outdone himself this time."

"Good evening," said a beautiful woman in an elegant gown. "My name is Sophia. Alberto here tells me we have some special guests with us tonight. But he was afraid he didn't get all the details."

I pulled out Dad's book. "My father led us right to your restaurant," I explained. "He wrote about everything he had—all eight courses for $2.25. Would you like to read his notes?" I held up the book to her, opened at the two-page menu.

She received it from me as if it were a sacred relic, looked at it, and slowly sat down. "Alligator pear salad! I forgot that used to be on the menu. It was my father's favorite creation. He always prepared those himself."

"So your father would have been here when my father came in?" I asked with growing excitement.

"My father came over from Italy in 1900, a young man full of dreams. He worked hard for many years, saved his money, and then bought this place, just a few years before your father came for his eight-course dinner . . ." she trailed off, her gaze far away.

Wiping her eyes, Sophia looked back at me. "Oh, I do apologize."

I covered her hand with mine. "It seems we're honoring two fathers here tonight."

"Yes, we are, aren't we?" she replied, gathering herself and returning my smile. "So let's do it right."

She got up, summoned her waiters, and the celebration began—all eight courses plus the best champagne in the house. As the parade of waiters danced around us, serving and entertaining, we could see the other diners clad in formal attire drifting out onto the patio, murmuring their curiosity at our exuberant feast.

When it came time to say *arrivederci* to this magical garden and pay for the bill, Sophia simply smiled and wouldn't accept my money. I realized then that we had both come full circle in a journey our fathers had begun.

As I got up to leave, we hugged one another warmly, two daughters of two beloved fathers—remembered, honored and celebrated.

Sheila Reid

Cushion Covers

Most of my treasured memories of travel are recollections of sitting.

Robert Thomas Allen

It was a quiet weekday morning when I boarded the train in Sopron for Budapest. The coach was sparsely occupied.

In a section by herself, sat a middle-aged country woman in the many-skirted costume of her district, her head covered with a woven kerchief. She was an unusual sight, as most Hungarian women shed their regional costumes decades ago. The woman sat half-turned, eagerly looking out the window as the train pulled out of the station. She drank in the bustle of the station like a child in front of a candy store. I thought that she might make an interesting companion for the three-hour trip to Budapest, so I politely asked if the seat across from her was free and she eagerly invited me to take it.

We began to chat and our conversation quickly turned to a discussion about our destination and the reason for our trip. I found out that she was an ethnic Hungarian living in the Transylvanian mountains of Romania. She had been visiting with her son, a university student in Sopron. I had to listen to her very carefully, because her dialect was different from any I had encountered and, of course, my Hungarian was rusty to begin with, having lived most of my life in Canada.

I told her that I had a son the same age as hers attending a university back in Canada. With this, she got very emotional as she told me more of her story.

"Our whole family is extremely proud of my son for getting a scholarship in forestry," she explained, her weather-beaten face glowing with pride. "It will provide him with a great future in our treed mountain region. He will have a good life."

She then went on to tell me how her whole family pitched in to provide for her son. Late into the night, she would sit with her daughters and her aged mother, embroidering cushion covers. An art that was passed from generation to generation to be practiced at leisure during the long winter evenings, now became a necessity—a lifeline.

When she had enough embroidery to fill a sports bag, she would take the train from her Romanian village into Budapest, carefully avoiding the customs officers at the border. Like dozens of others, she peddled her wares standing on busy tourist-frequented corners with one eye watching for approaching police. What she was doing was highly illegal, but there was no other way. Somehow she had to get a pair of decent shoes on her son's feet. As it was, his threadbare clothes were an embarrassment to him among the better-dressed Hungarian students.

On this trip she sold her goods in two days and bought the shoes. She then took the train to Sopron to deliver the shoes along with a small parcel of food from home. It was nice to have a short visit with her son, who spoke

endlessly about his studies. She listened with rapt attention even though she understood little of what he was
telling her. The main thing was that he was well, happy
and now had a future.

"I am very tired. I just hope I can keep this up until
he graduates," she whispered and hung her head as if
ashamed for being so weak. It was clear that the daily
struggle for survival had taken its toll.

She went on talking, her work-worn, brown gnarled
hands lying peacefully folded in her lap. Words tumbled
from her lips in a continuous stream.

Food was scarce, unemployment high and hope at an
all-time low among the people of her isolated village. Her
brother committed suicide last year because he couldn't
provide for his family. Of course, now his family is even
worse off. Everyone tries to help them, but there is very
little to go around.

"So you see, we have to do our best for my talented son.
No matter what it takes. All our hopes for survival are in
him," she said, her eyes bright with tears.

I took her hands in my white manicured ones. There we
sat, tears rolling down our cheeks holding hands. In that
moment, I could feel her anguish, her physical and emotional exhaustion, and my heart ached.

All my worries seemed to be inconsequential compared
to what this woman had to bear.

I don't know how long we sat there silently crying,
holding hands. Two mothers from two very different
worlds, sharing their love, hopes and fears—and caring for
their families. In Budapest, we parted with words of good
wishes, *"Isten aldja!"* God bless!

Then she disappeared into the throng of travelers, rushing to catch her connecting train back home to Romania,
where her mother waited, lovingly creating the next batch
of cushion covers for her son.

I return to Hungary every year and have spotted other Transylvanian women standing on street corners and in windy subway passages selling cushion covers. Smiling knowingly, I admire their fine workmanship and purchase a couple as souvenirs—for friends and relatives, but mostly to honor one family's heartfelt journey of hope and determination.

Eva Kende

Russian Peonies

Our journeying is a great-circle sailing.

Henry David Thoreau

A few years ago, my husband and I went on a trip billed as "The Waterways of Russia." We started in St. Petersburg and cruised across lakes and along canals until we reached Moscow a week later. Partway through the trip, the ship made a scheduled stop for a mandatory health and safety inspection. All of our other stops had been at scenic docks in populated areas, but this particular spot seemed to be a solitary dock in the middle of nowhere. One of the staff on board told us that there actually was a village at the top of the hill behind the dock.

We had been told previously that we wouldn't be allowed off since it was to be a very brief stop. However, as had been our custom, most of the passengers lined up along the railings of our three-story ship to watch it being tied securely with ropes. We were surprised to see several people from the village waiting along the embankment. They had brought homemade crafts and items from their homes to be offered for sale to the travelers. They were well aware that a ship would be stopping there every ten days, and they didn't want to miss the opportunity to make some much-needed money.

There were Russian flags, handmade shawls, kitchen utensils and various war medals. What caught my eye was an elderly woman dressed in a black dress and kerchief.

She was proudly holding out a large bouquet of fresh-cut pink peonies. I could sense the time and effort she had devoted to cultivating and nurturing these flowers in the hope that she would be rewarded for her efforts. Instinctively I leaned over the rail, caught her attention, and in the faltering Russian that I had learned on the ship, I asked her, "How much?" and held up one finger.

One of the crew members called up to me, "She says, twenty-five cents American." Again I asked her, "How much?" and made a circular motion to indicate the whole bouquet. The crew member translated, "Two dollars."

Immediately, I ran down the two flights of stairs to the main deck and hurried toward the old woman. I reached over the rail with my two one-dollar bills and she handed me her prized peonies.

When I got back to the upper deck, I could see the woman making her way along the dirt road. Halfway up the slope she turned toward the ship, clasped her hands as if she was praying, bowed, and then raised her outstretched arms towards the heavens. I watched as she continued climbing. When she reached the crest, she repeated the same motions before disappearing over the other side.

Once we were sailing again, I went around the ship and presented each of my fellow travelers whom I had come to know with a beautiful flower. Within a short while, I had just one left—for myself.

That night, my husband and I were out strolling under a moonlit sky in the fresh sea air. As we looked around, we noticed that every room on the ship had a window that looked out onto the deck and, on the ledges of many, propped up in makeshift vases, were my pink peonies.

Pink peonies and newfound friends, blessed by an old Russian woman on a hill.

Sandra Andrews

Sight Language

A painting is never finished—it simply stops in interesting places.

Paul Gardner

The Bangkok airport was stifling. And I was exhausted. All I wanted to do was get my boarding pass, make my flight to Chiang Mai and live through another day. Was that asking too much?

I had been traveling alone for three weeks in Asia, and I had always considered myself a real trooper—the "never-say-die" type of traveler who considers life an adventure. But this airport was making me nervous. It was teeming with people and gun-toting military men. I wanted out.

Finally, after a kick here and a shove there, I got my ticket. Dripping with sweat, I composed myself, gathered my bags and ran to the gate. There, breathless, I was practically knocked out by the rush of sweltering heat and the sight of the small plane sitting on the tarmac before me. Next worry of the day: Would this plane make it to Chiang Mai?

Strapped in for dear life, I looked out my window. I saw

a little boy, maybe six years old, walking hand in hand with the flight attendant toward the plane. Up they came, and even though there were about fifty passengers on board, many with empty seats next to them, the attendant asked if the little boy could sit next to me for the two-hour flight. She explained this was his first flight alone, and he was going home to Chiang Mai.

Sitting down shyly, he ran his hand over his simple clothes. He seemed to be thirsty, and before we took off, the flight attendant brought him some milk. He didn't look over at me at all. I noticed he had brought a pad of paper with him.

All of a sudden the engines started to roar, and before we knew it the plane was soaring in the air. I could see him grip the seat handles. I knew he was scared.

A thought came to mind. Perhaps if I gave him my pen, he could draw pictures to keep himself busy. I tapped him on the shoulder and offered him my pen. He didn't know what to make of this friendly stranger sitting next to him, but he gingerly took the pen and thanked me in Thai. I said, "You're welcome," in English.

I turned to my guidebooks on Chiang Mai. I was looking forward to spending time in this remote village in northern Thailand, and I read about its talented artisans, folkloric tradition, hill tribes, deities and religious symbols.

I was absorbed in my materials when I felt a gentle touch on my hand. I looked up to see the little boy staring at me. He pointed to his pad. He had drawn an enchanting picture of flowers, animals and trees. A big smile broke over my face, and he smiled, too.

It was time for a snack. I had peanuts and a soft drink; he had milk and candy. By this time we were sharing what we had, and the two of us ate a mixture of both. I went back to my reading, and he started drawing again.

Another gentle tap. I looked up to see him grinning

from ear to ear. Then I looked down. To my amazement, he had drawn a perfect picture of my face.

Tears welled up in my eyes. This boy, with talent as big as the sky, had shown, through the gift of a pen, the depth of his little soul. We didn't need words: We had invented our own language. We had crossed cultures and defied the word "barrier." We had done what many travelers do—opened our hearts to each other and instinctively realized that was enough.

The plane set down. The flight attendant came and got the boy. He looked back at me with a happy-sad face, as he gripped his new pen in one hand. I waved and held up my picture as he got off the plane and ran to meet his waiting parents.

Nancy Mills

The Guilt Trip

There is a wisdom of the head . . . and a wisdom of the heart.

Charles Dickens

Ah, the guilt of the traveling mother. Is there a more wrenching anguish?

My job required me to travel frequently and often for extended periods, making me even more vulnerable to self-doubt than the average working or traveling mother.

With every trip, it seemed that I was packing and hauling along an increasing amount of extra baggage. In addition to my briefcase, duffles and totes, I was carrying a heavy load of ambivalence and self-reproach. Over the years, the quiet claws of uncertainty were making their way into every aspect of my planning, packing and leave-taking. The pain of separation and concern about my family's well-being clouded the joy of taking off for those new worlds I was supposed to be exploring.

Often my flights would leave very early in the morning. I would tip-toe into my children's bedroom to say my silent good-byes while they were still fast asleep, inhaling

the familiar fragrance of shampoo in their silken hair, nuz-
zling my nose into their soft, warm necks and running my
fingers over their downy cheeks. Then, on the way to the
airport, I would burst into tears.

The intensity of my good-byes varied with every trip. I
learned that leaving a sick child or being absent for more
than a weekend took the heaviest emotional toll.

I suffered one of my worst bouts of guilt when my
daughters were three and six years old and I went to
Morocco for seventeen days on business—the longest I
had ever been away from home.

For weeks before my departure, I took extra precautions
to keep every microbe away from my children, to keep
them from getting sick. Compulsively, I spent every free
moment playing with them, cherishing their company. I
made endless lists and schedules for my husband and the
baby-sitter, stocked the cupboards and refrigerator to
overflowing and filled "goodie bags" with simple, gift-
wrapped treats to be opened each day I was away. But
even my best efforts didn't alleviate my guilt.

Although the pain of separation was slowly replaced
with the excitement of experiencing Africa, I would still
feel daily stabs of guilt. To comfort myself and to stay emotionally connected to home, I carried my family's pictures
with me everywhere I went, enthusiastically sharing them
with waitresses, guides and travel companions.

I even safety-pinned my favorite snapshots to the canvas walls of my tent when camping in the Sahara Desert.
One day I pulled them out of my backpack to share with
a nomadic Bedouin woman and her newborn baby as she
boiled water for tea over a wood fire. Together we smiled
and cooed over her child and the photographs of my
children.

In Marrakech, as had become my custom, I placed a
framed picture of my daughters on the bedside table in

my hotel room. For years I had performed the same nesting ritual in every new hotel, in every city: I would throw open the curtains, mess up the covers on my temporary bed and ceremoniously place framed snapshots of my children and husband all over the room. Perched on the nightstand, inches from my head, the smiles of my daughters would soothe me as I fell asleep.

I thought of them constantly. Shopping for treasures to take home, I managed to fill the small amount of free time I had on my first day in the city. In the bustling, colorful alleys of the Median I bargained for tiny embroidered slippers with turned-up toes, leather camels and exotic dolls. Finally, exhausted from the noonday heat, I returned to the oasis of my hotel room, eager for a few minutes of silence and a cool shower.

As soon as I opened my door, I could smell the fragrance of flowers. In a moment I saw them.

There, around the pictures of my children, redolent roses had been carefully arranged, transforming the bedside table into a beautiful altar complete with offerings. But from whom? This touching but mysterious ritual continued for two days—magical, fresh flowers adorning my children's smiles.

On my last day in Morocco I returned to the hotel late in the afternoon. As I stepped out of the elevator, I heard a rustling in the hall. A short woman with flashing brown eyes and a charcoal-colored bun quickly pushed aside her maid's cart and hurried to greet me. She had obviously been waiting for this moment. Motioning me closer with her keys, she unlocked my door. As I followed her into the room I was once again struck by the sweet smell of flowers, this time red, white and pink carnations.

The woman led me to the bedside table where she lovingly lifted the picture of my daughters to her chest and held it tightly. Then she raised the frame to her lips and kissed each girl's photo. I pointed to the flowers, bowed my head and tried to express my thanks with my hands pressed together in the universal gesture of prayer. Smiling, the woman then pulled a crumpled photograph of her own family from her apron pocket.

I took it, admired her four children, and held the picture to my chest. I embraced it as she had, gently kissing each child. I reached out to touch her arm in appreciation, and she hugged me closely. As we stood caressing in silent female communion, tears filled my eyes and my throat choked closed with emotion.

Using only gestures, our eyes and smiles, we told each other about our children. I felt blessed and quietly at peace. In that brief moment of sharing family pictures in a strange city so far from home, I realized that nothing has ever made me as happy—or as sad—as motherhood.

Once again, I was reminded that mothers all over the world work outside their homes, separated from their children. And we are not bad mothers because of it.

So it was that in a quiet room in Marrakech, a generous Moroccan mother helped me replace guilt with gratitude and grace.

Marybeth Bond

Reprinted with permission of Harley Schwadron.

Riding Tandem

When you follow in the path of your father,
you learn to walk like him.

A Shanti Proverb

In 1998, my father and I set out from Denver, Colorado, to take part in the Vietnam Challenge—a sixteen-day, twelve-hundred-mile bicycle trek from Hanoi in the north to Ho Chi Minh City in the south. It was my first time to Vietnam and my dad's second. He had been a fighter pilot in the Vietnam War, flying more than one hundred missions, and he hadn't been back since.

Since I am blind, my father and I rode a tandem bike. I wasn't always ecstatic, however, to be connected nine hours a day to my dad.

Not only did we have to ride together, our feet spinning on the pedals at an identical pace, but we also dressed the part. We wore the same tight uniforms and helmets and, when my sunglasses broke early into our trip, my dad came to the rescue with an extra pair of his "Coke bottle" prescription sunglasses.

"We're twins," my father needled.

"Yeah, right," is all I could muster. Regularly, a team-
mate would pull up beside us and yell, "Weihenmayer-
squared, how you doing?"

"I feel like a square in these dorky glasses," I'd mutter
back.

And yet, for all my misgivings about my father, as we
cycled forth I learned more and more about this rather private man.

While passing the former DMZ, the demilitarized zone,
my dad remarked, "I know this sounds corny, but even
after all these years, when I hear Kennedy's speech, 'Ask
not what your country can do for you but what you can
do for your country,' I still get choked up." He spoke the
words as if he were admitting a precious secret. And
maybe he was. I was astonished at my dad's ability to
hang on to his optimism, his faith in country, when others
around him became jaded.

I come from a generation of cynics. We were taught that
patriotism was for the naive, that patriotism had died in
the battlefields of South Vietnam. Even when I was
younger and "The Star-Spangled Banner" played before a
football game, my father would bellow out the words with
unabashed gusto, his bass, ex–Marine Corps voice drown-
ing out the mumbled sounds of me and my brothers. I'd
feel my brother's elbow in my ribs, and we'd both share an
embarrassed chuckle.

In college, after completing a history of war class, I
would argue with him, "You can't just blindly do what
your country tells you to do. You have to follow your own
conscience. You have to weigh whether your country's
cause is also your cause."

"Patriotism isn't learned in a textbook," he shot back
angrily. "What if every American put his own concerns
above those of his country? Where would we be now?"
While I had made the argument more out of an exercise in

historical debate, I was taken aback by the ferocity of his defense.

Halfway through the Vietnam Challenge, my dad and I faced our own challenge as we pedaled our tandem toward the Hai Van Pass. Rising 3,280 feet out of the coastal plains, this six-mile stretch of road with a 10-percent grade separated the former North from the South. It was, by far, the most physically demanding part of our entire ride. On this hot and humid day, despite our differences, we would need to be a team.

My father had been the captain of the Princeton football team. He admitted that he wasn't the best athlete, but perhaps the most "enthusiastic." Twice on kick-offs, he had hit his opponent so hard, that he knocked himself out. My dad loved a challenge, and the Hai Van Pass was that and more.

For a while, we climbed gradually, but then the road became progressively steeper. As I pedaled, I couldn't stop thinking of our experience the day before in the dusty parking lot of the My Lai War Crimes Museum. I recalled my father's words, his reluctant tears.

I had heard him cry only twice in my life, once when his father died and again after the death of my mother. But there he was, hot tears rolling down and burning into his proud face. "I am not a war criminal," he said. "I had a friend, Gus," he continued, his words coming in concentrated bursts, "he got married to the same woman three times. They kept splitting up and then getting married again. His Vietnam tour was done. He was going home, but on his last day he volunteered for one more mission." Dad took a deep breath. "Gus's plane was lost somewhere over North Vietnam. How can I believe that he died for nothing? I'm not proud of any war," he said softly, "but I am proud of my service to my country."

Listening to my dad against a backdrop of the Vietnamese anthem being piped out over loudspeakers, I was beginning to understand that, for my father, the meaning of patriotism was inextricably linked to the meaning of his own life. I awkwardly reached out and touched his shoulder. It was as though I was tenuously stepping out of one role and into another.

In the past, it had always been my father putting his hand on my shoulder. Just after I went blind at thirteen, our family started going on hikes together. My father would put his hand on my shoulder and inexpertly steer me over steep rocky trails. The system was imperfect, and at times, after a poorly placed foot, we would find ourselves bouncing down the side of a trail. In spite of the jarring force of our falls, I could feel my father still hanging on to my shirt—refusing to let go.

On the back of our tandem bike, facing the steepest section of the Hai Van Pass, this would be my chance to do something for him. I wanted my legs to be the force that would power our small team up the steep switchbacks to the top. "We'll go as slow as you want, but we won't stop," I commanded. But hearing my father's heaving breathing, I backed off. "We can stop if you want." He kept pedaling.

Each time we reached a switchback, the road would steepen further and I'd feel my father purposely weave our bike back and forth, creating mini switchbacks in the road. I'd pour my muscle and mind into pedaling until I felt the grade ease again. Then I'd attempt to relax and get into a new rhythm, waiting for the next rise. I wouldn't have to wait very long. Sometimes, I'd feel my father attacking the steep sections like he would an opposing lineman, exhausting himself in the effort. "Relax!" I'd coach. "Slow and steady until we get there."

"Another half mile," my father groaned, and I could tell he was barely hanging on. I was tired, too, and could feel my legs losing strength like a deflating tire. I could hear cheers carrying down to us from the top. It still seemed like a long way to go.

I maintained the rhythm of our pedaling. I wouldn't let

us quit. "Only a hundred yards," I heard my father gasp, and I could hear the cheers growing nearer. It was only a few seconds after that exclamation of confidence that we hit a huge rock in the middle of the road. My dad had been concentrating so hard looking up the road to the finish that he hadn't seen it.

Our bike toppled over. Both of us were too tired to react. I hit the ground, rolling through the fall, and was up in time to help my father, who didn't move quite so quickly. We pushed the bike the last few yards. "I feel a little dizzy, just a little dizzy," he admitted as we walked the bike through the flock of people who had gathered to greet our team.

Away from the crowd, I stood beside the tandem with a single, persistent thought in my head. The bullheaded optimism that had kept my father charging along through the years, even against a torrent of cynicism, had also burrowed itself into my life and had given me strength. My father and I do not have a "touchy-feely" relationship. Rather, in my family, love is expressed in subtler ways.

At the top of the pass, for only the second time on the trip, I put my hand on my father's shoulder. "Good job!" I said. "Great job!" I was talking to him, to myself, to the both of us. We had done it together.

At our last team dinner, Diana Nyad, the world's great long-distance swimmer, recounted some inspirational words from a conversation she once had with my father.

"I have lived through a war," my father told her. "I watched my son go blind. I saw my wife die in a car accident. Some people think I'm unfeeling. But what am I supposed to do? How am I supposed to act? Should I have given up? Should I have quit? Life is too precious, and all I can do is live it."

As I listened to Diana share my dad's words, I felt like I was emerging from a long dream. For over two weeks now, I had been connected to my father by the frame of a tandem bike, but I hadn't always been connected to his story. Like my father, I, too, had struggled with my blindness and with the crushing sadness of my mother's death. Like my father, I, too, had chosen to live, and in that way, I thought, my father and I were the same. Sitting at the dinner, reflecting on our bike ride across Vietnam, I was proud of my father, proud of myself, but especially proud to be my father's son.

Erik Weihenmayer

Boys, Again

From quiet houses and first beginnings, out to the undiscovered ends, there's nothing worth the wear of winning, but laughter and the love of friends.

Hilaire Belloc

We first met when we were six years old. Jim and I became best friends, spending our summers together in a town on the south shore of Boston, where Jim lived year round and my family rented a house during July and August.

In those early years, we went barefoot almost the entire summer, the soles of our feet becoming tough as leather, our arms and legs dark as chocolate from the sun, our hair bleached yellow-white.

Jim and I learned to sail at the local yacht club before we were ten, competing against each other in the walnut-sized sailboats known as "rookies," treasuring the blue pennants for first place, red for second. The year we turned eleven, our parents sent us both off to the same boys' camp in New Hampshire, where we grew to love the overnight canoe trips, the campfire cookouts, the smell of pitch pine.

When we were fifteen, we were accepted at the camp as counselors-in-training, an important advance in grade and rank, the first of life's promotions. But life's work still seemed far away, and after a year of counseling, we committed our vacations to travel and adventure.

We spent a summer in Nova Scotia and Quebec, taking odd jobs and camping along the way in an old canvas sheepherders' tent. In the summer of 1956, Jim and I drove across the country and worked in a lumber camp in the state of Washington. We worked another summer in a boys' club in the slums of London, a far cry from the camp in New Hampshire.

The year after graduating from college, our last summer together, we drove to Central America, where we rode a narrow-gauged train through the jungles of Guatemala, stopping at villages with Mayan Indians selling their wares beside the track.

After that, we went our separate ways. Jim took a job as a teacher at a school in South Berwick, Maine. I became a journalist and lived in Boston. We both got married the same year and both had two children, a boy and a girl. The children grew up and two of them got married, starting families of their own.

We sent each other Christmas cards but found it difficult to stay in touch, our lives diverging. Our careers took us in different directions, gave us different experiences, involved us in entirely different communities of friends.

The years went by. The ambitions of youth were tested, cast off—some in success, some in failure. We aged. Jim's hair turned snow-white; I went bald. I developed back problems, Jim had a bout with skin cancer. We both turned sixty.

And then, miles apart, we both woke up one morning

and knew it was time to retire. Separately, we came to the same conclusion in the same month. Both of us realized it was time to walk away from the jobs that had kept each of us engaged and excited for thirty-five years.

It was time to begin a new chapter of life.

I had heard about a research project in the badlands of Argentina—a team of paleontologists searching for the planet's oldest dinosaur fossils. And they were taking volunteers.

This Earthwatch project was more primitive than most. Volunteers brought their own tents and sleeping bags, lived in a barren area of the desert known as the Valley of the Moon. There was no electricity. No plumbing. No latrines. Just dinosaur fossils and occasional pit vipers.

On a whim, I called my friend of fifty-five years. We talked about our upcoming retirement, and I told him about the paleontology expedition. Then, on the spur of the moment, I asked him whether he would consider going on such a trip.

The answer was instantaneous and emphatic: Yes!

A few months later, just retired, Jim and I were pitching a tent along a dry riverbed at the foot of the Andes, pounding our stakes into the sandy soil with a large rock, the same way we had done as teenagers, traveling around the Gaspé Peninsula in Quebec.

Every day for the next two weeks, we hiked across the hardpack desert, searching for the fossilized remains of animals that had died there 240 million years earlier, dark purple bones in the white sand. We carried canteens of water and hunks of cheese in our knapsacks, just like the days we had hiked around the Grand Canyon. And in truth, the rugged landscape was very similar in both places—timeless and forbidding and very beautiful.

Late at night, lying in our sleeping bags, Jim and I looked up at the cold black sky, rimmed with stars, and talked about the time we had camped out in the Dakota badlands, far from any townships. We recalled how we woke up after midnight to hear a distant metallic sound, a faint clicking in the heavens, eerie and totally out of place in such a remote space. It wasn't until late the following day that we discovered the distant train track and figured out what that mysterious echo in the dark had been.

And as we had back then, Jim and I started to laugh. We couldn't stop. Our laughter rang across the desolate land and the years between us fell away, circles reconnected.

We were boys again.

Timothy Leland

One Small Step

It suddenly struck me that that tiny pea, pretty and blue, was the Earth. I put up my thumb and shut one eye, and my thumb blotted out the planet Earth. I didn't feel like a giant. I felt very, very small.

Neil Armstrong

By eight o'clock in the evening, the families of the astronauts were "collected" in their homes. They were ready to watch Neil Armstrong and Buzz Aldrin do what no man had ever done—walk on the moon. But it would not happen right now, after all.

* * *

In El Lago, Jan Armstrong sat on the floor facing the coffee table, staring at the television set, and laughed. "It's taking them so long because Neil's trying to decide about the first words he's going to say when he steps out on the moon," she said. "Decisions, decisions, decisions!" Nothing seemed to be happening, so she left the room.

In the Collins home, there was an atmosphere of jocu-
larity. The tension of touchdown had evaporated. There
was a prevailing note of impatience: Why were they taking so long?

Pat Collins thought it was a bit like labor pains: "God,
they come and they go. All this time and they're just getting ready to do it. When are they going to start the
countdown?"

In the Aldrin home in Nassau Bay, when it was learned
that Neil and Buzz hoped to step out of the Lunar Module
around eight o'clock, there was some banter about
upstaging the late show and preempting prime television
program time. Joan Aldrin was utterly relaxed. She
listened to some old Duke Ellington records. She seemed
to be in love with the world. "You know," she said, "this is
corny—but I love every minute of it."

At a quarter past eight, Mike Aldrin burst in: "Have we
missed anything?"

They had not missed anything; indeed half a billion
people watching television would have to wait a bit.

Until fairly recently it had not occurred to Neil
Armstrong that his first words, when he stepped on the
moon, would have a critical importance for history. But it
seemed to him that every person he had met in the past
three months had asked him what he was going to say or
had made a suggestion. In fact Armstrong had hundreds
of suggestions, including passages from Shakespeare and
whole chapters of the Bible.

As Eagle's astronauts fell behind schedule on their electrical checkout, there was some teasing banter in their
homes about Neil taking a long time to make up his mind
on what first to say.

The truth was that Armstrong and Aldrin had a lot of
work to do, and it was taking them longer to do it than
they and Mission Control had estimated in advance. Aside

from the system checkouts, there was the matter of donning the backpacks which would keep them alive when they stepped on the moon. The backpack looked—and was—a piece of equipment straight out of Buck Rogers; and although its moon weight was only a little over twenty pounds, it was awkward to put on, and each astronaut had to help the other.

In El Lago, hearing Neil quote the pressure at .1, somebody asked if the hatch could now be opened. Jan Armstrong nodded sagely and said, "There's not that much pressure," then went through the flight plan again and added, "Make up your mind what you're going to say."

Her son Ricky said, "Knowing Dad, you can't tell. It'll be something good, though."

Jan Armstrong bent down to explain to her son Mark why his father had to move around slowly: "The suit is very heavy and the sun is very hot, like Texas. He has to be careful because if he tears his suit, it could be very, very bad." Mark rubbed his eyes.

At 9:55:10 P.M., Mark pointed to the television screen. His father was coming down the ladder of the lunar module. "I don't see it," Mark complained. When Neil described the fine-grained soil, Mark asked, "How come I can't see him?"

In Nassau Bay, Joan Aldrin clapped her hands and said, "Look, look! Gee . . . I can't believe this."

In the Collins home there was a babble of conversation: "I see something moving. I can't stand it." "This is science fiction." "It looks like the North Pole." "Let's listen for his first words . . ."

Finally, at 9:56 P.M., Houston time, Neil Armstrong stepped out of the dish-shaped landing pad and onto the surface of the moon: "That's one small step for man, one giant leap for mankind."

* * *

A few months later, Charles "Pete" Conrad, the flight commander of Apollo 12, stepped on to the moon once again and this time, paraphrasing his famous colleague, added his own twist: "Whoopee, man . . . that may have been a small step for Neil, but that's a long one for me."

Neil Armstrong, Michael Collins and Edwin E. Aldrin Jr.
with Gene Farmer and Dora Jane Hamblin

More infamous than famous
were Neil Armstrong's early footprints.

Reprinted with permission of Leigh Rubin and Creators Syndicate.

Safe Journeys

A true journey, no matter how long the travel takes, has no end.

William Least Heat-Moon

I awaken early this last morning in Jerusalem, my mind filling with thoughts of all that must be done before we leave. I will finish packing when I return from the hospice, when the final leave-taking has become a reality. I lean back against the pillows and watch the pale rib of morning light streak across the black wood of Esther's piano to which a fine gray dust adheres. As always, I am startled at how the desert invades this city, the silt of its airborne sands settling everywhere.

A fringed black silk shawl drapes the piano. Probably it had belonged to her mother, reportedly an elegant woman, long dead when Esther and I met as students at the Hebrew University and fell into this loving friendship that has survived decades and distances.

We were oddly coupled, the beautiful, soft-featured, Italian-born Tel Avivian, fresh from army service, and I, the thin-faced, dark-eyed and dark-haired American graduate student, melancholic and awkward in the student society through which she glided with joyous ease. But we sensed an immediate rapport. Within days we had arranged to share an apartment, and through the years that followed we arranged, against all odds, to share our lives.

I returned to America. Esther joined the Foreign Office, but we spoke on the phone each weekend. She recounted adventures in Tehran, England, Paris, discussed the men who drifted in and out of her life. I married. She was exultant when my children were born, when my first stories were published. She later trained to become a psychiatric social worker, an ideal career for my gentle, caring friend.

Over the years, she came to New York; we vacationed together in Israel—our very young children as comfortable in her embrace as they would be later during their own student years in Jerusalem in this beautiful flat she furnished with such care. Here, we spent such happy hours, shared so many impromptu meals, so much talk, so much laughter.

I lie motionless beside my husband in Esther's bed and wonder what she and I will talk about on this last day. What if, after all these years, after all the laughter, the confidences and sharing of sorrow, the passionate arguments and the brief dark angers that are the stuff of friendship, words fail us? Will grief strangle idea and thought so my deathbound friend and I will stare across the Judean hills in mute despair?

Perhaps I had been wrong to come, although I had decided on the journey immediately, when Esther called to tell me she was dying, that the cancer that pebbled her lungs had, in wild and malicious avalanche, invaded her bones and liver. There was no hope. She had heard that in Holland they allowed death with dignity, administering palliative drugs that hastened oblivion. Would I go there with her?

"I'll come to Israel. We'll talk." My husband stared at my stricken face and was frightened. The next day her niece, Leah, called to tell me the pain had overwhelmed her. She had been admitted to the Hadassah hospice on Mount Scopus.

"There is very little time," Leah said sadly, warningly.

Hours later, we boarded a plane. I could not bear to let Esther go without saying good-bye and now, on this last day, I cannot bear to think of how I will say that good-bye.

I leave the bed at last, careful not to wake my husband. I do not want the solitude of my sorrow disturbed. Barefoot, I walk through Esther's flat, across the islands of sunlight on the polished floor of her consulting room. Her patients have been referred to other therapists but one man arrived for an appointment, holding a white box. When I explained that she was ill, he stared at me uncomprehendingly.

"*Sarton.* Cancer." I said the ugly word in Hebrew, repeated it in English.

His face collapsed and he held out the box, his hand trembling. "Tell Esther this is a gift from Elon. Perfume. From Paris." He descended the high stone steps with desperate swiftness.

I have, each day since, forgotten to bring her his gift, but today I will remember. There will, after all, be no tomorrow.

I prepare coffee, break off the heel of a baguette and carry my breakfast to the balcony that overlooks the neighboring courtyard—a mother braiding her small daughter's blonde hair, the two youthful soldiers who await a Jeep each morning, the gray-bearded man in sun-spattered prayer shawl and phylacteries who sways in prayer beneath the shade of a dwarf olive tree.

"Pray for my friend," I want to tell him. "She, too, watched you every morning."

Esther would laugh if I told her this. She is the secular daughter of an orthodox father and has not entered a synagogue for many years. She will tease me about it if it is a good day and morphine has not clouded her thoughts.

I toss the remnant of the baguette to the ground. A raven swoops down, grasps it between his talons and soars southward toward the desert. Esther may watch the flight from her hospice bed, situated near a window so that the scent of jasmine and sigalit overpower the odors of medicine and disinfectant. ("Weren't we lucky to get such a room?" We, her visitors, congratulate ourselves as though we are tenants in common in this, death's pleasant waiting room.)

I water the plants on the kitchen balcony. Blue flowers sprout from a cactus plant, a gift from a tall dignified widower, one of the many men who had loved her and whom she turned away. During our student days, tall youths had wept when they left her room. Occasionally on a Jerusalem street, a man would stop her, speaking urgently and softly as she shook her head. No, and again no.

I pluck away faded blossoms and withered leaves, dust the miniature bronze ibex, a gift to Esther from my husband in memory of a magic moment when we three had driven from Ein Gedi to Jerusalem at the twilight hour. Atop an incline, a majestic ibex had stood motionless, and we had watched in silent wonder until it streaked away.

I carry the ibex into the kitchen and place it next to the small copper candlesticks that had also been our gift to her. These are the only talismans of our friendship that I would claim.

My husband watches as I dress. We agreed that I would go alone to the hospice on this last day. He had made his own farewell the previous evening, pressing his hand to her lips because he has loved her all these years as he has loved no other friend of mine.

"Will you be all right?" he asks. "Take a cab. You'll be late."

I know that is not what he wants to say. He wants to tell me not to choke on grief, not to drown in my sorrow.

I rush down the high stone steps, and on the third floor the elderly chemistry professor, a beret perched on his snowy mane, stops me. He lived here when Esther bought the flat, he will live here when she is gone.

"How is *G'veret*, Esther?" he asks in his German-accented Hebrew.

Always she had shared her weekend newspapers with him, brought him groceries when he was ill. When she cooked her special delicacies, spinach pie or Tuscan stew, she carried a portion down to him. Each Rosh Hashana he had presented her with a bouquet of yellow roses, balancing the seesaw of gentle Jerusalem courtesy.

"The same," I tell him and tears fill his rheumy blue eyes.

"Tell her that I asked for her. Professor Weinglass from flat three."

I nod and dash out of the building, squinting against the morning brightness. At the greengrocer on Aza I buy a carton of cherries, newly in season.

"You picked a good box of fruit, *G'veret*," the mournful Yemenite proprietor assures me.

"They are for a sick friend."

"She should eat with appetite. God willing, she should live and be well," he says. "Twenty shekels."

"Amen," I reply, although I know that Esther will not live and be well because the God in whom she does not believe has willed otherwise. I give him twenty-five shekels and tell him to put the extra five against the account of a poor family. This is, after all, Jerusalem and I am, despite myself, in search of a miracle.

I buy the newspaper, hurry onto the waiting

number-eighteen bus and scan the headlines. Two soldiers have been killed in Lebanon. I fold the paper. I am too fatigued by the long days and nights of my friend's dying to think of the deaths and dangers that haunt this country every day.

The bus winds its way through the city, turning on King George to pass the Arab house where Esther and I shared a flat and gave parties still remembered by our university friends. On Jaffa Road, I stare out at the café where we sat over countless cups of bitter espresso. Then I turn away from the landmarks of our young womanhood and back to the newspaper. The soldiers were only nineteen years old. Esther is sixty-three. Death offers no equity—not in Israel, not anywhere.

At Mount Scopus, Hadassah Hospital glows golden in the sunlight. The guard who now recognizes me rummages perfunctorily through my bags.

"You go to the hospice," he says sympathetically.

I wonder if I should tell him that today is my last day in Jerusalem, the visit my last one. I say nothing and hurry through the lobby, past the synagogue where a minyan of young boys in shorts and T-shirts, Hasidim in black caftans, and soldiers in badly pressed uniforms intone the Kaddish. I wince, take the elevator to the second floor and follow the arrows to the hospice. Palm trees brush the glass ceiling that canopies the entry, and the air is thick with floral fragrance. In the common room, a huge television set is tuned to *Rechov Sumsum,* watched by the grandchildren of an old woman asleep in her wheelchair. A small girl watches with her head pressed against her dying grandmother's knees. In the communal kitchen, their sad-eyed mother, whom I have seen every day, lifts a monitory finger to her lips, although the children need no warning. They understand the courtesy that must be extended to the dying.

On the terrace, a frail old woman, her head encased in a peacock-blue satin turban (the "cancer *cloche,*" Esther wryly calls these head coverings and claims to be glad that she will never wear one, that she will die before she loses her thick copper-colored hair to the ravages of radiation), fingers a cherry from the dish on her table.

Malka, the tall social worker, approaches me.

"Today is your last day in Jerusalem, isn't it? Do you want me to be with her when you leave?"

"Oh, Malka, take care of her." My eyes burn. The sadness, simmering within me from the dawning of this day, threatens to spill over.

"Not to worry. I'll be close by."

Relieved, I hurry up the steps to Esther's room, and I see at once that she is having a good day. Already seated in a wheelchair, she wears a snowy-white silken robe, and her niece Leah is arranging cards on her bedside table.

Leah and I embrace. The small girl I knew during my student days is now a handsome woman, the principal of an elementary school, the mother of army-age children.

"Esther is feeling good today," she reports. "Tell her, Esther."

"Today I am wonderful. Shall we go to a café in Tel Aviv? Perhaps we should picnic at Ein Feshka, swim in the Dead Sea." She waves toward the undulating desert hillocks beyond which the waters of the Dead Sea foam.

"Not today," I imitate her false gaiety. "But Esther, look. The sigalit is in bloom."

My delight is genuine. The star-shaped flower is Esther's favorite. And now, serendipitously, it grows beside her bedside window, close enough for her to reach out and touch it.

Leah hurriedly prepares to leave, spurred by a sudden urgency to return to work, then hurry home and prepare dinner, to reclaim normalcy, away from this room where death encroaches.

She kisses Esther, and I follow her into the hall where we weep and embrace.

"Thank you for coming," she says. "It helped so much."

"I am sorry to be leaving," I say. "Before."

"I will call you," she promises. "When."

Before. When. Before she dies. When she dies. We speak in the cryptic code of the inconsolable, resigned to the inevitable but unwilling to articulate it.

I return to Esther's room and give her the cherries and the gift Elon, her patient, brought from Paris.

"Joie," she says approvingly of the perfume and dabs a drop behind each ear. "Come, let's go down and sit in the garden."

"You feel well enough?" It has been days since she left her room.

"I feel well enough. Bring my cosmetics case. And the cherries."

I put the soft green leather pouch on her lap, thrust the cherries into my own string bag and wheel her into the corridor. A nurse, wearing a jaunty red beret, and a young doctor, his head covered with a blue-and-white knitted *kippa,* smile at us approvingly of the perfume. Dov and Sarah, deeply believing caregivers to the dying.

"This is your last day in Jerusalem?" Sarah asks. I nod.

"Then I must wish you shalom. And a good journey." She reaches into the pocket of her white smock and hands me a laminated copy of the traveler's prayer.

I scan the familiar words. "May it be your wish, oh Lord, my God, to direct my steps in peace and uphold me in peace ..."

"Don't you have one for me, Sarah?" Esther teases. "I, too, will be making a journey."

Sarah blushes. Dov frowns, checks Esther's pulse, adjusts her IV.

"Mean of you," I say reprovingly as we enter the elevator.

"The dying have the right to be mean," Esther retorts, and we both laugh.

At ground level, I maneuver the chair through the common room past the small children who crouch in the play area, building a tower of pastel-colored foam blocks. Two cadaverous old men hunch over a card table and discuss politics as they slap their cards down. "Bibi." "Peres." "Levy."

The woman in the peacock-blue turban looks up as we make our way onto the patio.

"Such a beautiful day," she says. "Ah, the Jerusalem sunlight. I remember how it surprised me when I first came to the country. After the war. I came after the war, you know." She lifts the sleeve of her flowered robe. Pale blue numbers crawl up her stick-thin arm.

"I know," Esther replies gently. Her professional voice, cultivated over years of practice, years of listening. "How hard it must have been for you." The woman talks and talks, and Esther listens while I look out at the Judean desert.

"Take some cherries." She offers us her bowl. Her cherries are not as plump as my own, and I shake my head, but Esther presses my arm warningly and says, "Thank you," biting into one. "I love cherries."

"Eat and enjoy." A smile cracks the withered face. She is so pleased to have shared her life, her fruit with us. "I must go. My daughter is coming." She leaves, her dignity restored by generosity, her illness briefly forgotten.

I look at my dying friend and marvel at her wisdom.

"You knew exactly what to say to her."

"It's not so hard. The words come."

But for me it is hard. The words do not come. We sit in

silence. Esther lifts her face to the sunlight and closes her eyes.

"I am so tired. I want it to be over."

"You're not afraid, Esther?" My question is hesitant, daring. But we have always been honest with each other. Yesterday I had listened as her orthodox nephew read Psalms to her in melodic Hebrew. "In God I have put my trust. I will not be afraid," he had intoned and Esther had winked at me, knowing that like herself, I do not trust the God of that sincere young man in his black *kippa*.

"Of course I'm afraid," she replies now. "But enough. Give me my cosmetics case."

I hand it to her, and she arranges its contents across the wheelchair's steel tray.

Holding her hand mirror, she carefully outlines her eyebrows with the ochre-tipped pencil, applies blue eye shadow, dabs her cheeks with rose blush, brushes her skin with pressed powder and coats her lips to a creamy coral. She nods approvingly at this mask of health she has painted across her pain-paled face.

"Now I will do you," she says.

I pull my chair closer. The cosmetics are fragrant on her fingers, her touch is soft and light on my skin. I recall another day, decades past, when we had sat in a circlet of Jerusalem sunlight, and Esther had made up my face because I was traveling to Tel Aviv to meet a man I thought I loved. She had wanted me to look beautiful, to be happy—a good and generous friend then as she is now.

"There." She hands me the mirror. I frown because the new darkness of my eyebrows is at odds with my graying hair. I take a small collapsible brush from my purse, snap it open and attempt to conceal the silver tendrils.

"What a clever idea," Esther says, admiring the brush.

"American genius." I smile, rise to stand behind her and, slowly, I pass the brush through her still fiery hair, each stroke a gesture of love and leave-taking. We look across the desert hills and breathe in the scent of the sigalit as the brush moves in rhythm with the wind. I stop only when the lunch bell rings.

Malka motions us to a secluded table, sets Esther's tray down and hurries away so we will not see her tears.

"It was good you came. Good we were together."

"It was all good. All our years together." My voice is muffled and my eyes burn. My mind is crowded with memories of whispered confidences, bursts of laughter, mysterious tears. We are students sitting in a crowded café. We are young women walking down unfamiliar streets. We sit in a Jerusalem garden waiting, waiting.

"You'll take the ibex from my flat. And the copper candlesticks."

I nod and cover her hand with my own.

"Safe journey." Esther's voice breaks.

"Safe journey," I reply in turn and hold her close, my cheek resting on her hair.

And then, as though in a dream, I sit beside my husband as our plane soars above the Mediterranean. I read the wayfarer's prayer. I pray for all who travel forth on this day, for my husband and myself, and for my friend, whose fragrance is still sweet upon my skin, whose longest journey will soon begin.

Gloria Goldreich

$\overline{\underline{4}}$

MAKING A DIFFERENCE

You must be the change you wish to see in the world.

Mohandas Gandhi

The Nicholas Effect

We have only to follow the thread of the hero path.

Joseph Campbell

The night drive on the main road south from Naples to Sicily was like one of dozens we'd taken all over the United States and Europe—a divided four-lane highway, well-used day and night, traffic bunched in places, sparse in others.

We'd been playing twenty questions—my wife Maggie and I in front, and seven-year-old Nicholas on the back seat with his four-year-old sister, Eleanor. It ended when he'd beaten me with a question about Bonnie Prince Charlie.

We all enjoyed traveling. I've done a lot on my own, and as a family we'd walked on volcanic craters in California and the Icefields Parkway in Alberta, rafted in Idaho, and seen Indian rain dances in New Mexico. In Europe, Nicholas had stormed the invasion beaches in Normandy, hiked on the shoulder of the Matterhorn and visited Sleeping Beauty's Castle in the Loire Valley.

But of all places abroad, he liked Italy best. For his age, he'd seen a lot of it. He'd splashed in the sea at Portofino, taken walks around the Dolomite peaks and tramped around Pisa, Florence and Verona.

But this was the first time he had been as far south as Rome, and with a mind crammed with gods and heroes he was on edge to see it all. Earlier that day, at an ancient Greek temple in Paestum, he stood atop some steps and proclaimed with pride, "Look, I'm Zeus!"

Now both children were asleep, and we were enjoying the quiet ride. Suddenly our relaxed mood was shattered. A car that had been behind us accelerated and, instead of overtaking, ran alongside ours. A moment later the quiet was filled by loud, angry shouts. The words were incomprehensible, but clearly they were ordering us to pull over.

The menace in those roars told me that stopping would put us at the mercy of some very dangerous men. Instead, I decided to try to outdistance them. I pressed the accelerator to its limit. For a few moments we raced side by side. The shouts came again, then an explosion, quickly followed by another, and both windows on my side of the car were blown apart. Until then, I didn't know they had guns.

By now, however, we were doing what I had hoped—pulling away—and soon our assailants fell behind and out of sight. What a relief. We'd escaped after all.

A few minutes later, Eleanor woke for a moment but went right back to sleep. Apart from that the children hadn't stirred. It seemed a blessing at the time. They had missed the horror. What a tale we would have to tell them the next day. And how they'd regret having missed the excitement.

We raced on looking for a gas station or somewhere to call the police. As it happened, we came across an accident, and the police and an ambulance were already there. A policeman shouted at us to keep moving, but I pointed to the damage on our car.

As I got out, the interior light shone on the children. I noticed that Nicholas's tongue was sticking out slightly. Gripped with fear, I looked closer and saw blood on his hair. He didn't move. Maggie cried out in horror.

Almost in disbelief, the policeman shouted to the ambulance men who, just as shocked as we were, carried Nicholas's limp body into their vehicle. I picked up his blanket, a small piece of sheepskin he'd slept with almost every night of his life, and they laid it next to him.

Eleanor, frightened and confused, wanted to know what was happening. Maggie picked her up and held her tight. "Nicholas has been shot," she replied. "We're going to get him to the hospital."

A young Italian man helped us by acting as an interpreter. As the ambulance sped off, he handed Maggie his rosary.

At the hospital, we were told that our son needed special care, and they would have to take him to a much bigger hospital in Messina on the island of Sicily. We were asked to stay behind to make a statement to the police as Nicholas was driven away into the night.

When we arrived in Messina hours later, he was in the intensive care unit surrounded by tubes and equipment, but we were not allowed to go in to see him. Eleanor, tired and bewildered, sat on Maggie's lap as the neurologist slowly and carefully explained the gravity of the situation. The bullet had lodged at the stem of the brain. It was too deep to operate on. He was in a coma, and the only hope was that his condition would stabilize and that in time they might be able to do something. The outlook was very bleak.

The next day, we tried our best to remain hopeful. We

waited around helplessly, but his condition didn't change. At all times, whenever she asked, we tried to tell Eleanor exactly what was happening. "Is Nicholas going to die?" she asked once in a breaking voice.

It was a question I'd been asking myself from the beginning, and I knew I had to answer it for her the way I was answering it for myself. "We don't know, dear. Those doctors we saw today are giving him all the help they can. And all those nurses are helping, too. We must just keep hoping." I tried not to dramatize it or cling to her too closely but I put my arm around her, hoping she wouldn't see my tears.

The following day, the doctors asked to see us. Gently, they explained that Nicholas's brain had died. Only a respirator was keeping him breathing. Our little boy was gone.

Maggie and I held hands as we sat there, thinking of our lives stretching ahead without him. We had expected great things of him. His teacher said she always knew that he was her teacher. "He was the most giving child I had ever known," she added.

All at once it became quite clear that even in death he could continue to give. "We'd like to donate his organs," we told them. That beautiful body was no longer of any use to him, but it could be to others.

We took Eleanor to our hotel room, sat her down next to us on the bed and told her what had happened.

"Won't I ever see him again?" she asked quickly.

"Nicholas is an angel now. He'll always be with us, all of us," Maggie told her. "He'll always love you, and you'll always love him. You can think about him any time you want to."

The decision to donate, which had seemed so obvious to us, electrified Italy. The president and prime minister each saw us privately, talking to us tenderly like family members. Wherever we went, mothers and children and burly men smoking cigarettes stopped us in the streets to shake hands silently, tears in their eyes.

A man telephoned the hotel one night to say he and his wife couldn't sleep for thinking about us. In Messina, an old man in the street gave Eleanor a stuffed animal and the police bought her ice cream at the best place in town. When we needed some clothes for Nicholas to be buried in, the owner of a department store offered anything we wanted, and we dressed Nicholas just as he had dressed himself at home when he wanted to look his best—in gray slacks, a blue blazer and a tie with Goofy on it.

Everything was done in a manner befitting a proud nation. When his body arrived at the San Francisco airport in the middle of the night on a plane belonging to the Italian president, the eight-member Italian military guard insisted on performing the full honor ceremony due a national hero.

I think perhaps they felt his presence, as I did, when I spoke later at his funeral. "Your radiance is still with us, little boy," I said. "But now it's time to sleep. Good night and sweet dreams."

Since then, we have received hundreds of letters. Every major newspaper in Italy and every television station carried the story. The whole country seemed to grieve. Children wrote stories and poems. Streets, schools, parks and the largest hospital in Italy have been named for Nicholas. "They speak of him with what I can only call reverence," an American journalist in Rome told us.

Within a few months of returning home, we were invited to Italy for a ceremony to honor his memory. Our visit gave us the opportunity to meet the people who received his organs.

Maria Pia Pedala was only nineteen years old and had been in her final coma when she received Nicholas's liver.

Andrea, fifteen years old, had already had six operations on his heart, all of which had failed. Silvia, for many years a diabetic, had been in repeated comas. Anna Maria and Tino, two children who received Nicholas's kidneys, had spent hours and hours three days a week hooked up to dialysis machines. Until they received our son's corneas, Francesco hadn't been able to watch his children play games, and Domenica had never seen her baby's face clearly.

Since then, organ donation rates in Italy have more than doubled so that literally thousands of people are alive who would have died.

Italians call this "the Nicholas Effect," but it went far beyond Italy. To this day, we meet people in this country or hear from people overseas who say they received a new heart or lungs from someone who was moved by his story.

A forty-two-year-old American called the house one night to say he recently went blind and that sometimes he thinks of suicide. "But the thought that Nicholas helped those people to see again is giving me the strength to resist despair," he said.

We have never regretted our decision to offer Nicholas's organs. In fact, as I went into the hospital room on that last day to say good-bye, the first thing I saw on his pale face were his freckles and I thought, *I wish they could have used those.*

I'm still at a loss to know what alchemy turned this small tragedy into a global event. But it is clear that for some reason Nicholas's story has lit a spark of love in millions of hearts around the world. To try to make sure as much good as possible comes from it, Maggie and I still travel across North America and Europe talking to audiences of every kind about the importance of organ donations.

The urgency is clear. Every day fourteen Americans on

those long waiting lists die. Many are children, some just babies, dying because of the failure of one organ. In virtually every other country, the story is much the same.

On the final night of one of our many visits to Italy, after an exhausting day of meetings and speeches, we returned to our hotel and were met by a man who asked me to go with him to a club. It sounded outlandish at that time of night, but he was on a special mission. Two musicians had written a song for Nicholas and they wanted me to hear it, he explained.

As I went in the disco, the music and dancing stopped. Suddenly two young men started playing guitars and singing a song. The only word I could make out was "Nicholas" but the emotion was intense. At the end, the audience spilled on to the tiny stage, cheering, hugging and crying. The love in that room was overwhelming.

And there have been other results we could never have foreseen. Maria Pia, the nineteen-year-old who had been at the threshold of death, burst back to full health with her new liver, and a year later she got married.

"Nicholas is always with me," she told us. Every day she puts a fresh flower in front of the photograph we sent her. She also had a baby boy—a whole new life that would never have been—and, yes, his name is Nicholas.

Reg Green

Abou's Baby

There's someone out there who needs you. You must live your life so that person can find you.

Jan Phillips

I remember the baby, clenching his teeth on the spoon. He kicked his feet and brushed the spoon away with his hand. His mother pinched his cheeks, forcing open his mouth, and slid in a spoonful of protein-enriched porridge. The baby pushed out the porridge with his tongue and cried.

He was a little over a year old, but he didn't look like my girlfriends' chubby babies back home. His arms were so thin, they hung off his bony shoulders. Like many of the babies I worked with in Niger, he had severe diarrhea, and as a result, he had become malnourished.

"He is stubborn," the mother said, looking at me. Her name was Abou. She had a weary face, with dark circles under her eyes.

I was worried. I had been working at the rural dispensary for almost a year, and I knew from experience that when a severely malnourished child refused to eat, he or she would probably die. Sometimes the mothers thought it was cruel to force a child to eat. Most of the women had never been to school and believed that malnutrition was a "disease" that a baby caught.

For several weeks, Abou made the long trek from her village to the dispensary just to weigh her son. The baby would lose weight one week, gain weight the next. With every visit she would complain, "He refuses to eat. Give me medicine to make him eat."

It was something I heard often, too often. Despite my lessons on diarrhea, malnutrition and the three food groups, the women still believed that vitamins were the cure for malnutrition or a child's "lack of appetite."

When Abou stopped coming, I feared the worst. With over four hundred malnourished babies to keep track of, I frequently did not find out until months later which babies had survived and which had died.

Several weeks later, on a cold day in February, I was sitting on the top step of the dispensary. It was the Harmattan season, and the wind was blowing so hard that red dust and sand had caked in the creases of my eyes, the collar of my shirt and the part in my hair.

It had been a bad morning. An old woman had brought in a severely malnourished baby who was blind in one eye, and I suspected the blindness had been caused by a vitamin deficiency.

I was depressed and homesick. It was taboo for an adult to cry in public, but I knew that it would be one of those days when the minute I was safely inside my house, I would burst into tears. I felt helpless and angry—there seemed to be little I could change about these babies dying so needlessly and I was mad at the world for allowing such crushing poverty.

I started asking myself the same questions I'd had since the first day I arrived in the village: *What am I doing here?*

How am I going to change anything? Who do I think I am? I was
ready to pack my bags and go back home.

Finally, it was noon and time for the afternoon siesta.
Just as I stood up and began wrapping a turban around
my face, I heard a squeaky, high-pitched voice shouting
my name. It was Abou, walking toward me. I was relieved
to see a little bundle on her back—the baby was still alive.
She was balancing a pot on her head and carrying something else in her hand, but I couldn't see what it was
because the wind was blowing sand in my eyes.

When she got closer, I saw what she was holding: a
chicken. She took the pot off her head, put down the
chicken and raised her fist in a salute. "Greetings on your
work," she said. She took the baby off her back and placed
him on the bench next to where I was sitting.

"Watch this," she said. She took the top off the pot and
began feeding him the baby porridge. And he ate. His
brown eyes wandered nonchalantly, as if he didn't
remember—just weeks before—how violently he had
refused food. His mother and I looked at each other and
laughed with joy.

Then Abou handed me the chicken and said, "Thank you."

I hadn't done any more for her than I had done for any
other woman who had come to the dispensary. In a country as poor as Niger, where people rarely have the opportunity to eat meat, I didn't want to accept the chicken. But
I knew that it was also considered an insult to refuse food,
so I thanked her for the gift and she left.

About a year later, Abou passed away and the baby
came to stay with his grandmother who lived just across
from me. I saw him take his first steps, and I took a picture.
In it, he is wearing a crocheted knit hat and sweater, and
he actually looks quite chubby. His grandmother is smiling, and he has the same stubborn expression he had the
first time I saw him.

Looking at his face, I recalled his mother's generosity and persistence. She had given me something I greatly needed—the feeling that I had in fact "done something" and the encouragement not to give up.

After that time, I still had many moments when I felt disillusioned and ready to quit. But then I would notice something that, like Abou and her baby, would bring me hope—a mother breast-feeding as she knelt down to pray, an old man sitting under a tree playing with his grandchild or a flower growing in the middle of a barren field.

Elizabeth "Hadiza" Schrank

Earning My Wings

How wonderful is it that nobody need wait a single moment before starting to improve their world.

Anne Frank

In 1978, I became a flight attendant for a major airline. Earning my wings was the culmination of a childhood dream that I had set for myself after my first plane ride at the age of five. Like so many others before me, I fell in love with the romance of airplanes, adventure and helping others.

I have flown hundreds of flights since graduation, but one stands out among the many.

We were flying from Los Angeles to Washington, D.C., when I answered a lavatory call light in the coach cabin. There, I found a young mother struggling with her infant. Everything was a mess, to say the least, and the mother, who was near hysterics, told me that she had no more diapers or other clothing onboard the aircraft.

Through her tears, she informed me that they had missed their flight the previous night in Los Angeles and because she had very little money, she and her son had spent the night on the airport floor. Since she hadn't expected to miss the flight, she was forced to use up most of her supplies and whatever money she had to feed them.

With the saddest eyes I have ever seen she continued. She told me that she was on her way to New Hampshire to deliver her son to the family that was adopting him. She could no longer support the two of them.

As she stood in front of me, crying, holding her beautiful son, I could see the despair and hopelessness on her face. And, as a mother of three beautiful daughters, I could feel her pain.

I immediately rang the flight attendant call button and asked for assistance from the other flight attendants. They brought cloth towels from first class to assist in cleaning up both mom and the infant. I ran and got my suitcase; because this woman and I were about the same size, I gave her a sweater and a pair of pants I had brought for my layover. Then I asked several families if they could spare extra diapers, formula and clothes for the child. After the young mother and her son had changed their clothes and the baby had gone to sleep, I sat with her, holding her hand, trying to provide some support and comfort for the remainder of the flight.

Once we landed, I walked them to their next flight, which would take them to their final destination: separation. I briefed the gate agent and the new flight attendant crew on the situation and asked them to give her special attention.

With tears in my eyes I gave her a hug and told her, "You have shown me the true meaning of courage and a mother's love. I will never forget you."

As she thanked me for all I had done she said softly, "You're not a flight attendant, you're a sky angel." Touching my flight attendant wings, she continued, "And these are your angel wings."

With those words she turned and walked down the

jetway, her child in her arms, and boarded the plane for New Hampshire.

Though I am no longer a flight attendant, my "angel wings" are still on prominent display in my office. And each time I see them, I am reminded of that young woman, her infant son and the gift she gave me on that special day—that we truly are all spiritual beings traveling in human form.

Robin Chapuis

CLOSE TO HOME JOHN McPHERSON

"... Spare diaper, ma'am? Stage three or stage four? Bless you ma'am. Spare diaper? Spare diaper, sir?"

Miles

That best portion of a good man's life—his little, nameless acts of kindness and love.

William Woodsworth

One day about eight years ago in the departure lounge of a flight from New York's LaGuardia airport to O'Hare in Chicago, I spotted a young boy in tears and obvious emotional distress. His mother at his side also appeared upset. Being a parent, I was naturally curious if I could be of assistance.

As it turned out, the flight was full, and they couldn't sit together. The boy was terrified to be separated from his mother. Those were the days when the first-class cabins were not always full and Nancy, the special service representative working with me that afternoon, seated mother and son up in first class.

In the short time we had to chat, we found out that Miles and his mom were returning to their home in Kansas City. They had spent the last two weeks at the Ronald McDonald House at Long Island Jewish Hospital. Miles is a surviving twin (his brother died at birth) and has had serious health problems with internal organs. In spite of his thirty-one major surgical procedures, his long-term prognosis was still in doubt. He would be back through LaGuardia many more times.

During his numerous trips, the friendship and bond between Miles's family and the special services staff grew closer, and we'd stop in on Miles during his stays at Ronald McDonald.

Miles particularly enjoyed his flights through LaGuardia as it allowed him time to spend time in our VIP lounge, where we have an entire wall filled with autographed pictures of the many celebrities who frequented our office. We soon added Miles's picture to the wall of fame.

Miles's hero, and the person he most admired, was country singer Garth Brooks. Miles would just sit and stare at Garth's picture.

One day, Mr. Brooks was traveling from LaGuardia to Nashville and was relaxing in the lounge waiting for his flight to depart. As he looked at the collection of photographs for any new additions, Garth inquired about the youngster with the big smile. We told him about Miles and the fact that he was currently recuperating from yet another procedure at Ronald McDonald. We also told him how much Miles loved and admired him.

Mr. Brooks left the lounge and headed off to the gate where the rest of his party was waiting.

A few minutes later he was back with his guitar and penned a few words of encouragement inside the guitar case. He asked us to please deliver the guitar and his cowboy hat to Miles at the hospital.

That evening, Nancy and Sam took Garth's guitar and hat to Miles. It was like the gift of life.

At first Miles couldn't believe that it was really a gift from his hero. As he comprehended that it was not a dream or a joke, he beamed a wide eternal smile. It was as if any discomfort he was having just disappeared.

On subsequent trips through LaGuardia, Garth would inquire about Miles, and about six months later he asked us to help him contact the family. Garth was going to be performing in Kansas City and he wanted Miles to be his guest. Not only was Miles seated in the front row, but he and Garth also had a lengthy private meeting backstage after the performance.

Although Miles would undergo many more treatments after that special evening, his broad smile greeted us with every subsequent visit, the face of an ailing boy transformed by the joy of a stranger with a guitar.

Roy Mingo

The Gift of Sight

The real voyage of discovery consists not in seeing new landscapes, but in having new eyes.

Marcel Proust

I will never forget the look on Stevie Wonder's face. In appreciation for Stevie lending his name to our efforts to cure world blindness, I had presented him with a small token of our gratitude—a book.

The book contains some of Picasso's greatest works in relief. It was created specifically for the vision-impaired. I got it at a sculpture garden for the blind in the Picasso museum in the south of France. The book is stark white, and after several pages in Braille, there are fifteen to twenty embossed pieces showing the master's genius.

Because Stevie had always been blind, I wasn't sure if he would be able to recognize and appreciate drawings and symbols, a skill sometimes absent in people who are blind from birth. I placed his hands on the book, and he began to turn the pages, closely examining each one.

"Wait a minute, let's go back a few pages," he smiled. To me, the expression on his face at the sudden recognition of one of the artworks triggered a memory from a few years before . . .

I had just arrived in Haiti where I was to live and work for the next few months. I was there performing eye surgery and examinations for the poor in downtown Port-au-Prince and at an outreach clinic in the small village of Leogane, about twenty miles away.

The front portion of the house where I was staying in Port-au-Prince was used as a small business for the blind, where children and some older people could work filling little stuffed animals. It was there that I first saw Angeline, a beautiful nine-year-old girl who wore the same thread-bare red dress every day.

What kind of life could a blind child like her look forward to? I asked myself. All I had to do was look around the room to see her elders at the same task after so many years.

At the clinic in Leogane, scores of people needing eye care would assemble before dawn under a thatched covering. As medical care was not available, they waited all day to be seen. I was the only doctor at the clinic, and I would see patients from morning until after dark. We tried not to turn anyone away because many of them had walked for miles.

One day, to my surprise, our last patient was Angeline. She was barefoot and wearing the same red dress. I brought her in to my examining room and found that, while she was blind, her cataract condition was treatable by a relatively simple twenty-minute operation—one that costs about thirty dollars in the developing world. In fact, twenty million men, women and children around the world are needlessly blind from these cataracts.

The following week, Angeline came back to have her cataracts removed. Everything went smoothly but, in the middle of her operation, the power went out and I had to finish the surgery with a person holding a flashlight over my shoulder.

Shortly afterwards, Angeline came back to have her eye patch removed. As I peeled away the covering, I could sense her fear but then, as she slowly opened her eyes, I was thrilled by the expression on her face, the very same one that I was now witnessing on Stevie.

A few weeks later, we fitted her with a pair of glasses, and after that, I didn't see her at the stuffed toy room anymore.

On the morning that I was leaving Haiti, Angeline appeared at my doorstep. Proudly, she stepped forward in her red dress and presented me with a small gift—a face carved into a coconut husk.

"Your face was the first I ever saw," she said, "and I will never forget it."

I couldn't hold back my tears as I hugged her sweet soul good-bye.

As I gaze at Stevie's book of sculptures and recall Angeline's carving, I am grateful. For while I may have given sight to many, they in turn have provided me with something I truly needed—clearer vision.

Rick Weiss, M.D.

The "Sleeping Room"

After a long flight—which included various delays, a substituted aircraft and a replacement crew—I finally arrived in Forth Worth on my way from Boston.

While waiting for my next connection to Houston, I called my friend Scott, who works at a large hotel chain. I explained that I desperately needed a room. I had an early morning meeting and apparently every hotel was sold out. With my after-midnight arrival, I doubted that even Scott would be able to find me a room. He told me to check my voice mail upon my arrival in Houston.

Because of further delays, we finally landed well after midnight. I called in for Scott's message. He suggested another hotel in the same chain although he wasn't sure if they'd have a room.

I reached the hotel at 2:45 in the morning. My meeting was scheduled for 8:30 A.M. and it was thirty miles away.

I presented my credit card for identification, but the front desk clerk apologized and told me that he didn't have any rooms. However, as he had received a call from Scott, he held the "sleeping room" for me. I took the key and dragged myself to the elevator. I was exhausted. The sleeping room would have to do—at least I could grab a few hours of sleep on its small bed.

When I opened the door, I was met by a large pair of long-horn antlers hung over a leather bar. The room could have been designed by Ernest Hemingway. Animal skins and leather adorned the walls. The room was vast. It must have been twenty-five hundred square feet. The bar alone was fifteen feet long. This was some sleeping room—Scott had "stuck" me in the presidential suite!

On the coffee table I discovered a note from Scott, apologizing because he could not find a "roomier" suite. Next to the card was an assortment of Texas beer, a large bottle of tequila, a bowl of blue corn chips, a gallon of salsa and two pounds of guacamole.

I called the front desk.

"Any problems, Sir?"

"Yes! I cannot possibly eat or drink all this stuff. Can you send someone up to help?" I replied.

Minutes later and all through the night, security guards, housekeepers, kitchen staff and even the front desk clerk himself rotated through the suite to join in the feeding frenzy.

At sunrise, I showered and was getting ready for my meeting when the phone rang. My meeting had been canceled. To make matters worse, the budget for the entire program had been eliminated! I wasn't too happy.

Then, at that same moment, the bill for my room was slipped beneath the door. I looked at it.

$1,954!

My heart stopped. And then my eye wandered down the page.

Toward the bottom were the signatures of all the staff who had joined me earlier that morning and a stamp that read: PAID.

I guess it's true—everything *is* bigger in Texas!

Jim Feldman

A Cruise and a Promise

No pessimist ever discovered the secrets of the stars, sailed to an uncharted land, or opened up a new heaven to the human spirit.

Helen Keller

Although I had been on many cruises, they had all been to the Caribbean—this was my first trip to Alaska.

The first evening, I headed down to the dining room and was seated next to a young man and his parents. Michael was in a wheelchair, and it appeared that he had lost his left arm.

But my first thoughts weren't about the wheelchair or his disability. I had finished graduate school in 1985, and I didn't think we would have anything in common. Sitting beside him, I wasn't sure what we would talk about.

I was wrong. We actually had a lot in common. Mike was majoring in business administration with a concentration in marketing, and I held an MBA from Loyola University in Chicago. We did the usual comparisons about classes, professors and some marketing theories, but what impressed me more than anything was Mike's handle on life.

Mike excused himself after dinner, and after he wheeled himself out of the dining room, his parents, Gary and Doreen, explained some of the details surrounding Mike's accident.

Their son had been a full-time student in his senior year at the University of California in Riverside. One sunny Saturday afternoon just after Thanksgiving, Mike was riding a motorcycle back to campus when he was struck head-on by a car that had crossed over into his lane. The eighty-three-year-old driver had fallen asleep at the wheel.

Mike was left a double amputee—he lost his left arm at the shoulder, and his left leg above the knee.

That Mike even survived the accident was a miracle in itself. He also punctured his lung and suffered multiple fractures of the skull, jaw, vertebrae and chest. He had received twenty-four units of blood and had been in a coma for six days.

Unfortunately, Mike had developed a rare medical condition called heterotopic ossification, which was why he still couldn't be fitted with prosthetic limbs.

Mike's parents had taken him on this cruise as a celebration. After ten months in hospitals and rehabilitation facilities, Mike would be returning to school to finish his business degree.

The next day I attended a wine-tasting session and Mike was there. We sat together, and afterwards, we decided to go to a nearby lounge to talk. Looking around for possible seats, Mike noticed some empty high-backed bar chairs, and he easily hopped up into one.

Noticing my amazement, he quipped, "I'm a lot taller than I look." It turned out that he is actually six feet, four inches.

Mike explained that the most difficult part of dealing with the aftermath of the accident was having to depend on other people. I could tell he was a fiercely independent person, and he mentioned that going back to campus would give him a chance to regain some of that independence.

That evening after dinner, Mike's mother showed me copies of some of the articles that had been written about Mike. When I took them back to my stateroom to read, I gained even more admiration for Mike and the struggles he had been through.

At the time of the accident, Mike had been a full-time student and his student insurance would only cover a thousand dollars a year for wheelchairs and prosthetic limbs. A new wheelchair alone could run in excess of six thousand dollars. With the severity of Mike's amputations, they estimated that a prosthetic leg could run about thirty-five thousand dollars and a suitable prosthetic left arm would be around eighty-five thousand dollars. And because of Mike's age—he was twenty-six at the time of the accident—his prosthetic limbs would have to be replaced every few years.

Because the woman who hit Mike had only minimal insurance coverage, Mike's family had set up a trust fund in his name and had worked extremely hard to raise funds to cover the costs of his prosthetic limbs. They had made it their goal to have funds ready when Mike was finally able to be fitted with prosthetic limbs.

Even though this was his first cruise, Mike made his way around like a pro using his nonmotorized wheelchair. He disembarked at every port and explored each small town by himself.

Having worked in the travel industry for ten years, as we neared the last day, I decided that when I got back home I would see if I could get a cruise donated to Mike's trust fund. The cruise could be raffled off and the proceeds would go directly to the trust.

When we said good-bye that last morning, I promised

Mike I would keep in touch, and that I would try my best to get a cruise donated for his fund.

Mike thanked me and then assured me that he would graduate the following year.

As soon as I got back to work, the first cruise line executive I contacted generously donated a seven-night cruise. When I received word from the cruise line, I couldn't reach Mike, so instead I called his mother. Later Mike phoned to thank me, and confessed that he didn't think he would hear from me again as many people had made promises and then not followed through.

The raffle fund-raiser was an unbelievable success: Mike's family and friends sold nearly twenty-five thousand raffle tickets. Then, after successfully completing his first quarter back at university, Mike underwent an extremely difficult and painful surgery to get fitted with a prosthesis. Finally, on April 21, 1998, Mike took his first steps with his new prosthetic leg.

Unfortunately, right before his last quarter of school, Mike developed bone spurs from his new leg. Just weeks before his graduation, Mike was refitted with another leg, and had to learn how to walk all over again. Despite all these obstacles, Mike still managed a 4.0 GPA!

In June 1999, less than two years after meeting Mike on that Alaskan cruise, I was traveling again, but this time from Chicago to Riverside, California, for Mike's graduation.

Seated in the audience that day, nothing, not even sweltering temperatures in the nineties, could lessen my excitement. I listened impatiently to all of the speeches and then, as they began awarding degrees, I kept my attention on the front stage area. I waited eagerly to hear Mike's name being called and, finally, three magic words rung out: "Michael Gary Durnell."

Tears streamed down my face as I watched Mike slowly and proudly walk across that stage on his new leg. He beamed with joy as he approached the gathering of university officials and shook each of their hands.

I knew my young hero would have more surgeries to face, but on that hot summer's evening, we had much to celebrate.

And it all began with a cruise and a promise.

Cindy Bertram

An Unknown Soldier

I expect to pass through this life but once. If therefore, there can be any kindness I can show, or any good thing I can do to a fellow human being, let me do it now.

William Penn

One day, while changing flights in Chicago, I called my wife to let her know that I would be home shortly.

As we were talking, I overheard a young soldier on the phone next to me leaving a message, "Mom, I don't know. They just told me that they won't change the ticket without more money . . . and I don't have it." He paused for a moment before continuing, "Okay, I'll try to stay here by the phone. Please call back soon. The number is . . ."

The soldier hung up, and with a worried look on his face, he stood next to the phone bank, nervously waiting for the phone to ring.

I said good-bye to my wife and then turned to the anxious young man. "How much do you need, soldier?" I asked.

"Sir, I'm twenty dollars short of getting home."

I reached into my pocket and took out my wallet. "For giving to our country, I am honored to give you this twenty dollars."

A big smile of relief came over him as he took the money and said, "Thank you, sir."

"Now, go home," I smiled back.

And with that, he shook my hand, grabbed his duffel bag and dashed off to the gate and on to his waiting family.

You can't get much more than that for any amount of money.

Terry Paulson

Nathan's Upgrade

Sometimes when I consider what tremendous consequences come from little things . . . I am tempted to think there are no little things.

Bruce Barton

"Mr. Degner," he began, "I'm Tom Fury. You probably don't remember meeting me and my family back in November. We were going to Miami and the flight was overbooked."

I confessed that I couldn't recall the occasion.

"You made an announcement asking for volunteers willing to give up their seats for free tickets and a later flight. My wife, Ann, went up to your desk and told you that the four of us—myself, my wife, our daughter Mariah, and our son Nathan—would be willing to go later.

The story still didn't ring a bell.

"Well," he went on, "we gave you our tickets but about fifteen minutes later, you came back and said that you wouldn't need our seats after all."

At this point I still was unsure just where my former

customer was going with his phone call. Was he angry that his family didn't get their free tickets?

The man continued, "So you gave our tickets back and then you told us that you had 'upgraded' our seats to first class as a way of showing gratitude for our willingness to be bumped. Now, I know that this was something you didn't have to do—you could have just as easily left us with our original seats. Now do you remember us?"

"Yes, I think I do recall meeting you." I didn't really, but as he seemed pleased and not upset about something I had done, my biggest reaction was a sense of relief. "I'm glad you enjoyed those seats so much," I said.

"Oh, we did! That flight to Miami was wonderful," he replied. "We were so excited. Ann and Mariah sat next to each other and Nathan and I were right across from them. We laughed and talked all the way to Florida. It was just fantastic."

"I'm really glad that you and your family were happy with the seats, and I thank you for taking the time to call—"

"There's something more," he said. I noticed a sudden shift in the tone of his voice.

"Just after we got home from our vacation . . ." I could hear the strain of tears and pain in his voice as he continued, "Nathan was out riding his bike and . . ." he hesitated, "the driver of the car didn't even see . . ."

He couldn't finish his sentence but I knew what had happened. My eyes welled up as I waited in silence.

A moment later, the boy's father went on, "That trip was the last week the four of us were together. We'll always remember that flight to Miami, all of us sitting in those first class seats. We were so happy and Nathan had so much fun. It meant so much to him. You helped make that time special, Mr. Degner. Ann and I just wanted to say how much we appreciate the gift you gave us."

I was speechless. I breathed in deeply and, somehow, I found the words to express my sympathy for his terrible loss and thanked him for sharing his story with me.

After we said good-bye, I sat down and cried for this little boy and his grieving family. I hadn't realized how much their upgrade had meant to them on their final trip with their son. It was, after all, just a routine procedure that I gave little thought to.

A few months later, Nathan's father visited me at the airport. He and his wife and daughter were taking their first flight since the accident. I shook his hand warmly and thanked him once again for the phone call. He, in turn, gave me a small photograph of Nathan.

It has now been several years since that brief visit, but Nathan's picture has been with me at work ever since. I keep it as a monument to a boy who is no longer with us, and a constant reminder that we never know when even the smallest gesture can touch others in an unexpected and extraordinary way.

Jeff Degner

Mission to Mexico

We all have the extraordinary coded within us—waiting to be released.

Jean Houston

My parents first met when they were teenagers, competing at an equestrian riding event. They got married in 1968, and shortly after that, my father enlisted in the air force and was stationed in Okinawa, Japan, during the Vietnam War.

Lonely, without her man and desperate to begin their new life together, my mother set off with a one-way ticket to Okinawa, armed only with her bouffant hairdo, patent-leather shoes and sewing machine. She served in the Red Cross as a "donut dolly," bringing coffee and donuts to the American servicemen who were being evacuated out of the jungles for medical reasons.

Dad was honorably discharged in 1970, and they both returned to their hometown of Monroe, Washington. Mom worked as a social worker in a drug rehabilitation center, and Dad ran a motorcycle shop and later sold ads for a local radio station; together they next founded and became the pastors of Rock Church.

In 1997, they heard about a community living around a garbage dump in Mexico. Moved by their plight, my parents flew down to Puerto Vallarta and spent a month doing whatever they could to help Pastor Saúl González in his efforts.

"Take me to the place where no other Americans will go!" Mom exclaimed to Pastor Saúl. He could not remember any ordinary traveler asking such an absurd question while visiting in Puerto Vallarta.

The next afternoon, we waited outside our hotel for the driver to come. An old fifteen-passenger van pulled up, and we climbed aboard the white, rusty and worn vehicle. The original interior had been removed and the new seats were set in place without being secured.

"Watch your seats," was all the driver could muster as we set out with smoke from the exhaust pipe trailing behind us. On our way, we drove though traffic and past barrios, merchants and shanties. Off "the strip," we were surrounded by poverty. Dirt and sewage was everywhere. Asphalt and cement gave way to dusty unpaved roads.

Finally, we arrived at the dump site. We watched as people sorted plastics, metals, wood and anything the garbage truck dropped off. Their hands were wrinkled from years under the hot tropical sun while their faces contorted from wincing all day at the brightness.

And then, out of the clouds of thick dust, emerged children of all ages, dressed in leftovers from the sun-worshippers of the north. From every direction they came—walking, running and skipping. They approached the van, their seemingly bright teeth contrasting with their dark filthy skin. There were hundreds of smiling faces, for every Thursday the same van would come from the local church and feed them. Every Thursday these children expected a meal, and none missed the opportunity to eat a meal prepared properly.

Mom got out, and with the help of a translator, she started talking with them. She found out most of them ate from the garbage dropped off from the hotels. She discovered that most of these kids' mothers and fathers worked here sorting garbage by hand for little or nothing but a roof over their heads. She learned there was no fresh water to drink, only water thickly infested with E. coli and various other parasites that left lesions on the children's legs and skin.

"No child should eat out of a garbage dump," said my mother. She turned to me and my sister with big tears in her eyes and continued, "We must do something for these hard-working people, we must give them hope."

Appalled at what we had witnessed, my parents shot some video to show to our congregation back home.

"I've watched a four-year-old girl fight a buzzard for a sandwich," Mom exclaims on the tape, while standing on a pile of debris. "I've seen a boy with worms coming out of his mouth. I have chosen my life project, and it's in a garbage dump."

On their return, Mom and Dad raised thirty-seven hundred dollars to build two showers. They convinced the owner of their favorite hotel in Puerto Vallarta to offer the use of its water truck to supply the showers and give the people at the dump some clean drinking water.

Over the next two years, my parents collected more money for food, clothing and school supplies. They also raised funds for a van so Pastor Saúl could deliver food to the dump. They named their charity Mission to Mexico.

Their most ambitious project was a fifty-thousand-dollar facility that would act as a school, clinic and kitchen. This past January, as everyone was ringing in the dawn of the new millennium, my parents went down to

Puerto Vallarta to work at the dump. During their visit, they did find some time for romance, celebrating their thirty-second wedding anniversary.

Planning to return again in three weeks, they set out to catch their flight home. When they got to the airport, they realized that Dad's passport had expired, but somehow airline officials let them on anyway and they boarded Alaska Airlines flight 261—a flight that never made it home.

At 4:36 P.M., Mom and Dad's plane crashed into the sea just off the coast of Los Angeles, and my parents joined the list of great servants who have graced God's green Earth.

My mother and father traveled the globe many times throughout their lives. However, as I reflect back, there were very few times when they traveled for their own pleasure. Mostly they traveled to give life where life was needed.

On February 12, 2000, over three thousand mourners attended a memorial service for my parents. On March 27, I flew down to Puerto Vallarta accompanied by my wife and sister, and more than thirty church volunteers. On our third day, we traveled to the dump, stopping along the way to give out milk and bananas to an elementary school, as Mom and Dad had often done.

Later that evening, as I was preaching at Pastor Saúl's church, we were all overcome with grief. Wiping my tears, I noticed a white-haired woman approaching the pulpit. She stopped in front of me, reached out her leathered arms, and as I bent down to accept her hug, whispered, "Mi niento"—"My grandson."

Jeff Knight

Peace Pilgrim

Free of earth, as free as air, now you travel everywhere.

Friends of Peace Pilgrim

Born in 1909 on a small farm in the eastern United States, Mildred Norman grew up with modest roots, and, like many people, soon acquired "money and things." In her thirties, she set out on a life of increased simplicity, volunteering for peace groups and working with people who had physical and emotional challenges.

Then, on January 1, 1953, she took the name "Peace Pilgrim" and began her pilgrimage for peace. Relying upon the goodness of others, she vowed "to remain a wanderer until mankind has learned the way of peace." It would be a pilgrim's journey undertaken in the traditional manner: on foot and on faith.

The birthplace of her pilgrimage was at the Tournament of Roses Parade in Pasadena, California. She walked ahead along the line of march, talking to people and handing out peace messages, and noticing that the holiday spirit did not lessen the genuine interest in peace. When she had gone about halfway a policeman put his hand on her shoulder, and she thought he was going to tell her to get off the line of march. Instead he said, "What we need is thousands like you."

She spent hours being interviewed by reporters and having her picture taken by newspaper photographers. The story of her pilgrimage went out over all the wire services and radio and television newscasts.

Peace Pilgrim walked alone and penniless and with no organizational backing. She walked "as a prayer" and as a chance to inspire others to pray and work for peace. She wore a navy blue shirt and slacks and a short tunic with pockets all around the bottom in which she carried her only worldly possessions: a comb, a folding toothbrush, a ballpoint pen, copies of her message and her current correspondence.

At Tijuana, Mexico, just across the border from San Diego, she was received by the mayor, and he gave her a message to carry to the mayor of New York City. She also carried a message from the California Indians to the Arizona Indians.

In Arizona, she was arrested by a plainclothes policeman while mailing letters at the local post office in Benson. After a short ride in a patrol car she was booked as a vagrant and put in jail.

In court the following morning, she pleaded not guilty and her case was immediately dismissed. In her personal effects, which were taken overnight, was a letter that had great weight in her release. It read:

The bearer of this note has identified herself as a Peace Pilgrim, walking coast to coast to direct the attention of our citizens to her desire for peace in the world. We do not know her personally as she is just passing through our state, but since undoubtedly it will be a long, hard trip for her, we wish her safe passage.

It was on official stationery and signed by the governor of the state, Howard Pyle.

While she was being released a court officer remarked, "You don't seem to be any the worse for your day in jail."

"You can imprison my body," she said, "but not the spirit."

She averaged twenty-five miles a day walking, depending upon how many people stopped to talk to her along the way. On very cold nights, she'd walk through the night to keep warm. When the days were very warm she would walk at night to avoid the heat.

Once a six-foot man, confident he could out-walk her, made it for thirty-three miles. When he gave up, his feet were blistered and his muscles ached. He was walking on his own strength; she wasn't. She was walking on that endless energy that comes from inner peace.

She never experienced any danger on her walks. One time a couple of drunks followed her in a car, but when she moved off the road, they left. Only once did anyone ever throw something at her: A man in a speeding truck threw a fistful of crumpled dollar bills. She simply gave them to the next church where she spoke.

In the early years, most of the time she was offered food and hospitality by people she didn't even know. She accepted everything as an offering sent from the hand of God. She was equally thankful for the stale bread she received at a migrant worker's home as she was for the sumptuous meal presented to her in the main dining room at the Waldorf-Astoria Hotel.

Once a sixteen-year-old Mexican boy, who had heard her on the radio, raced out as she passed his home and excitedly extended an invitation to stay for the evening. His family lived in a poor itinerant sharecropper's cabin, but she was treated as their honored guest. After a dinner of tortillas and beans, the family rolled up their only rug and placed it as a blanket upon their only bed. In the morning, before departing, they fed her another loving meal.

One bitter cold morning, a college student in Oklahoma gave her the gloves from his hands and threw his scarf around her neck. That night, when the temperature had dropped below zero, an Indian couple offered her shelter.

When she first started out, her tunic read "Peace Pilgrim" on the front and "Walking Coast to Coast for Peace" on the back. Through the years, the message on the back changed from "Walking 10,000 Miles for World Disarmament" to "Walking 25,000 Miles for Peace."

She finished counting the miles of walking in Washington, D.C., in the fall of 1964. "Twenty-five thousand miles is enough to count," she said. "It kept me tied to the main highways where mileage is recorded on road maps, but they weren't good places to meet people, just good places to count miles."

Although she continued to walk daily, speaking became her first priority. By 1981, Peace Pilgrim was crossing the country for the seventh time. She had walked through all fifty states, and had also visited Canada's ten provinces and parts of Mexico.

And then, on July seventh, as she was being driven to a speaking engagement in Indiana, she was involved in a head-on collision and died instantly. Or, as she would have said, she had made "the glorious transition to a freer life."

In an interview the day before her passing, Peace Pilgrim spoke of being in radiant health. She was planning her itinerary beyond the current pilgrimage route and had speaking engagements through 1984.

"You seem to be a most happy woman," the interviewer remarked.

"I certainly *am* a happy person," she replied. "Who could know God and not be joyous? I want to wish you all peace."

Friends of Peace Pilgrim

Harold's Wish

I first met Harold in August 1997. He was an eighteen-year-old Native American boy. He was a very quiet young man who came to our hospital in Yankton, South Dakota, because his lymphoma had metastasized quickly to his brain. As a result, his eyesight was fading fast, and with each passing day, Harold was dying.

Though I had worked as a nurse with many cancer patients over the years, Harold's composure touched me deeply. He was so young, yet never asked for anything and never complained. Moreover, he trusted us implicitly; his faith in us never wavered.

One day, while some other nurses and I were helping Harold pack up his things, I asked him a very hard question, "If you could have one wish, what would it be?"

Harold sat back on his bed, his brow moving pensively over his eye patch. Finally he turned to us and answered softly but with certainty, "I would like to see what an ocean looks like."

We all glanced at Harold before finally meeting each other's eyes. We wanted to give him something special, but how could we make his wish come true?

Later that day, as we gathered for a quick dinner break in the conference room, we mulled it over and decided that somehow we would grant Harold his wish.

For about half an hour, we discussed how we could raise enough funds to realize Harold's dream before it was too late. We formed a committee, and decided to host a raffle and sponsor a big bake sale. One nurse volunteered to furnish the raffle tickets; another offered to paint signs for advertising around town; still another promised to alert the local news media of our mission.

His condition was deteriorating rapidly; we didn't have much time. We targeted October 8 as the date for Harold's trip, which gave us about seven weeks to raise enough money.

Within days, Harold's trip grew into a crusade as word spread like wildfire through our close-knit community of 14,000 people. Prizes for the raffle flooded in alongside contributions to our "wish fund." A local homecoming queen rallied the students in her high school to contribute a dollar apiece; by the end of the week, they gave us eight hundred dollars.

We slated our Friday bake sale to run from 7 A.M. to 4 P.M. By 10:30 that morning, everything had been sold, and all our prizes raffled off. A local Lutheran church matched our bake sale profits and added another five hundred dollars to the fund.

Area businesses pitched in with donations, and a wish-granting organization agreed to give us two airline tickets to California and two hundred dollars in spending money. The support of our community was astounding. By the end of our campaign, we had raised more than three thousand dollars!

In September we visited Harold and his mother at their home. Still as a blade of grass, Harold sat there while the other nurses and I told him that his wish was about to come true.

Looking at us briefly, he shook his head. "No," he said. "No. I can't go."

"Yes, you can, Harold," we said. "You don't have to do anything but go, put your feet in the ocean and enjoy yourself."

We explained that Ellen, our head nurse, had a brother living in Sacramento who would pick them up at the airport and host them for their four-day trip.

So on October 8, the four of us nurses took the day off, bought Harold a camera, some new clothes and got them packed up.

When it came time to put them on the plane, we cried as Harold hugged us from his wheelchair. He didn't say very much. He just hugged.

Moments later, they headed toward the gate, and we watched as we sent him off to California with the three thousand dollars our community had raised tucked snugly in his pocket.

As their plane taxied down the runway, we pressed our noses to the glass like little children, straining to watch the plane until it disappeared from sight.

Harold and his mother Annette were met in Sacramento by Ellen's brother Pat. He would be their tour guide for the next four days. Accompanying them was Pat's friend Morgan, another Native American, with whom Harold quickly formed a bond. Though they had never met before, the four were soon driving off to the ocean that Harold had longed to see.

Four days later, we waited anxiously for Harold and Annette at their arrival gate. As we watched her push his wheelchair through the ramp, he was smiling from ear to ear. For the first time since we'd known him, soft-spoken Harold did not stop talking. The Golden Gate Bridge, Alcatraz, the friendly people, the fishing boats bobbing on the waves.

When we asked him about the ocean, he replied simply

and contentedly, "It goes on and on until it meets the sky."

Harold's sight deteriorated rapidly after that. By Christmas, he was completely blind. Soon, he was bedridden, and his health began a rapid downward spiral. He stopped his chemotherapy treatments and stayed home during the last two months of his life.

On March 6, 1998, two weeks before his nineteenth birthday, Harold passed away. He left behind his mother, five brothers and three sisters.

At his funeral, all of us nurses sat together sharing this last celebration of his life. We were glad he wasn't in pain anymore and honored when Annette recognized us as not only caregivers, but as his friends.

After the service, Annette approached us as we began to walk away. "You know," she said haltingly, "I had never seen the ocean until I went with Harold." She paused, tears gathering in her eyes. "Thank you for giving us both that gift. I will cherish it forever."

Harold's dream had become our dream, and despite his passing, Harold's memory lives on—in his display of courage, trust and faith under the cruelest of circumstances—and in the enthusiasm generated by a community eager to make his final wish a reality.

A few days ago, I received a call from Annette. It was Harold's birthday. She told me that she had ordered a headstone with his picture on it. She had put some money down and planned to pay the rest on a monthly basis. Shortly afterwards, I found out that one of the sisters at the convent affiliated with our hospital had helped with the bill, without Annette knowing.

And so the kindness of Harold's community continues, even though he is not here in person, but watching from afar.

Cheryl Slowey

A Christmas Gift

We can do no great things—only small things with great love.

Mother Teresa

It was a half-hour before midnight on December 24, 1989. I was a ticket-counter supervisor for a major airline and was looking forward to the end of my shift at Stapleton International Airport in Denver, Colorado. My wife was waiting up for me so we could exchange gifts, as was our tradition on Christmas Eve.

A very frantic and worried gentleman approached me. He asked how he could get home to Cheyenne, Wyoming. He had just arrived from Philadelphia and missed his connecting flight. I pointed him to the ground transportation area. There he could either hire a limousine or rent a car from the various agencies.

He told me that it was extremely important for him to be in Cheyenne for Christmas. I wished him well, and he went on his way. I called my wife to let her know I would be home shortly.

About fifteen minutes later, the same gentleman

returned and informed me that all the buses were full and there were no cars or limousines available. Again he asked if I had any suggestions. The most logical option was to offer him a room in a hotel for the night and get him on the first flight to Cheyenne in the morning. When I suggested this, tears starting running down his cheeks.

He explained that his son was seventeen years old and weighed forty pounds. He had spina bifida and was not expected to live another year. He expected that this would likely be the last Christmas with his son and the thought that he would not be there to greet him on Christmas morning was unbearable.

"What's your name, Sir?" I asked.

"Harris, Tom Harris," he replied, his face filled with desperation.

I contacted all of the ground transportation providers and the car rental agencies. Nothing. What was I to do? There was no other choice.

I told Tom to go to the claim area, collect his luggage and wait for me. I called my wife Kathy and told her not to wait up for me. I was driving to Cheyenne, and I would explain everything in the morning. Something had come up that was more important than our exchanging gifts on Christmas Eve.

The drive to Cheyenne was quiet, thoughtful. Tom offered to compensate me for my time and the fuel. I appreciated his gesture, but it wasn't necessary.

We arrived at the airport in Cheyenne around 2:30 A.M. I helped Tom unload his luggage and wished him a Merry Christmas. His wife was meeting him and had not yet arrived.

We shook hands. As I got into my car, I looked back at him. He was the only customer in the airport. I noticed how peaceful and quiet this was compared to the hectic, crowded airport in Denver. Pulling away, I waved good-bye and he waved back. He looked tired and relieved. I wondered how long he would have to wait for his wife to pick him up. She was driving quite a distance.

Kathy was waiting up for me. Before we went to bed, we traded gifts and then our conversation concerned Tom. We imagined his family on Christmas morning as Tom and his wife watched their son open his last Christmas presents. For Kathy and me, there was no question that driving Tom to Cheyenne was the only option. She would have done the same thing.

A couple of days later, I received a Christmas card with a picture of Tom and his family. In it, Tom thanked me for the special gift he had received that holiday season, but I knew the best gift was mine.

Bob White

5

THE HEALING
PATH

We must find our touchstones where we can.

John Berryman

Bigger Than Life

Courage is the price that life exacts for granting peace. The soul that knows it not, knows no release.

Amelia Earhart

Treading slowly up the formidable slope of Japan's Mount Fuji, I felt equally challenged by the weight of the secret I was carrying. With only time separating us from the summit, I reflected on the genesis of our journey.

My wife Kelly and I have always enjoyed hiking, ever since we first met back in college in San Francisco. Visits to her hometown in Lake Tahoe for a weekend of trekking helped form the foundation of our relationship.

We continued our outdoor excursions throughout our courtship and into our marriage, including hiking trips abroad. Although each experience had a special significance, we tended to travel to areas with volcanoes. In fact, I had proposed to Kelly at the top of Hawaii's ten-thousand-foot volcano Mount Haleakala.

In the spring of 1992, we spent a month backpacking through Europe, which was our idea of living life to its fullest. Upon our return home, we decided to try to start a family.

Less than a month after we got back, Kelly began feeling strange. Her heart was racing at an abnormal rate. At first her general practitioner thought she might be stressed and offered her the card of a psychiatrist.

But Kelly was not stressed. Her thirty-year-old body had been attacked by a rare devastating virus, which had scarred her heart, disrupting her electrical cycle and causing her heart to race at speeds that could have easily resulted in death. For the next two and one-half years, Kelly endured months in the hospital, harsh medications, the implantation of a cardiac defibrillator and other invasive procedures.

During this nightmare, Kelly struggled each day, both in and out of the hospital, to try to resume her regular exercise regime, which had been so central to her life. We never knew if Kelly would be able to travel or hike in the mountains again. Her cherished high-altitude treks were replaced by short assisted walks, sometimes only as far as the nurse's station and back. As her health failed, I found myself having to carry her up the stairs in our home as she was too fatigued to manage this on her own. Eventually, we learned that her heart was so damaged that she would need a heart transplant or she would die.

We waited anxiously and then, in November 1995, Kelly received the most precious gift—a new heart.

Although the emotions of receiving a new lease on life were exhilarating, her body soon began rejecting her new organ. Despite heavy doses of medication to combat her latest challenge, Kelly immediately began to resume her walks. Starting off slow, she paced her activities as her medication tried to restabilize her body. Six months after her transplant, Kelly received a clean bill of health. Her body was no longer rejecting her heart.

With a new lease on life, Kelly was like an animal released from its cage. Each morning she would faithfully set out on a walk to satisfy the minimum daily requirement she set for herself. Because her new heart no longer had nerves to signal when to speed up or slow down, it would take Kelly's heart several minutes to start beating fast enough for her to catch her breath. Walking uphill was a formidable task.

Soon her walks grew into more challenging hikes. Less than ten months after her transplant, Kelly shocked the medical community by traveling to Yosemite, California, and climbing to the top of the famous Half Dome, a twelve-hour, seventeen-mile ascent of more than forty-one hundred feet to an elevation of nearly nine thousand feet.

A year later, Kelly set out to conquer Mount Whitney, the tallest mountain in the continental United States. Kelly led her five-person support team on a three-day, twenty-mile hike to become the first recorded heart transplant recipient to summit and the only person to have reached the almost fifteen-thousand-foot summit with two different hearts! She was back.

A week later, Kelly returned to Europe to spend some time traveling with her family. It was as though she felt a big clock ticking and needed to cram as much adventure and life experiences into her new life as possible.

News of Kelly's accomplishment spread throughout the country and world. Kelly became an inspiration to many, including a special family back East who had read about her tremendous feat.

Less than a week into Kelly's European trip, I received a message on our voice mail, "This call may sound unusual but I think you have my mother's heart." The message took me by such surprise that I thought I was going to swallow my own heart.

The caller, Greta, explained that she and her grandmother had read of Kelly's accomplishment and, based on some of the details in the story, they realized that Kelly was the recipient of her mother's gift. After sharing the emotional news with Kelly, we composed a truly heartfelt letter to Greta expressing our appreciation for the decision they made to share her mother Carol's life.

A few months later, Kelly and I read about a young Japanese girl who had flown to California to wait for a heart transplant, as Japan did not have a transplant program. The newspaper continued with reports on the status of the little girl, but after waiting for several weeks she passed away. She was only eight.

Shortly after she died, a law was passed that made it possible to perform heart transplants in Japan but only in certain restrictive circumstances. With our firsthand experience, we decided to travel to Japan to do what we could to shed positive light on the benefits of a transplant program. We needed to share our success story with the Japanese. We thought that the best way to do so would be to hike their tallest and most famous mountain, Mount Fuji.

Ever since Half Dome, Kelly and I had made a tradition out of blowing bubbles and making wishes when we achieved certain milestones, especially when we summited mountains. Prior to our departure, and unbeknownst to Kelly, I contacted the daughter and sister of Kelly's donor to invite them to send a wish, that I could take to the top of Mount Fuji.

The daughter and sister were delighted to answer my invitation. But the daughter had a very special wish, a request so big that I needed to keep it a secret from Kelly until we completed our climb to the top.

As we left the mountain hut on Mount Fuji to complete the final ascent to the peak, my mind was focused on

Kelly's health and strength. Would she have the energy to reach the peak?

As we set out, the sky was clear under the light of a full moon. What light the full moon did not provide was offset by our headlamps as we negotiated our way through the cracks in the frozen lava. The hike was very steep with lots of loose rocks. Kelly had just been weaned off one of her major drugs, which was causing her muscles to cramp and fatigue. Midway up the final leg, Kelly began to take frequent rest stops. Her breathing was labored and fatigue was setting in. The challenge of the hike and our lack of sleep were starting to take their toll.

Since safety has always come first, I was very concerned about my plans for sharing my special secret. After each rest, Kelly rallied to resume her pace. As we approached the summit, cold winds, heavy rain and a thick fog had set in, but Kelly was determined to reach the top.

At 4:30 in the morning, after hours of trudging through darkness, we finally reached our goal. Slowly, Kelly passed through the Tora, the temple gate at the summit. She raised her arms in victory. She had made it. Tears of joy filled her eyes.

As it was very cold, we decided to move quickly into the mountain hut. I prepared some hot soup for Kelly to warm up. Gradually, she regained her energy. This hike had been far more challenging than we had expected.

Recognizing that we still had a long hike back, I closely assessed Kelly's strength before determining if she could handle the surprise I had been so closely guarding. I decided to take things slowly.

First, I shared some gifts. I handed her a charm of Mount Fuji to add to the bracelet I had given Kelly after her transplant. She was committed to filling the bracelet with charms from each of the mountains she wanted to conquer. This was her third charm, her third mountain.

Then I gave her a red glass heart from one of her best friends, T. J., with a note, "Although I was not with you on the hike I was with you in spirit all the way." T. J. had been very concerned about Kelly, and this was a symbolic and supportive tribute to my wife's triumph.

Finally, it was our time to blow wish bubbles. We put on our gear and ventured outside. While trying to protect Kelly from the howling wind, I positioned her at the top of the steps to a shrine. I took out our bottle of bubbles and held the wand in front of Kelly's shivering lips. Suddenly, a strong gust did the job for her as the bubbles floated off on their own. Our tradition carried on, and I knew I could now begin to share the special secret.

Calmly, I explained that I had been in contact with Greta and Nancy, Carol's sister, and that I had invited them to send us their own wish wand and a wish. Kelly's tears started flowing. I passed her the family's wand.

With their wand in her hand and Carol in her heart, Kelly attempted to blow, knowing this time that the wind would do most of the work. It did. And finally, surrounded by wishes, bubbles and prayers, I decided I could divulge the fullness of their secret wish.

I took a piece of paper out of my pocket and told Kelly that Carol's family had a special request. I looked carefully into Kelly's eyes and continued, "Greta asked us if we would do them an honor and disperse Carol's ashes from the summit."

Kelly burst into tears. She looked over to the small pouch on the shrine next to me and asked if those were the ashes. But she already knew. She held her hand to her heart.

Recognizing the dignity and importance of her impending task, she shook with tears, releasing her fears and inviting the fullness of her gift of life. She knew that, in this small pouch that I had so carefully guarded, were the ashes of the woman who had given her life.

I then presented Kelly with a photo of Carol that Nancy had sent me. Overlaid on the picture was a prayer, which I had received from Greta. Kelly cautiously glanced at the prayer card. She was frightened. The prayer was read at Carol's funeral. It was one of Carol's favorites.

I guided Kelly over to the edge of the summit where we both sat down on the lava gravel next to a small wooden platform. There I read Carol's prayer aloud.

Neither the altitude nor the strain of the hike could have taken her breath away to the same degree as experiencing this moment. We both cried and hugged.

And then, meticulously, I removed my gloves and opened the leather pouch. As I started to unfold the white handkerchief, Kelly reached over to help.

Together, we scattered Carol's ashes. Miraculously, the heavy fog and rain clouds that had enveloped us parted for just a brief moment. Suddenly, we could see the valleys and mountains ahead, light where once there was darkness. A sense of fulfillment and deliverance warmed our bodies.

Carol was now free to the wind, once again of the air, part of life. And suddenly the burden my wife had been carrying was lifted—she had given something back to Carol. Kelly could now move on. Breathing in deeply, she, too, was free and feeling very connected to something that was truly a miracle, something bigger, much bigger than life.

Craig Perkins

Road to Reconciliation

A journey is best measured in friends rather than miles.

Tim Cahill

I was in Vietnam from 1970 to 1971. I was a nineteen-year-old grunt—a foot soldier. I spent most of my time in the field scrounging through the jungle and rice paddies, looking for the "enemy." In February 1971, barely six months after my arrival, my platoon was out on a reconnaissance in the central highlands. I saw a clump of grass on the road and in the millionth of a second it took me to say to myself, *Hmm, I better not step on that,* I stepped on it. The next thing I remember I was on the ground screaming and writhing in pain.

I had placed my foot on what we called a "toe popper," an antipersonnel land mine. I lost my right foot and part of my right calf. Although it was a very traumatic experience, I also felt tremendous relief and happiness—I knew it was my plane ticket home.

Back in the States, I was fitted with an artificial leg and I threw away all my souvenirs of Vietnam—my photographs, my uniform and my Purple Heart. They had no value to me. They reminded me of something of which I wasn't really proud and I had one constant reminder: one artificial leg.

Twenty-six years passed, and I never once thought about returning to Vietnam—until I received a newsletter from an organization called World T.E.A.M. Sports. In it, they announced their upcoming Vietnam Challenge. I had never heard of it before.

A team of Americans, Australians and North Vietnamese veterans and civilians would ride bicycles down Vietnam's main freeway, freeway One, from the north to the south, a distance of twelve-hundred miles. Being a cyclist and a fan of a good challenge, I knew that I wanted to go, and I applied.

I was accepted and a flood of emotions filled my heart and soul. Wonder and excitement. Hesitation and fear.

The possibility of meeting a former North Vietnamese soldier fascinated me. Maybe, just maybe, we shared similar feelings. Thrown into war, how did he feel when he was being attacked? What was it like fighting us?

I was also curious about my fellow veterans. I had had nothing to do with Vietnam veterans for twenty-six years. What would it be like to travel with a whole group of them?

Four months later, I found myself on a plane with more than thirty team members heading back to a place I knew only as a war, not a real country with real people. As I looked at the faces of the other veterans, I wondered if that's how I must have looked. How would the North Vietnamese people react? How would we react?

Upon our arrival, we were warmly greeted by open arms, flowers and gracious smiles at Hanoi's airport. After a few days in the capital, we were ready to hit the road.

On the first day of January 1998, I was riding out of Hanoi with my eighty American and Vietnamese war veteran teammates. The energy in the air was ecstatic. Before I knew it, I was waving to hundreds of cheering Vietnamese citizens, holding hands with a former North Vietnamese soldier.

His name was Tran Van Son. He was my age, and like me, Tran had also lost his right leg to a mine. But unlike me, he also lost six immediate family members in the bombing raids on Hanoi. He said he used to be filled with hate for Americans, and he nearly lost his spirit hundreds of times.

As Tran opened up to me, I felt my own heart unfolding. One day, I heard that he had slipped in the shower, and his leg was hurting him. I offered him some gel liners and stump cushions to ease his pain. He put them on and gave me a "thumbs up." He smiled his magnificent smile. And that was enough.

We had a connection, a special connection. As language was a barrier, we often relied on a smile or a hug to convey our camaraderie. Over the miles, we found that we could just let go, relax and enjoy each other's company, even without words.

In Vietnam's national cemetery in Hue, Tran and I were talking about his prosthesis. I knew that he could benefit from some of the new technology that was available and I was doubting the capability of his artificial leg. He mentioned that he had run the New York City Marathon twice. I was amazed. He obviously loved running as much as I did, and if a new leg could bring him a fraction of the joy I felt, then maybe I could arrange for a new prosthesis for him.

As I pondered the possibilities, he asked me, "Are you a fast runner?"

"Yes," I replied.

Then he said, "I do one hundred meters in fifteen seconds."

"You gotta be kidding." I was shocked.

He shot back, "You, me, race right now."

And so we did.

We staged a little one-hundred-meter race in Vietnam's equivalent of Arlington National Cemetery. We sprinted neck-and-neck down the improvised course, to the cheers of veterans from both sides. It was a tie, and at the finish line we hugged each other in a spirited moment that cut across history and brought much-needed healing.

In that instant, I mentioned to Tran that maybe some-day he would be able to come to the United States, and we could run the New York City Marathon together. We smiled at the possibility and knew that somehow we would make that dream come true.

From that day on, Tran and I "talked" daily. I couldn't help but feel awed that twenty-eight years ago Tran and I might have tried to kill each other. And we were fast becoming the best of friends. I felt like I was the luckiest person alive.

When I returned home I talked with my friend Jim, who owned the company where my prosthesis was made. I told him about Tran Son and how he should have a new prosthesis and running foot. Jim agreed, and we started making calls that night.

In April of 1998, it was Tran's turn to travel to my coun-try. My family and I waited for him at the airport in Sioux Falls, South Dakota, and my heart fluttered when I saw the face of my smiling friend come through the gate. I real-ized that I actually knew this man. He was my friend. This Vietnamese man was my friend, and now our friendship would continue over here.

We got Tran a new prosthetic leg and lightweight flex foot. Seeing him on his state-of-the-art leg brought tears to my eyes. Tran had given me so much, and now I was happy to give something back to him . . . and, in many ways, to his country, Vietnam. In three short days, Tran and I were once again running together, more comfortably, and this time in my hometown.

It was an honor for us to have Tran Son staying at our house. My wife Robin and I noticed how Tran brought out the best in our two teenage daughters. They seemed to blossom when Tran was with us. He had three daughters of his own, and across the miles, he treated mine as his own. We were his American family.

He spoke eloquently at our daughters' school about forgiveness. Despite all that had happened between our two countries, despite all of his loss, he found the place in his heart to forgive. We were so proud to know this man who had traveled so far to be with us and share his gentle sense of dignity and grace.

In November, Tran flew back to the United States, this time to New York City. But this time he was there to meet me when I arrived at the airport. When he saw me walking through the gate, he ran to greet me, his head bopping up and down, that ever-present smile on his face.

Together, we ran the New York City Marathon. Through five boroughs and a little over twenty-six miles, we cherished each other's company and recalled our journey through his country. After all the horrific and heartrending moments we had endured, a marathon was somehow the easy part.

As we headed toward the finish line in Central Park, Tran's innocence prevailed. Even though it's not permitted, he stopped to ask an official if she would take our picture below the banner. She couldn't refuse his beaming face. And so my new friend and I finished our race, triumphant hand in triumphant hand, just as we had started our journey in Hanoi so many months before.

Daniel Jensen

The Strand

And the day came when the risk it took to remain tight in the bud was more painful than the risk it took to blossom.

Anaïs Nin

"But who will push the hair out of your eyes?" my lover tenderly asked.

In the six months that we had been together, to say that our relationship had been a tumultuous one would be a glaring understatement. Certain doom and separation lay always around the next bend. At the same time, something wise, loving and profound lay buried deep and fast just beneath the surface of our chaotic affair. Our saving grace, it seemed, was the single lock of golden hair that remained fastidiously in my eyes—a single strand that she repeatedly and lovingly would swoosh away with a brush of her hand and a nurturing smile.

She was my saving grace. I was simple and soft. She was passionate and alive. Somehow, it seemed, almost in defiance of the thirty-five years in which I had mastered cowering and avoiding life, she appeared. From that moment, nothing in my world had been the same. And so it was, on this Tuesday morning as I sat on her bed and told her in trepid detail about "the call."

The call. It had been from my brother the night before. One of those calls that sets your heart pounding even before you pick up the receiver. One of those calls you have been secretly dreading for months, and yet were never surprised when it finally came.

The call. My father was sick. He had been sick. But this was different; things looked bad. Could I come home? My mind immediately contrived a thousand excuses. The kids. My business. What other excuses could I possibly come up with? What better excuse than the one that really was my driving force—fear.

I hadn't been "home" in three years. Truthfully, I hadn't planned on returning home until my father had finally died, making that sorrowful journey of the prodigal son, home to a place that was anything but home. Home to where my young body had grown, but my soul had withered and died. Home.

It was a complete surprise, then, to hear myself saying yes when she said, "Let's go." What was it about her that made the scariest things seem not only doable, but somehow adventurous, invigorating, even healing?

Within two hours we had packed her little red roadster, loaded the CD player and were on our way into the oblivion of my childhood past. I had no idea what healing would take place there. I had no sense other than the fear—and the extremely comforting reassurance that she would not let me lose myself. I was safe.

That night we drove through the red clay of Alabama and Mississippi. Further west into the raw, urban energy of Memphis. Night fell on us as we tooled, top down, through the dark, starry expanses of Arkansas cotton fields. It was still all an adventure, happy and carefree. We laughed, we sang. We stopped for the night, wanting to rest ourselves before the next day's travels.

The following morning, however, the dread had set in. All sense of adventure lay behind me, back to the east where safety lived. Where I knew who I was, where I belonged.

How could I go to this place that held so much sorrow, such loss, such fear? How could I hold the hand of a man who was never demonstrative? How could I fight back the angry words that lived in my head? How could I go back to the darkness, when I had struggled so long and so hard to find my way, solo, back into the light?

I wanted to run, and in truth, she would've let me. Instead, something wise inside me told me to talk. *Just start talking,* it whispered. Tell the stories. And in the hours that followed, as we drove farther and farther north, she simply listened—listened to stories that even my heart was afraid to hear. Stories, bittersweet, of laughter and pain. Of triumph and humiliation. Stories typical, and yet profoundly unique. When I needed to cry, she let me cry. When I needed to laugh, she let me laugh. When I needed to sing, she let me sing. And in my moments of silence, she held my hand and sang to me.

When at last we arrived, we sat for what seemed like hours outside the hospital entrance. She told me if I needed to turn around and drive back home, we would do it. Her permission to run gave me just enough courage to stay. Together we walked arm in arm through those doors, claiming whatever lay behind them. If it was pain, I would accept pain. How little I trusted the universe then.

We found my father's room, and together, for those three days, spent the duration in much the same way travelers idle their time in airport lobbies. Amid the sounds and smells that only hospitals can claim we talked some, laughed some, and simply watched life in whatever form it took move gracefully, and not so gracefully, past us.

My father was in pretty much the state I expected him to be. The stroke had stolen his voice several years earlier, so communication was a strain. Wisely, I chose not to attempt to talk, but instead simply sat and held his hand, and I let whatever feelings and emotions that arose wash over me. I was through fighting, battling, thinking. I wanted to let go and simply love this man. Only I didn't know how.

And always in the periphery, she was there. Simply watching, witnessing. Holding me in love and compassion. Holding me and my father. He took to her immediately.

I was the serious one, but she could make him laugh. She brought him toys, and even jokingly agreed to wrestle the nurses who were late bringing him breakfast. She was a godsend. An angel in disguise.

For three days, she helped me do what children of ailing parents do. We waited. We had the conversations that must be had. Do we or do we not resuscitate? How to divide the land? Sell the house or keep it? I sat through all these conversations, numb, bitter, but wondering. Was this all there was?

I took her to the house I grew up in. I was ashamed. It was dark and cave-like. I was afraid she would think less of me, think somehow that this was all I could ever be. Funny the thoughts that come to you in moments like this. I was afraid she would think I was incapable of vision, of wonder, of love. I was afraid she would judge me by my past.

On that last day, I sat again on my father's bed. I held his hand because that was all I could do. Yet, somehow, it was satisfying, quietly endearing. It was enough. Finally, finally, I began to feel the shift. To feel the years of bitterness move slowly away, begin to break apart, like ice from the top of a mountain as spring heralds imminent change. I began to let go. To say good-bye, but in that good-bye, to finally say hello. Hello to what was, not to how I expected everything to look and feel. I found myself gently squeezing my father's hand.

To my amazement, in that instant, my father's demeanor completely changed. In that very moment, he reached up, and with a hand gnarled and withered with age, he brushed that single golden strand of hair from my eyes. With a gasp I looked up at my lover's face and saw the tear in her eye.

I was loved. I was treasured. And six hundred miles from where I lived, I was at last, finally, home.

Dante Jericho Schmoeker

Bud

Each journey is an experience of the past.

Robert Better

When the crowded bus squeezed through Florence's city gates and jolted to a stop, an elderly woman pushed her way inside. Her grey hair was pulled back tightly into an uncompromising bun. A dark dress covered her matronly figure. She looked about the same age as my mother, and I stood up and gave her my seat. A gold tooth flashed as she smiled her thanks at me.

My mother also smiled as I lurched across the aisle to stand next to her. Age was the only thing she had in common with this Italian woman.

Mom's white hair was fashionably short, her knit shirt and golfing skirt as distinctly American as my blonde page-boy and summer khakis. We looked as out of place as we felt.

We didn't talk much.

Any visit to a relative's grave is hard. Even after fifty years, memories flood back. It was easier for me. I never knew my father. But my mother was going to visit her husband's grave.

For as long as I could remember, she had avoided every-thing associated with death. At thirteen, she had buried her mother and at twenty-three, her first husband. Weary of the pain of funeral rites, she had not been to a funeral or grave since. Neither had I.

But when I learned business would take me to Italy, I immediately planned to visit my father's grave. To my surprise, my mother wanted to join me.

The American Battle Monuments Commission sent a brochure with directions to the cemetery. They were simple and clear on paper: "Florence Cemetery is located on the west side of Via Cassia, about seven and a half miles south of Florence . . . The bus station provides frequent bus service . . ."

It was easy to find the huge bus station in the center of Florence, but we couldn't figure out where to catch the right bus until the woman at the tourist information win-dow finally found one going to Via Cassia.

Even though the bus windows were open, it was get-ting hotter as the sun climbed higher in the sky. Mom's hair was beginning to mat. I reached down and squeezed her shoulder. She patted my hand, and I repeated the silent prayer of the traveler who can't speak the language, "Please, God, let us be on the right bus."

We were looking for the unmistakable symmetry of an American military cemetery. "The bus stop is conve-niently located just outside the gate," read the pamphlet. But what if the folds of the hills hid the cemetery from view?

We'd planned to buy flowers at one of the many stands near the bus station, but by then we were too confused to add another task to our journey. *Firenze,* the Italians call Florence—the city of flowers. Few flowers bloomed by the dusty roadside on this hot July day.

My father must have known these hills, this heat. In

July 1944, the American Army had reached the outskirts of Florence as they fought their way north from Rome. I was not yet a year old; he was twenty-three. But I would grow older, and he would not. He was killed on July 13, 1944.

The bus emptied as we drove farther and farther from Florence, but the elderly Italian woman still sat across the aisle in the seat I had given her. I envied the comfort of her routine. She knew where she was going.

Maybe she would also know where we were going.

"*Cimitero Americano?*" I asked her.

She frowned in puzzlement and shook her head with an apologetic smile. She couldn't understand my pronunciation, but our hotel clerk had written down our destination. I handed the paper to her. She read it and looked quickly from me to my mother. Then, in a few gestures, she indicated that she would tell us when to get off.

In the end, there was no choice. When the bus reached the small town at the end of the line, it dropped the three of us, the last of its passengers, and headed back to Florence.

We stood together in the glare of the July sun. Pleasant stucco homes painted in soft pastels lined each side of the road. The woman pointed down the road, moving her arms to show it was a long walk. She looked troubled.

"Taxi?" means the same thing in English and Italian.

So did her answer. "*Solo Firenze.*" Only in Florence.

Mom angrily wiped her eyes, furious with herself for losing control. With a fierce determination, she set off down the road in the noonday heat.

"*Scusi, mia papa . . .*" I didn't know enough Italian to say more than "Excuse us, my father . . ." but the woman understood. She would have been in her early twenties during the war. She must have known many men who died too young.

She caught up with my mother, motioned us across the

street to a pale blue house, and urged us to go in. In that hot, foreign town, it was impossible not to follow her.

We entered a kitchen—cool, dark and high-ceilinged. A younger woman stood at the counter, fixing lunch. At her mother's quick explanation, she made us welcome.

The four of us, two mothers, two daughters, sat around the kitchen table. A kitchen table is a familiar place. I don't know who began to cry first, my mother or the elderly Italian woman. And, as they shared the unspoken pain of their memories, their daughters cried with them.

When the tears finally stopped, the two Italian women began an urgent discussion that ended only when the daughter got up and left from the house. She returned five minutes later with the joyous sound of car keys jingling in her hand.

It was a short ride to the cemetery, less than ten minutes by car. They let us out at the gate, and my mother and the elderly Italian woman embraced. They came from two different parts of the world; they could not speak the other's language; they would never see each other again. But they had one thing—and everything—in common. In their youth, they had shared the horrors of a world at war.

Inside the cemetery, we found ourselves on American soil, speaking in English. Because we were next of kin, the caretaker offered to drive us back to Florence. On a map he found my father's gravesite and drove us to it.

Row after row of graves lined the hillside with military precision, each section identified by a letter of the alphabet. On each soldier's headstone was carved his name, rank and military unit, his home state and the date of his death. The rows of crosses were broken occasionally by the Star of David or the crescent of Islam.

In Section F, Row 9, Grave 35, I met my father for the first time since he came home on a seven-day pass when I was a week old. He lay between a staff sergeant from New

York and a "Tec 5" from Oklahoma. I stared at his head-stone, trying to imagine the journey that had taken him to that spot, trying to connect with a man who was never given the chance to share my life.

After a few minutes, I walked over and sat down in the shade of one of the tall trees that bordered the graves. My mother needed some time alone.

As I sat there playing with a blade of grass, I looked over at my mother. Had our visit caused her too much pain? Was she sorry we came?

A few minutes later, she turned and walked over to me. I took her hand and asked her if she was feeling sad.

"Sad?" she asked, shaking her head and smiling at me. "No . . . today was filled with such joy. I had the chance to be with Bud again."

JoAnne Stewart Wetzel

The Little White Chapel

The events in our lives happen in a sequence in time, but in their significance to ourselves, they find their own order . . . the continuous thread of revelation.

Eudora Welty

I love to go on road trips. It doesn't matter where.

One Sunday afternoon, my best friend Evelyn and I decided to drive from our hometown of Phoenix, Arizona, to a gem and mineral show a couple of hours away. Evelyn was excited about expanding her rock collection. I was just thrilled to be heading out on a new adventure.

After a while, we turned onto a deserted stretch of highway and passed a large white sign on the side of the road. It stated simply: Pause, Rest and Worship.

"What's that?" Evelyn asked. It was strange to see a sign like that in the middle of nowhere. What did it mean?

About a quarter mile down the road, we spotted a small white chapel sitting by itself in a field. As we drove past, we wondered: Who would build this tiny church out here—and why? We turned the truck around to find out.

As we started down the dusty trail and got closer, we noticed how small it really was. It wasn't much bigger than a playhouse, maybe eight feet across and twelve feet deep. There were little flowers planted around the outside and a little white cross was perched on top. There wasn't a sign or any literature telling us what it was called or describing its history. Was it in fact a church? Were we on private property? Should we be here? Would it be all right if we went inside?

Cautiously, we got out, looked around and walked toward the chapel's tiny door. It was open. We stepped inside.

There were four wooden pews, each would seat two people. I sat down. As I admired the simplicity and the beauty of the little chapel, I beheld its beautiful stained glass windows. A sense of profound calm came over me. All was quiet. Still. Peace.

I noticed a plaque hanging on the front wall. I got up and walked toward it. It was from the man who had built the chapel.

This was his farm. He had built this chapel to celebrate all of the many blessings that God had given him in his life. He had lived a very long and happy life, blessed with a wonderful wife, many healthy children and a farm where he had worked and lived.

On the altar at the front of the chapel lay a guest book with its pages open. Written at the top was a note: "Rest, pray, enjoy the chapel. Stay as long as you like."

As I turned the pages, I noticed the countries: Japan, Israel, France, Brazil . . . people from all over the world had found their way to this little white chapel.

I looked around for a place to leave a donation. There wasn't one. This man just wanted to share his special place with strangers who might need a brief respite on their long journey.

It has now been two years since my visit to the little chapel, and this is my first Christmas without my mother. I lost her last year to heart failure. We were very close and I miss her so very much.

As I was out shopping for presents, I suddenly stopped and the reality sunk in. Mom wasn't going to be here to get her present this year. She wasn't going to help me cook the turkey. She wasn't going to look across the table and smile at me as if to say everything would be all right.

I wanted to see her face when she opened up her gift. I wanted to cook with her and receive her warm smile. For the first time, I would spend this holiday without my mother, and it would be that way for the rest of my life. I was feeling very alone and wasn't sure how I was going to make it through the season.

At that moment, I looked up and right in front of me, on a display table, stood a small white ceramic chapel.

Immediately, I was taken back to my little white chapel in the dusty desert. Once again, I could feel the peace of its refuge, the strength of its love. I recalled the man who had built it out of gratitude for life's blessings, and then I remembered my own life's blessings. Suddenly, I felt myself smiling my mother's smile, and like the little chapel, I know that she, too, would always be there with me on my journey through life.

Dawn Rambin

The River of Life

Journeys bring power and love back into you.

Rumi

It was one of those picture-perfect days in south Louisiana. My husband, Milton, and I decided to ride our motorcycle in the unusually warm February weather. Mardi Gras in New Orleans can bring out the adventure in anyone, but that morning we wanted to escape the crush of crowds and drive away from the city.

The ferry ride across the Mississippi River was lovely, with a chill in the air and the sunny promise of warmer temperatures by midday. We were the last vehicle onboard as the ferry sounded its horn. Our motorcycle was ushered to the right of the large, flat boat. I watched the riverboat worker untie the enormous rope that fastened us to the dock and walked to the rail for a better view.

The Mississippi is as muddy as it's rumored to be, and I stared into the brown swirls. Debris was scattered as far as I could see, driftwood and seaweed floating among the waves.

We reached the levee on the west bank and I climbed on

the back of our Harley, hugging Milton's waist and happy to be on the road again.

Two children had also left their vehicle, and I heard their young voices call to their mother who motioned from a rusty pickup truck. "Let's watch 'em take off!" called the young girl to her older brother. I waved to them and gave her a thumbs-up sign. She rewarded me with a timid smile.

We cruised along at sixty-five miles an hour on the country highway past haunting bayous. Soon, the traffic began to resemble a rush-hour commute. A bend in the road revealed some Mardi Gras floats tying up the road.

"And we thought we were getting away from it all," I grumbled to my husband.

We explored the next small town, and I came upon a shop named Bryson's Angels. The fragrance of jasmine and roses enveloped me as I walked in. A lovely woman bid us welcome and, as I browsed around, I noticed a basket with purple cards that had a stylized drawing of an angel on the front. I casually picked one up, wondering what they were for.

The owner explained that there was a message on each card. I peeked at the one in my hand and felt myself tearing up as I read a wonderful message about being open and willing to fill the space within me with God's love.

Somehow the conversation turned to the history of this woman's shop.

"I was a social worker," she explained, "and five years ago something happened that changed my life. You see, my son died and. . ." She paused, searching for the words to continue.

"My name is Rose," I interjected softly. "What's yours?"

"I'm Lisa," she replied.

I took her hand. "You don't have to explain, Lisa. My daughter, Gina, died when she was three years old."

With that, we hugged each other and over the next while exchanged the kinds of details about our lives that only mothers who have known this kind of pain can express with an economy of words and an abundance of compassion in our eyes. We wanted each other to know about our lost children, to reach out and touch the places in our hearts where they reside, without disturbing the fabric of peace we had found.

Lisa explained that the shop's name, Bryson's Angels, was a combination of the names of her two children, Bryan and Jason. Then she offered me a card. Inside the card was a poem that began: "I'm standing upon the seashore; a ship at my side spreads her white sails to the morning breeze and starts for the blue ocean. . . ." The cover showed a small ship bobbing in the waves.

We gave each other one last hug and, in that moment, we both understood that Jason and Gina had arranged this meeting, steering us to meet on that day.

Riding home in the twilight, the wind dried the tears that stung my cheeks. Milton and I followed a winding road along the river, with the gentle levee to our left and beautiful plantation homes on our right. As we coasted along, I recalled the day, almost twenty years before, when I was staring out of a hospital room window at the same river some one hundred miles upstream. A nurse had told me the most horrific news of my life. My beloved daughter had passed away. I wanted to run from that room onto the levee, and drown myself in that rushing current.

But now, the feeling that Lisa and I had shared, that our children were waiting for us and guiding our paths, glowed in my heart. And I knew that there were angels along the river of life.

Rose Marie Sand

Seven Days and Seventy Miles

We must travel in the direction of our fear.

John Berryman

I approached the wooden suspension bridge with extreme caution while daring to view the fierce rapids below. My legs trembled as I crossed to safety on the other side praying that my guardian angel was sure-footed. It was a mission almost impossible, but I met the challenge with sheer will and determination to achieve my goal.

Nothing could have prepared me for the rugged terrain of Chile's Torres del Paine National Park in Patagonia. The unpredictable weather is notorious with fierce winds and temperatures that fluctuate from freezing to eighty-six degrees Fahrenheit. Steep rocky slopes, ankle-deep mud, entangling vines, fallen tree trunks, boulders, rapids and narrow mountain passes made me wish I had been born a combination monkey, mountain goat and pig. I asked myself why I was taking these risks reminiscent of an Indiana Jones escapade. But of course I knew the answer.

In February 1992, my seventy-three-year-old husband, Larry, was backpacking on his own through Torres del

Paine along this same seventy-mile loop. Larry loved the outdoors and often backpacked in the Sierra. Larry enjoyed challenges, whether in his career as a top sales- man for Pitney-Bowes, water skiing or backpacking in Africa or Indonesia. He was very enthusiastic about this trip, and I was eager to meet him, on February 11 in Santiago after he was finished, to continue touring together through Chile, Argentina and Brazil.

I arrived in Santiago as we had planned. Larry's sched- uled flight arrived, but Larry didn't show up. The travel agent checked the airline but found no record of him being on that flight. I contacted the American Embassy.

The park rangers began a search using military police and air force helicopters. For three long weeks of sleepless nights, loss of appetite and many anxious moments with- out hope, I remained in Santiago. With no sign of Larry, I returned to California. And then, on Friday the thirteenth of March, I received the telephone call: Larry's body had been found.

Two German hikers remembered talking to him and reported it to the American Embassy. The searchers con- centrated their search in that location until, eventually, he was found in a rocky area near the river. The cause of his death was never determined.

In the days and months that followed, I felt lost, over- flowing with questions that seemed destined to remain unanswered. I wanted to get a sense of what my husband was feeling in the minutes, hours and days before he had died. I wanted to see what he had seen and experience part of what he was seeking along the trail. I realized that I wanted to complete the hike Larry had begun and to visit the place where he had died.

I made arrangements for the seven-day trek with two guides, Roberto and his wife Berit, who had agreed to carry my packs for me and set up camp each day.

In February 1996, I began the journey back and, in many ways, forward.

The beginning of the hike was easy, through gentle farmlands surrounded by wildflowers and grazing. I soon realized that was only a teaser when, the following day, we traversed a narrow mountain pass where a hiker had been killed two years before. Berit helped me across this treacherous area. And then things got worse.

Next day the rain turned to sleet, and the path was dangerously muddy and slippery. I was very cold and began regretting my desire to make the trip. I was haunted by the memory of Larry's death while struggling through this horrendous day. Only my commitment to follow in Larry's footsteps kept me going.

The following day, after ascending cliffs and descending over rocks, we arrived at the spot where Larry's body was found. As I approached, I could picture Larry struggling in the difficult terrain. If only I could have been there to help him.

My adventure had been fraught with mixed emotions: saddened by Larry's loss, yet angered by his desire to attempt such a difficult hike alone. As I fought my way through the mud and vines, I thought of how exhausted he must have been at the same location burdened with his heavy pack. At times when I had to crawl over boulders, I wondered how he managed the task and marveled at his tenacity.

I created a makeshift marker out of some stones and lovingly placed pink wildflowers between them. I sat in silence, and soon my tears weren't of sadness but of joy in celebration of the wonderful life we had together. There was a sense of relief and contentment as Berit and Roberto hugged me.

I found myself fondly recalling the ways in which Larry had instilled in me his love of adventure as we traveled

throughout the world. When I married him, I didn't realize that I'd be like Jane to Larry's Tarzan when we visited
the jungles of French Guyana and Ecuador. When we
traveled by dugout canoe in torrential rains, battling
mosquitos to meet with Indian tribes and accompany
them on a blowgun hunt. In Rwanda, where we climbed
the Virunga Mountains to track mountain gorillas. In
Indonesia, where we watched Komodo dragons, the
world's largest monitor lizards, mating and fighting.

Perhaps this was why I had the courage to attempt this
most difficult of journeys on this, the fourth anniversary of
Larry's death and my sixty-fourth birthday—Valentine's
Day. From Larry, I had learned to persevere in difficult circumstances and to accept the challenges with a sense of
humor and always with a strong sense of adventure.

Now, I felt that I could hold his hand, at least spiritually,
and bid him farewell. Finally, I could move forward, grateful for where Larry's path had led me. This journey was a
summation of Larry's life spent tirelessly in pursuit of
challenges, both intellectually and physically with endless
enthusiasm. These seven days and seventy miles were a
tribute to Larry's boundless spirit.

I got up and started walking. From here the landscape
would become more rugged. Every muscle ached and I
was emotionally drained, but I knew I would reach the
end of this trail for Larry—and for me.

Adele Carney

A Place for Our Tomorrows

Light tomorrow with today.

Elizabeth Barrett Browning

In June 1987, just days after our sixteenth wedding anniversary, I was diagnosed with breast cancer. I was only thirty-seven years old and frightened.

What do you mean, I won't live forever? I still had a seven-year-old son to raise . . . and I'm not finished having children yet! How can the very thing that gave sustenance to my child now betray me?

We struggled with decisions and finally chose a radical mastectomy with elective chemotherapy. We put our faith in God's hands and prayed for a cure. My chances of survival were good, but we were wrought with the pain of wondering about our tomorrows.

Surgery went fine. Chemotherapy—well, what can anyone say about chemotherapy . . . it's a necessary evil, but a minor inconvenience in view of the other options. Slowly, the weeks became months, the months became years, and we tentatively celebrated each holiday and anniversary as it came along.

In April 1990, I was about to celebrate my fortieth birthday. I was always wary of birthdays but my husband Doug was different—he wanted to celebrate in grand style.

We flew out to Miami on Friday evening, and to my surprise, we were met at the airport by my dearest high school friend, Karen, who I had not seen in many years. We partied and stayed up well into the night. I was so happy to see her and very grateful to Doug for arranging this reunion.

The next morning we drove around "seeing the sights" and ended up down at the docks. We admired all the boats and especially the cruise liners. We boarded one of the ships and had our photographs taken onboard. We met the cruise director, and then Doug wandered off to check out the ship.

As the time drew closer for the ship to embark, we seemed to linger longer than I thought was safe.

"Come on, Honey, let's go," I implored.

"Just a minute, just a minute," he replied.

Many minutes later, the ship was just about to set out, and I was panicking to get us off before it left. As the last announcements were made for only passengers to remain on board, Doug smiled at me lovingly and said, "Don't worry, Dear, we're on the passenger list. Happy fortieth! Let's put our fears behind us and cruise into the future with abandonment!"

I didn't know what to say. This was his surprise gift to me.

Before leaving the ship, Karen presented me with a dozen roses to decorate our room and a bottle of champagne to toast to our new "beginning."

On our way to the Caribbean, Doug gave me daily gifts, gestures of his love—books of poems about the sea and music to celebrate the start of our carefree lives. For the formal gala, he surprised me on deck, looking handsome in a new tuxedo he had bought just for the occasion. That evening, I fell in even deeper love with my husband—this precious man whom I had known ever since we were high school sweethearts.

On our last night, we decided to savor our final tropical sunset. Doug collected the petals from Karen's roses, and I grabbed the bottle of champagne.

As we looked out toward the vast open sea, the wide and bountiful ocean of hope that lay ahead, we raised our glasses in a toast. We gathered some petals and cast our dreams into the wind.

Just at the moment when the flowers and glasses hit the water, a school of dolphins broke the surface and we felt a wondrous sense of release. Finally, we were free! We had thrown away our fear and pain, and found a place for our tomorrows.

Joyce Vullo

$\overline{6}$

ON LOVE

All travel is the exploration of love.

Duncan Fallowell

My Traveling Companion

Traveling in the company of those we love is home in motion.

Leigh Hunt

I've spent most of my career as a traveling salesman, and I know that there's nothing lonelier than a bunch of salesmen eating their meals in a motel coffee shop.

One year, my five-year-old daughter pressed a gift into my hands. The wrapping paper was all twisted, and it was bound together into a shapeless mass by at least a mile of tape.

I gave her a big hug and sloppy kiss—the kind that all daddies give—and proceeded to unwrap the little package she had bestowed on me. The contents hidden within felt kind of soft, and I was very careful not to cause any damage. With excitement radiating from her face, little brown-eyed Jeanine stood attentively beside me in her too-small pajamas while I completed the process of unraveling my surprise.

A pair of black, beady eyes peeked out from their papery hiding place, then a yellow beak, a red bow tie and orange feet. It was a stuffed toy penguin that stood about five inches tall.

Attached to its right wing with still wet paste was a tiny, wooden sign, and a hand-painted declaration, "I Love My Dad!" Beneath it was a hand-drawn heart, colored with crayon.

Tears welled up in my eyes and immediately I gave it a special place on my dresser.

Seldom did much time pass before I had to leave on another business trip. One morning when I was packing, I tossed the penguin in my suitcase. That night when I called home, Jeanine was very upset that the penguin had disappeared. "Honey, it's here with me," I explained. "I brought it along."

After that day, she always helped me pack, and saw to it that the penguin went in along with my socks and shaving kit. Many years have gone by since then, and that little penguin has traveled hundreds of thousands of miles all across America and over to Europe. And we have made many friends along the way.

In Albuquerque, I checked into a hotel, dumped out my bag and dashed to a meeting. When I returned, I found the bed turned down and the penguin propped up on the pillow.

In Boston, upon returning to my room one evening, I saw that somebody had perched it in an empty drinking glass on the nightstand—it never did stand up that well. The next morning I left it sitting in a chair. Again that night it was in the glass.

Once, at New York's Kennedy airport, a customs inspector coolly asked that I open my bag. And right there, on top, was my little pal. Holding it up, the agent quipped, "That's about the most valuable thing I have seen in all my years on the job. Thank God we don't charge tax on love."

Late one night, after driving over a hundred miles from my previous hotel, I unpacked my luggage only to discover that the penguin was missing.

Frantically, I phoned the hotel. The clerk was incredulous and a bit aloof. He laughed, saying it hadn't been reported. Nonetheless, a half hour later, he called back to say that my penguin had been found.

The time was late, but not that late. I got back in my car and drove the couple of hours to retrieve my two-toned touring buddy, arriving near midnight.

The penguin was waiting at the front desk. In the lobby, tired business travelers looked on at the reunion—I think with a touch of envy. A few of them came out to shake my hand. One man told me that he had even volunteered to deliver it to me the very next day.

Jeanine is in college now and I don't travel as much anymore. The penguin spends most of its time sitting on my dresser—a reminder that love is the best traveling companion. All those years on the road, it was the one thing I never left home without.

Edmund W. Boyle

Cycle of Love

*A journey is like a marriage. The certain way
to go wrong is to think you can control it.*

John Steinbeck

The moped wasn't much to look at, but it ran. The tires
were completely smooth, except for the occasional patch
of cord showing through. The front wheel was definitely
not round. The frame was rust and blue, and I could make
out remnants of a *P* and an *O*. It looked Italian—I figured
it had to be a *Piaggio.*

The agent in charge of the small stand of ancient
mopeds pulled the wooden plug out of the fuel tank,
peered in, sloshed the gas, and asked, "How far?"

"About an hour," I replied.

He laughed, slapped me on the back, and said, "Oh,
sure. You'll make it!"

And so I hopped on and began my two-wheeled exploration of Cuba, first inland, past green fields and skinny
cattle, then back toward the sea. Up the coast there was
supposed to be a quiet beach, but for a few miles I saw
nobody as I picked my way through sand and around

potholes. Encountering an ancient flatbed truck headed the other way, I waved at the half-dozen people hitching a ride aboard it. A couple of them politely waved back.

When I passed a small group of pedestrians, they laughingly hailed me in Spanish, wanting a ride. But I doubted my rattling steed could carry another pound, so I declined with a nod and puttered on.

I rounded one corner to find a strange apparition floating toward me. It looked like three farmers and a bushel basket of fruit levitating on a light blue cushion of air. When they got closer, I realized they were all piled onto a moped remarkably similar to mine, but older and going faster. Suddenly I felt stingy about having refused pedestrians a ride in this land of poverty and gracious manners.

There was a beautiful beach at the end of the road, a deserted one: sand, sky, trees, ocean, birds and total silence. For the hundredth time since coming to this island, I wished that I could paint. Eventually, I turned the moped around and headed back the way I'd come.

At a villa, two women smiled and waved for a ride. But between the two of them and their burdens they probably topped four hundred pounds, so I just smiled back and puttered past.

Onward the *Piaggio* grumbled, and then I saw her. A white blouse, shoulder bag, sandals and a thousand-watt smile. She was beautiful. She waved for a ride, and I stopped like what I was—a man entranced.

She laughed and ran up. I hadn't really considered where I might put a passenger on the rattling contraption, and I greeted her in masterful and eloquent English: "Hi . . . er . . . hello . . . umm . . . I'm not really sure where you can sit. . . ."

She laughed and chatted for a bit in the most musical Spanish. I didn't understand a word. To be honest, it didn't matter. It was the way she smiled, the way she moved those brown hands and arms while she talked, and those laughing dark eyes. I would have listened to her happily all afternoon.

She sat down on the rack and put her arms around my waist. My brain short-circuited, but I applied the throttle and set off.

I wrote those next fifteen minutes into my memory with indelible ink. I pressed on between sea and greenery with her arms around me. She laughed and waved to friends and pointed out sights in Spanish. Conscious of her precarious perch, I picked my way around the most obvious road hazards and kept the speed down.

All too soon, I felt a pat on my shoulder and saw her arm point to an apartment complex festooned with laundry. I slowed to a stop, and she got off and stood beside me. She was looking for words with which to say good-bye. I took off my cap and stuck it on her dark curly hair.

"See you later!" I said. But I never saw her again.

I don't remember the rest of the ride, except that the *Piaggio* made it back on whatever fueled its faithful soul.

"How was your ride?" my wife asked when I returned.

I am intrinsically an honest man, but pragmatism ruled my decision; no way was I going to tell my wife of sixteen years the whole truth about my motorcycle excursion.

"It was fun . . . roughly what you'd expect," I replied, trying to sound relaxed, even bored.

"Where's your hat?" she asked with uncanny perception.

Shamefaced, I told her the whole story. She laughed and teased me, and made me a tall Cuba libre with real Cuban rum. We reminisced about the year we met and the carefree summer we spent rambling around southern Ontario on my old Honda. We remembered the reasons we married and found some new reasons why we stay that way.

We left Cuba warmer, wiser and younger. I had found a new love, lost it and renewed an old love. And none of it might have happened without that *Piaggio*.

Felix Winkelaar

Bill

I would love you all the day, every night we would kiss and play, if with me you'd fondly stray, over the hills and far away.

John Gray

It began on board a luxury 104-foot trimaran called *Cuan Law.* I had an assignment to write a story on scuba diving and bicycling in the British Virgin Islands.

The enchantment of these romantic isles took over the instant I bounced down the rollaway steps of the little prop plane that brought me to Beef Island from San Juan, Puerto Rico. The night air was pleasantly humid with the fragrance of exotic flowers whose names I knew only from perfume bottles. Beneath the lilting dialogue of the baggage crew, the hums, buzzes, chirps and whirs of night creatures gave exotic mystery to the dark.

Outside the tiny terminal, a lanky islander in a white shirt over neatly pressed khakis pushed himself away from a van and approached me with a smile.

"Hey, Miss, you be goin' to de *Cuan Law?*"

At my nod he swooped up my duffles and gestured toward the van.

Moments later, I could see a rubber inflatable raft tied to a small cement dock. A tan, blond fellow in shorts barely long enough to be decent greeted me with a smile, accepted my luggage from the driver, handed me into the raft and pointed it toward a string of lights in the bay.

He said his name was Bill.

Within minutes I was being welcomed aboard the largest trimaran I'd ever seen. Scuba tanks were neatly arranged on the deck, mountain bikes leaned against safety lines, and Japanese lanterns cast soft shadows on padded benches and varnished tables. Inside, a half-dozen people lounged in the large saloon, sipping drinks and chatting. Bill introduced me to the group, then wrestled my duffles to my cabin.

In the days that followed I got to know a couple from Tennessee, a pair of doctors from Texas, a single accountant from Minneapolis and Bill.

At first he was just one of six crew members aboard *Cuan Law*, helping me into my dive gear and leading dives. He'd point out creatures that I would have missed, like a palm-size octopus and needle-like trumpet fish. Mornings often were spent ashore on mountain bikes, exploring tiny back roads clogged with herds of goats, passing cheering children who thought the safety flags on our bikes meant we were in a race.

I soon became aware that Bill remembered that my dive vest was the pink one, and that I preferred white wine as a before-dinner cocktail. During one particular bike ride, when we found ourselves separated from the rest of the group, Bill volunteered that he had "run away from home" and a confining eight-to-five job in the Midwest. He was fulfilling a dream of living on the Caribbean and doing as much diving as possible. He'd been on the boat just over a year, and he loved it.

We exchanged tales about my nomadic life as a travel writer and his duties as a dive instructor and paramedic. After dinners served *alfresco,* we fell into a pattern of meeting on deck when Bill finished work. With others murmuring in the darkness around us, we'd gaze skyward, vying to identify amazingly brilliant constellations undimmed by city lights or pollution. The warm Caribbean breeze caressed us, making it inevitable that we would end up together.

In the days that followed we became better acquainted, sharing moments and experiences without any frantic necessity to cement a bond. On the Saturday that I left, Bill shouldered my duffles and dropped them in the dinghy. We talked of writing and keeping in touch. But I was certain that after a few postcards or perhaps a phone call or two, the friendship would fade into a lovely memory of a delightfully shared week.

Back in Los Angeles, I wrote my thank-you to the yacht's owners, enclosing an envelope for Bill with snapshots we'd taken while I was there. One Sunday morning several weeks later I received a phone call from a rushed-but-cheerful Bill, who'd managed to sneak a moment from the precious few he had ashore to get in touch with me. I was surprised at how glad I was to hear his voice.

Shortly after that, I received a small package from the British Virgin Islands marked fragile. Slowly and carefully, I unwrapped its contents to find a perfectly formed shell swathed in cotton. Wrapped in tissue inside the shell were a pair of tiny gold earrings in the shape of the shell. For the first time, I let myself realize that this was more than a friendship.

To facilitate the long-distance courtship, Bill began recording audio tapes and sending them to me once a week. He suggested I do the same. Telephone communication, besides being expensive, was difficult because Bill's time ashore usually involved greeting guests and bringing them aboard, leaving little time for personal pursuits. There was no phone on the boat. The tapes filled in the gaps, and helped us learn about each other's families and backgrounds.

Four months after I had returned home, Bill announced on one of his tapes that he had three weeks off, during which he intended to visit his parents in Florida. He also wanted to spend some time with me in Los Angeles.

While I was enjoying our fun-from-afar relationship, I was uneasy about anything closer. As the survivor of a previous long-term relationship, now ended, I was fearful of anything that even hinted of commitment. I used the excuse of travel assignments to gently say no. Bill was disappointed, but accepted my reply optimistically.

During his Florida vacation, we talked often. I met his parents by long distance and wondered if I'd made a mistake in telling him not to come. By the time he was back on the boat and our blizzard of letters and tapes had resumed, I knew that he'd be welcome in Los Angeles the next time he asked.

It was ten months between the time I said good-bye to Bill on *Cuan Law* and when I picked him up at Los Angeles International Airport, he was as tan and blond and blue-eyed as I had remembered. We'd decided to spend five days of his thirty-day vacation together to see how things went. As it turned out, one month was not enough.

Before he went back, Bill decided to leave the boat when his contract expired and move to Los Angeles. Within six months of his return, we were engaged, and the following June we were married. We honeymooned aboard *Cuan Law*.

If it hadn't been for my incurable wanderlust, I never would have met my husband. If it hadn't been for his patience, ingenuity and inventive communication techniques, we never would have gotten together. If it hadn't been for the gentle charms of the Caribbean, I'd probably still be single.

The very things that attracted me to Bill for a shipboard romance were what seemed to make him unsuitable as a permanent mate. China blue eyes, sun-blond hair, an all-over tan and a nomadic lifestyle? *Hardly the stuff on which to base anything long-term,* I kept telling myself.

We recently celebrated our ninth wedding anniversary. Thankfully, Bill was smarter about relationships than I.

Judy Wade

Moses pens his personal ad.

Love on the Edge of the Grand Canyon

Sometimes things happen to bring people closer for other reasons altogether.

Christopher John Campbell

I was seven when Jane Chaddock Davenport reached ninety. She was my great-grandmother, a beautiful woman with large violet eyes, exquisitely groomed white hair, and magnificent hands, veined and transparent, which she enhanced with antique rings. She gave me one, an oblong purple amethyst set in heavy gold, which I love more as I get older. She wore brocade dresses with lace petticoats. The shoes on her little feet always matched her satin hair bands.

She liked to talk to me. I loved to listen. She told me many things, once about a love affair she had years earlier "on the edge of the Grand Canyon." She explained that she was much younger then—only seventy-four.

"On the very edge," she repeated in her crystal-clear, yet moss-soft voice. "It was very romantic. I looked straight down the canyon walls—a thousand miles below. We were passionate then and unafraid, being young."

At the time, I had no idea what she was talking about. I only imagined my exquisite and delicate great-grand-mother in passionate embrace with a mysterious stranger on the very rim of the Grand Canyon, while a sunset of glorious oranges and golds spread across a darkening vastness. Holding hands, they dangled their feet over the edge, rapt in beauty. Then, when there was only black and silver and silence all around, they made love.

Many years later, my husband Alex and I were on our honeymoon, driving across the West. Late one afternoon, we found ourselves at the entrance to Grand Canyon National Park, and we decided to stay the night.

We followed the signs to the central complex, where a new hotel blazed in the center of what seemed to be a parking lot. Newly arriving travelers, all with reservations, crowded the lobby. The harried man at the desk was sorry, but there were no more rooms.

"I know that hotels always have an extra room for an emergency," Alex insisted. "Say a VIP arrives unexpect-edly. Give us that room and we'll pay for it." Alex was in no mood to drive any farther.

"Sir, we would give you a proper room if we had one. But we have only one room left, one we never rent any-more. It is in the Old Inn, and people don't like it, so we don't bother to show it."

"Sounds perfect," Alex said.

A bellboy called ahead and then, gathering our bags, led us to the Old Inn. We followed him through its lovely old lobby and then down the corridors to the back of the building. We finally arrived at our room, its dimensions worthy of the Grand Canyon. The bedroom was the size of a ballroom, and the bathroom was as big as your run-of-the-mill living room. The tub itself was about seven feet long and four deep.

Everything was ready for us by the time we got there:

large towels in the bathroom, bed turned down, curtains pulled. A fire had been lit and was burning cheerfully. The room was large but had a cozy feel to it: natural wood, green-and-white chintz and an antique silver mirror over the dressing table.

"Nothing wrong with this," I said.

The bellboy silently accepted his tip, put another log on the fire and left us.

I decided to take a hot tub. It took some time to fill, but soon the heat was loosening the tensions of the day. After a while, I remembered the sunset.

The window was right beside the tub. I only had to pull back the curtain and look out: sky orange and gold, shot through with giant splashes of green and purple. A star. A half-moon, green in the golden air. I looked over to the far side of the Grandest Canyon of them all. The edge was still visible. My eyes climbed slowly down to a silver ribbon, running in the already black canyon bottom. I got up on my knees to see better and gasped.

Grabbing a thick towel, I tumbled out of the bath and ran into the bedroom. Our bed was set right against an enormous window. I jumped on it and threw open the curtains. Sure enough, the bed, too, was right over the canyon.

I knew immediately that this had been my great-grandmother's room all those years ago.

Speechless, I beckoned Alex. The pull of the dreadful height got to us. We lay on our stomachs to look. There was no rim on this side—nothing between us and the bottom. Only an awesome down. "Down a thousand miles," as my great-grandmother had described.

Alex looked at me and I looked at him.

That evening, we left the curtain open, and looked out and then down, straight down, as Great-grandmother Jane and her lover had done, on the very edge of the Grand Canyon.

Jane Winslow Eliot

Our Contingency Plan

Travel is more than the seeing of sights; it is a change that goes on, deep and permanent, in the ideas of living.

Miriam Beard

Our long-anticipated trip to explore America began leisurely in early August. Driving Highway 2 from Montana, we'd mosey to Niagara Falls, weave into southeastern Canada, and meander south to Key West. Then we'd zigzag across the southern states, and see the West coast before springtime tugged us home. We were confident. Forty years of marriage and eighty-five thousand miles of travel in our twenty-foot RV proved that we could conquer the challenges. Weren't we dreaming of seeing the same things and enjoying togetherness?

Before we left home, friends teased us, "If you have an argument, there's only your three-by-four bathroom to get away from each other."

We laughed, "We have a 'contingency plan.' If either of us tires of traveling, we've agreed to come home. We'll never be more than two weeks away."

Ever-changing vistas and interesting destinations constantly delighted us, and frequent phone calls eased homesickness. Our Montana license plates held a mystique, drawing people to us like bees to honey. But we always hurried onward to find the highlights I'd compiled in twenty-two pages of single-spaced, typewritten research.

Art found antique merry-go-rounds for me to ride. I felt like a teenager as he proudly gave me the huge stuffed animal he'd won at a county fair arcade. Exploring museums and joining square dance groups had mitigated our "togetherness." Yet after scarcely ten weeks, I was ready for that "contingency plan."

While I prefer to think that I'm a planner and organizer, Art claims that I'm just plain bossy. A little praise for my growing skills at map-reading might have cheered me up. Instead, we often went astray when he didn't follow my "navigation" suggestions.

Art's favorite part of the day was his midmorning stop at roadside coffee shops or quaint diners. I gained unwanted pounds so he could eavesdrop shamelessly.

As we bypassed historic sites on my list like lighthouses and Hyde Park, I became less content to say, "Oh, well, we can't see them all." Impatiently he hastened us onward.

By sunset each day, our RV neighbored up with other RVs, often like the junior cousin beside a really big motorhome. We enjoyed the evening campfires, swapping yarns and information with eager strangers. But the next morning, I regretted leaving behind those one-night friendships.

When we missed the witchcraft history of Salem, Massachusetts, because he zoomed past the off-ramp, I hunched over the atlas in the bathroom that night, plotting a route home.

"Just think, within six days we can be back in our normal routine," I said over breakfast.

Realizing that I wanted to turn homeward that very day he said, "No way!"

"I'm sick of laundromats and moving every day and weird traffic directions. I don't even get to decide when to cook or when to go to the bathroom!" Bottled up resentments rushed in a torrent. "I want to do things my way. At my speed. Why can't we stop in one place for a week?"

"Be sensible," he said. "What about Gettysburg and Harpers Ferry? I thought you wanted to see the Blue Ridge Mountains and the Everglades?"

"I don't care anymore! I'm sick of coffee breaks, donuts and sweet rolls, and moving, moving, moving! I'm ready to go home!"

"You wanted to visit an antebellum plantation. And snorkel in Florida. And pick up seashells."

"What about our agreement?" I asked.

"I'm seeing New Orleans," he declared, as I scrambled to get my seat belt buckled.

We headed south from the beautiful campground, sunshine splashing our windshield, silence shrouding us. Before midmorning coffee time, Art spotted a flea market. Like a homing pigeon, our RV scrunched the gravelly road and was parked.

"Want to go have a look?" he asked sheepishly.

Before I could decline, he was already striding toward a table piled with hand tools. Grudgingly I followed. No longer an avid tourist eagerly inspecting treasures and trash, I'd become a cynical soul, wallowing in self-pity.

And then a small, plastic sculpture of a little boy and a little girl looking at each other with love-struck awe caught my eye. How dare they try to attract me? Today I didn't believe in love, and this flea market wasn't my idea of a lover's lane.

But five words printed on the statue's base stopped me, and I started giggling. I paid the owner and quickly caught up with Art, handing him my treasure. His puzzled frown eased. We grinned and read the words aloud: *"Together we can make it."*

Scrapping our contingency plan, we started a new morning ritual. Linking hands, we gazed at that statue sitting sublimely on the RV's dashboard, and repeated its message—"Together we can make it"—sometimes confidently, other times questionably, but always with hope in our hearts.

Ten years later we still have the statue, our memories and each other. "Together we can make it." Anytime, anywhere, in our RV.

Mona Leeson Vanek

"If we had followed the yellow brick road,
we'd have been to Oz hours ago. But *noooo*!
We just *had* to listen to someone without a brain
who *insisted* he knew a shortcut!"

A Fair Price

There are two ways of spreading light: to be the candle or the mirror that reflects it.

Edith Wharton

A few years ago, as a college student, I journeyed to Kenya on a mission team with a social service organization. The goal for the ten of us was to construct a school classroom for a Masai village and to share crafts, games and skits with the local Masai children.

None of us had ever traveled to Africa before, and the deep colors and vibrancy of the landscape and people made a profound impression. We visited Lake Nakuru, which blazed pink from thousands of teeming flamingos, gazed at the infinite abyss of the Great Rift Valley, felt the dust rise up from stampeding game through the plains of Masai Mara, and jangled our teeth and bones loose riding in the back of our van across the cratered, red dirt roads.

Our driver, Frances, was a black-skinned Masai man with a brilliant smile and tumbling laugh. Often he would stop to show us a puff adder or flame tree, and his knowledge of wildlife and tribal politics created a window for us into local culture.

On a typical day Frances would deliver us safely to the Masai compound where we worked. Each morning, hundreds of blue- and red-sweatered children lined the roads, clapping and singing as our van rumbled up the hill. In the afternoon, our team swung hammers and hauled sheet metal up rickety scaffolding. Slowly, our classroom began to take shape.

One evening, Frances needed to deliver a Masai chief to the local hospital clinic and asked if anyone wanted to accompany him. I volunteered, and once our errand was completed, we began the fifty-minute journey back into town. I knew Frances was married and asked him how he had first met his wife.

"I was fifteen years old when I first met Mary," he told me. "She was collecting water at the town well with the other women. I was with my friends and showed off in front of her as boys do, but we never spoke. The first time I saw her I thought she was an angel. She was so beautiful, and her smile lit up everything and everyone around her."

He paused to hide a smile of his own before he went on.

"The problem was that Mary is a Kikuyu, and I am a Masai. The two tribes have a history of hatred and bloodbaths. They do not intermarry or trust each other. They do not even speak."

He explained that two years went by before he saw Mary again. He was then seventeen years old and about to leave for Nairobi to attend the schoolteachers' college. They spoke for a long time. He wanted to ask where she stayed so that he would not lose her again, but he admitted that his ego got in the way. Instead, he decided to give her his address in Nairobi feeling that if she really liked him she would write.

She did.

After two years of correspondence, they loved each other deeply and wanted to get married, but both of them worried that their families and tribes would shun them for their relationship. Nevertheless, with great humbleness and anxiety, Frances approached her parents to ask how much of a bride-price they wanted for her.

In Kenya a bride-price, or dowry, is often the only means a family has to gain wealth. A healthy, hard-working female might bring many cows. Status is very important.

He was nervous and said, "I am just a poor school-teacher, and I haven't much money. But I love your daughter and want to marry her. I will pay anything you ask."

Mary's parents looked at him and replied, "There is much to do to plan a wedding. This is a celebration! We will discuss the bride-price when the two of you are settled."

Frances smiled at me as we rounded a bend and braked for a herd of skinny cattle. His eyes shone in remembrance as he continued, "That was unheard of. A marriage *never* occurs without payment first. And between Kikuyus and Masais . . . it was an exceptional situation."

A year went by before they had their first child. He returned to Mary's parents and again inquired of the bride-price. As he and Mary were so busy with a new baby, they told him that he should wait until things calmed down a bit.

Several more years passed, and they had another child. He returned again to Mary's parents and insisted that he needed to settle his debt. Once again, he said that he was a poor schoolteacher without much money, but that he was so happy and in love that he would pay anything.

Mary's mother asked him, "What do you think is a fair price?"

Frances laughed and replied as a joke, "A lifetime of love and devotion from your loyal son-in-law!"

Mary's mother smiled softly and whispered, "It is enough. The bride-price has been paid."

Frances was silent for a time, and tears spilled over his cheeks as he drove.

"Have you ever told your wife exactly how you feel?" I asked suddenly. "Have you ever said, 'The first time I saw you I thought you were an angel. You were so beautiful . . .'"

Frances snorted. "Of course not! Masai men don't talk like that. All women know if they're beautiful. They just need to look in a mirror. Besides, we've been married now for fifteen years. It would be silly to bring all that up now."

"Frances!" I exclaimed. "You have to tell her. Especially if you've been married so long. Can you imagine the look on her face if you walked in one day and said, 'Listen, Mary . . .'"

Frances shook his head. While he had been so open, perhaps I had overstepped the boundaries. Suddenly my ideals and youthful romanticism collided sharply with the ways of east Africa. We rode the rest of the trip in strained silence.

For the last days of my stay, Frances was cool and didn't have much to say to me. I wanted to break the ice but thought that perhaps I had already said enough.

As our mission team waited to clear customs in the Nairobi airport, a commotion broke out as a man ran toward us. "Kristie!" he called out. "Is there someone here named Kristie?"

I turned around and faced the stranger with surprise.

"I have a message to you from Frances," he panted. "He says to tell you that he talked with his wife . . ."

Kristie McLean

L'Air du Temps

Think not that you can direct the course of love;
for love . . . directs your course.

Kahlil Gibran

In the picture, the one my ex-husband's girlfriend ripped in half, I am wearing a white blouse and yellow gathered skirt that billows over full petticoats like an open parasol. I am sitting on the edge of a fountain in Paris, and I'm laughing—laughing because I've had a summer of freedom, I'm seventeen and I'm in love with the boy taking the picture. And we're in Paris.

I wonder about the petticoats. I don't remember packing them into that heavy, brown leather suitcase I lugged all summer, but the picture says I did. Surely I didn't starch and iron them, as fashion required back in 1955, to make the pastel skirts appear to float. Where would I have found the starch and the iron? Yet there I am, fluffy as a peony.

With every step the boy and I took, wandering the Latin Quarter, drenched in romance and innocence, we sealed our fate. I had my first taste of champagne and watched a dancer swathed in leopard skin slither across the stage of the Moulin Rouge.

That evening I wore the pink linen dress my mother had made with loving care before she sent me off to a summer in Europe, thinking I would be protected from change because I was part of such a trustworthy, well-escorted group of students. The dress was so tight around the waist—stitched so at my insistence—that I could take only shallow breaths, and I never wore it again.

I had arrived in Paris on a train of World War II vintage, crouching in the dust under the compartment's wooden seat. Sheltered by my friends' legs and blankets, I rode there all night, cramped and drowsy as the wheels clickety-clacked over the rails of western Europe. I was hiding from the conductor because I had lost both my passport and my train ticket from Copenhagen. As the train rolled into the old, echoey, smoky station and my friends whispered that the coast was clear, I crawled out and stretched, giggling. "Anybody got a comb?"

One girl rummaged in her purse and pulled out a handful of papers. "Look at this! Your passport and tickets! I had them all along."

I laughed. What did I care about inconvenience? This was adventure—and Paris.

On the Champs Elysées, the boy and I walked for miles, dodging traffic as if we were citywise, rather than small-town kids who'd never been anywhere. We climbed the Eiffel Tower, gazed at the Seine, watched the torch lighting at the Arc de Triomphe tomb, ate *jambon* and *fromage* and ice cream at sidewalk cafés. We tossed coins in every fountain we saw, always with a wish to return.

With the last of my money, I bought a miniscule bottle of perfume, L'Air du Temps. By dabbing my wrist sparingly, and only on special occasions, I made it last for months.

We went to the Louvre, and the boy sang, "Venus de Milo was noted for her charms, but strictly between us, you're cuter than Venus, and what's more you've got arms . . ." I thought it was charming.

He saved the champagne bottle from the Moulin Rouge, and when we were aboard the ocean liner sailing home, far out to sea, he wrote our names on a paper, put it in the bottle and corked it. Then he tossed it overboard—and kissed me. I was dazzled.

Many years have gone by. The boy and I got married, and after nineteen years and four daughters, we ended up in a bitter divorce.

But the girl in the snapshot, the one my ex-husband's girlfriend ripped in half, doesn't see that. She's dazzled by a future that shimmers bright as the fountain spraying behind her. All the tears and pain destined to divide us lie ahead—and yet I wouldn't change a thing.

Because, once in a while, I catch the scent in a perfume shop or from someone walking by. I recognize it instantly and smile. It's L'Air du Temps, and I'm in Paris again, and seventeen.

Marilyn McFarlane

CLOSE TO HOME   JOHN McPHERSON

"Roger, never mind! I found the airline tickets under my blouse on the bed!"

A Gallic Good-Bye

I haven't had a perfect moment yet, and I always like to have one before I leave an exotic place. . . . But you can never plan for one. You never know when they're coming.

Spalding Gray

It must be genetic with French men. No matter what their station in life, they all seem to be capable of the grand romantic gesture.

Late one afternoon I stood on the deck of a large cruise ship docked in Marseilles as passengers toting parcels streamed back aboard chatting about their day in port. Two aproned French women, one bent with age, sold fresh irises and lilies from large buckets next to the gangway. Children deftly steered bicycles among cargo stacked on the quay that was waiting to be hooked by a large crane and swung into an open hold.

As I leaned against the ship's rail, mildly engrossed in the busy scene, I watched the dark-eyed operator in his little enclosed cubicle atop the crane. Skillfully he handled the levers that caused it to swing into position. After a moment his glance took me in. On the next pass, the glance was accompanied by a smile. I smiled back. Between maneuvers he managed to doff his beret. I waved. He blew a kiss. I caught it in my heart.

While he worked, I watched, smiles and mouthed kisses flying back and forth in a flirtatious game. By the time he deposited the remaining bulky bale into the hold, our eyes were inseparable. And then the sharp blast of the ship's whistle said it was time to go. The last passengers straggled aboard and the gangway was removed. I felt a little stab of sadness as he turned the crane away with never a backward look.

Then suddenly he swung the giant hook down to the quay one last time, near to the old flower women. As they looked up, he called out and waved a fistful of francs. Quickly the pair put the remaining flowers in a single bucket and looped its handle over the crane's hook. With the ship inching away from the quay, he swung the bucket of flowers to the liner's rail and presented them to me.

Thrilled, I cradled the blue bundle against my yellow summer dress as a tear slid into my smile. He grinned and then waved one last time, before our ship slipped sweetly into the twilight.

Judy Wade

"Mom, when we go to Europe can we just
skip the history?"

Travels with Mama in the Old Country

You will find as you look back upon your life that the moments when you have truly lived are the moments when you have done things in the spirit of love.

Henry Drummond

"*Ciao*, Cecilia," shouted my mother, as we looked down across the steep vineyard. "Where are you?" she cried in Italian.

A door from a lone hut nearly lost in the great green vines opened. A humped figure dressed in black waved. Her dress was muddy, her shoes torn. At ninety, this frail woman still worked among the grapes of Massa Marittima, the Tuscan hill town where my mother was born. She hobbled towards us, leaning deftly into her cane.

"*Bella, cara, tesoro,*" said this strange bundle of crumpled black reaching up to caress my face. She was calling me "beautiful, dear, treasure." I bent down to kiss my great aunt. Once, more than half a century ago, she had held my mother's little-girl hand in the piazza. Now, her hand clasped mine.

In the days that would follow, many more hands would clutch mine and lovingly stroke my face. My mother had finally lured me to Italy to meet the relatives. At the time, I was twenty-three and not particularly keen about vacationing with my mother in the old country. But when she insisted on paying my way, I could scarcely resist. And I was at least faintly curious about her place of birth.

My mother, the fifth of seven children, was christened Ida Pia Elica Elena Ornella Androvandi. Honestly, she does have all those names. As a child, I used to impress friends by rattling off her name-litany as a tongue twister. But that was all that I'd concede was different about my mom. I preferred her to be 100 percent American, not Italian-American, as she would identify herself.

I never could understand why she was, well, so darn Italian. You know, kissing everyone and making such a big fuss about the family. As for all these people back in Italy with odd names—they were her relatives, not mine.

Her childhood had been so poor: not enough to eat, living in two small rooms, no running water, no electricity, only owning two dresses and no other outfits when my grandmother took her brood to a new life in America.

They had settled in southern Illinois in 1923, where my grandfather had been working in a coal mine for several years. In this "New World," my mother, at age nine, had enough to eat but not much more. In all her girlhood, she never had even one doll, ever—a fact she told me every time she reminisced about her childhood.

I, in contrast, had a new doll every Christmas. My growing-up was a carefree and secure existence with two younger sisters and a brother in a well-off Milwaukee suburb.

"Joy-a, get into the car." After only one day in Italy, Mother had taken to pronouncing my name Italian-style. "We're going to drive Cecilia back to Massa Marittima and then meet your Aunt Anita." She was in her element. At last, she was opening the doors of her childhood to me. Clearly, Mother was in command.

For one thing, she knew the language. I didn't. What's more, people in Massa Marittima treated her like visiting royalty, hugging and kissing her, calling her name as she walked the cobbled streets, bringing her gifts of welcome. She'd been back several times and had become a kind of town heroine. And because I was her daughter, I, too, was instantly beloved.

I was impressed.

I was also astonished by the beauty of Massa Marittima, a walled, medieval stone city teeming with arches, alleyways, stepped passages, red-tiled roofs, green shutters and wrought iron balconies rimmed with flower pots. Below, olive groves, vineyards and wheat fields reached ten miles to the Mediterranean Sea.

Massa, as locals call their hometown of ten thousand, was immaculate, just like my mother's house in America. And many of its people had her same handsome features: fine bones, narrow hips, straight noses, blue eyes, smooth light-olive skin. And the women, petite like her, were "dressed to kill," as mother says and does. That meant looking *molto bella*," especially when promenading arm-in-arm in the piazza at dusk. "All eyes notice you here," Mother warned, frowning at my Bermuda shorts and tennis shoes as we strolled into the main square.

How proudly she showed me the nooks and crannies of her memories—the big stone basins at the foot of the hill where she washed clothes as a small girl, the huge clock tower with its sweeping view of the valley—and her favorite place of play, the so-called "Five-Hundred Steps," a steep, wide passageway leading to the new city.

And then, of course, there were all the *parenti*—relatives.

Each morning over cappuccino in the piazza, we'd review who was who.

"Let's see," I mused, "the old woman in the hospital with the broken hip is Maria, another great aunt. Narciso is the man with the little farm who gave rabbits to GIs during World War II. He's your cousin and, therefore, my second cousin."

"No, no," she interrupted. "In Italy, you don't have second or third cousins—just cousins."

Before long, the names of my mother's relatives no longer sounded so foreign, Mazzini, Liana, Sergio, Cesare, Bruno, Fulvia, Nuncia and a whole string of others were now my family, too. I liked having an Italian-American mamma. In Massa Marittima, she was bequeathing me my inheritance.

One day, my mother announced she had something special to show me—the tiny two-room apartment where she had lived with her four cousins and two brothers. It was on the fourth floor of a run-down building at the end of Via Bogetto, an area where the poor miners lived when my grandfather was a young man.

"We're lucky," she said. "The rooms aren't occupied. They're going to be renovated." She opened the door. "This is where I took my very first breath," she said excitedly.

I entered cautiously, not anxious to confront what I thought were bleak memories. There they were: the walls and floors of my mother's childhood, as dark and dreary as I had imagined. And here was the hearth where she severely burned her elbow, and the tiny back window where my grandmother sat wet-nursing other women's babies to earn a few lire.

I couldn't wait to get out, to leave this moldering old building that testified to my mother's dismal start.

Yet my mother lingered cheerfully, recalling instead

games she had played with her "toys"—pebbles from the street—and the good minestrone her mother cooked and how all her sisters and brothers giggled together on one mattress. Finally, outside again in the bright, fresh air that was Massa, she sighed happily. "It's fine to return to the past, but I live for today," she said simply. *"Andiamo!"* Let's go.

My mother is now seventy-something and still, like me, making almost annual pilgrimages back to Massa. She remains a happy woman, full of life and Italian embraces. In fact, in all the years that I've known her, I've only seen her cry once.

It happened about a year ago, on her birthday, when I gave her a present I had bought in Italy. When she saw what was in the box, tenderly she lifted the gift and clutched it to her breast. *"Bella, bella,"* she murmured tearfully over and over.

At last, my mother had a doll.

Joy Schaleben Lewis

7

A MATTER OF PERSPECTIVE

Traveling does what good novelists do to the life of the everyday, placing it like a picture in a frame or a gem in its setting, so that the intrinsic qualities are made more clear.

Freya Stark

The Real Hero

It is Day 118, and I am alone in the middle of the Pacific Ocean aboard my vessel *Reach*, attempting to be the first person to row around the world. Heading westward from California, I have covered almost five thousand miles so far and the closest person to me now is probably a thousand miles away.

I am being tossed around in my small cabin, hunched over my laptop computer. Sweat drips from my forehead onto the keyboard as I wait for the satellite terminal to download an incoming message from my wife Stacia, sharing a few warm adventures of our two-year-old twin daughters back home.

During these thirty seconds of download time, I am usually like a six-year-old on Christmas morning. But today is different. I am wallowing in self-pity.

As the "RECV DATA MSG" light continues to blink, I begin a mental list of the things I want to lament about: sun blisters, unfavorable currents and winds, jellyfish stings, saltwater sores, burning wrist and elbow joints, sleep deprivation and the ever-present loneliness. I can chew on any one of these and feel the strength seep out of my body. I hear it escaping like a deflating bicycle tire.

It feels good to whine, even though I know that the boat will feel twice as heavy to row and it will be much harder to sleep.

I shake my head back and forth as I glance up for reassurance at the five words I scribbled above the hatchway with a blue indelible marker, "You Chose To Be Here." That doesn't help. In fact, I feel worse. Probably because it's reminding me that I can choose my own attitude right now, and right at this moment, I feel like simmering in my self-pity.

The light stops blinking. Finally, I can open up the file. It is the expected message from Stacia, but it contains something extra, an additional message from a couple in Chicago, sent to her and now forwarded onto me. Tossed around in water four miles deep, I read on:

> *I saw your story on television and find your spirit incredible. My wife is in the hospital and it has been a good escape to follow your progress while she is having a bone marrow transplant. We find inspiration in your journey, and we pray for you daily. Best of luck.*
>
> *Rick and Susan*

Find *my* spirit incredible? Find inspiration in *my* journey? Wishing me luck?

I can't believe it. There is a woman I don't know across the Pacific Ocean, past the railroad tracks and wheat fields, lying in a hospital bed on probably the most frightening and threatening journey of her life. Yet she and her husband are gathering the strength to step out of their world and wish me luck on *my* journey.

I stare at the computer screen, my mouth open. I scan their message quickly one more time just to make sure it said what I thought it had said. It did.

I am embarrassed. Shame swells up inside me. Whining

about the wrong direction of the wind while Susan's got needles stuck in her body by people she doesn't know and whom she has reluctantly been forced to trust. I have a couple of blisters and a few aches and pains while Susan's lying in darkness and can't move. She's got cancer. I have a jellyfish sting on my foot.

In that moment, those four loving sentences from Susan and her husband span across the miles, from her bed to my boat and directly into my heart. They slap me upside my head with the truest illustration of absolute courage.

I read the message three more times, turn off my computer, step out onto the deck and gaze out to the northeast, towards Chicago.

I know Susan's out there, going through more hell than I have ever experienced, drawing her inspiration from this sniveling whiner.

I crawl back inside the cabin, log out from the satellite and put my computer back into its watertight case. I fix dinner, sit against my single-side band radio and eat in silence surrounded only by the slapping waves of the ocean and the courage of a couple in Chicago.

With dinner settling in, I plop myself down on the sliding rowing seat, grab my two ten-foot spruce oars and begin to pull. The boat feels lighter. My destination feels closer.

It is easy to forget that there are thousands following this voyage. I pull today with rekindled spirit and strength. Today, every pull of the oar is for you, Susan. I send blessings and strength to you both, on the wings of every sea god I can muster. Thank you, Susan. Thank you for reaching out and showing me how to pull. *You* are the real hero.

Aloha,
Mick.

Mick Bird

Names have been changed.

A Passport from the Elements

*The traveler must be born again in the road
and earn a passport from the elements.*

Henry David Thoreau

It was two in the morning when we landed at Biak, an
island off the north coast of Irian Jaya, the Indonesian half
of New Guinea. We were lucky to be on this flight.

Arriving at Bali's airport ten hours earlier, Jill and I had
signed onto a long list of standby passengers. For hours,
we sat on our backpacks near the ticket counter, clasping
our hands together whenever the agent for Garuda Air
looked our way, beseeching him to find us seats. If we
didn't get on this flight, we'd miss Jill's brother's wedding,
and it would be three days before there'd be another
chance to fly home. Our hopes ebbed as passengers began
boarding. Then, fifteen minutes before departure, the
agent waved us to the counter, took our tickets, rushed
our packs onto the conveyor belt and suddenly we were
on our way home.

Several hours later, as we approached the airport in
Biak, the loudspeakers announced in Indonesian, English

and four other languages, "Passengers must disembark during refueling."

Wandering groggily into the terminal, we followed the crowd to a lounge. As Jill sat on one of the plastic chairs and closed her eyes, I steered over to the gift shop.

On the counter was a rack of postcards of local tribes-people: men in feathers and face paint, bare-breasted women in front of grass huts. One card in black and white showed a woman holding up her outspread fingers; six of her digits were missing above the first joint. On the back it said that when a relative died, women cut off a finger in mourning. Below the postcards was a display case full of an assortment of stone axes chipped from grayish-black rock, with various prices depending on their size. Stone axes in an airport gift shop! What would it be like to visit highland tribes whose elders could still remember the days before first contact with the outside world in the 1930s?

A guitar twanged. In a corner of the lounge were three men in paint and feathers, looking more or less like they'd stepped out of one of the postcards. One strummed the guitar, another shook a gourd rattle and the third was shuffling barefoot on the cool linoleum floor. Behind them, the tall windows of the terminal looked into a perfect darkness marred only by the red and white lights of a solitary airliner gathering speed on the runway. The men began singing exuberantly in a language I'd never heard, the music vaguely reminiscent of a Hawaiian folk song. Jill opened her eyes, and I stood by her listening, exhilarated and full of longing. The world was a huge place; there was still so much we hadn't seen, hadn't even imagined—all our travels had made only a thin line around an immense globe.

Back on the plane, Jill curled up with her head on my shoulder and dozed off. I was wide awake as the stewardesses secured the cabin doors, and we lifted into the air once again, leaving the lights of Biak behind, plunging east into darkness. Another nine hours and we'd be in Hawaii, a few more to Los Angeles, another hour up to San Francisco, then catch the Airporter bus for home.

I pulled my passport from my shirt pocket. The cover was slick from wear, the gold-lettered "United States of America" eroded half away, the travel-worn eagle ghost-like against the dark blue background, the arrows and olive branch clutched in its talons erased to mere outlines. Thumbing through the pages, I looked at all the visas: purple triangle for Uganda, red rectangle for Brazil, blue circle for Panama and a black one for Kenya. More than just a testament to the places I'd been, they stood for colors of experience, new shapes of thinking.

Turning to the front, I gazed at myself three and one-half years younger. How far had we traveled since that picture was taken? Forty thousand miles? Fifty? But the success of the journey didn't depend on the number of miles covered or countries visited. It had more to do with how much I had, and how much I would let myself be changed by the experience.

"Why are you traveling?" Dwarko had asked at Bodhgaya in India. Maybe I'd never have the whole answer, but here was part of it: I traveled because I wanted the dust of India and the sun of East Africa to stain my skin; because I wanted the rhythms of Brazil to weave their vibrations into my bones; because I wanted images of the Himalayas to engrave themselves not only on my retinas, but on my soul; because I wanted to drink from the Amazon and the Ganges, the Napo, the Nile, the Tapajos—I wanted the waters of the world to mingle until something new was distilled in my blood.

All that was part of it, and there was something else, too. Dwarko in India, our friend Badr in Egypt, the dancers of Bali, a hundred musicians in Brazil—they had brought something buried in my heart to light and into focus. It was only through seeing my reflection in the looking glass of other cultures that I'd finally been able to explore the dark continent I held inside.

The outer journey and the inner one were stitched together by a certain inevitability, a shared momentum. Without travel, I might never have discovered my own deeper desires, my own story. Without travel, I would never have known how many ways there are to live a human life, would never have sensed how many possibilities there are without seeing them lived out in other cultures.

I had something of my own now, something that could never be taken away. I felt a new face, or an old one long hidden, emerging, and had the odd sensation that the next time I looked in a mirror I'd find myself gazing into the eyes of a stranger I'd been waiting to meet for a long time.

Arthur Dawson

Pilgrimage to Lourdes

The use of traveling is to regulate imagination by reality, and instead of thinking how things may be, to see them as they are.

Samuel Johnson

Sitting in the airport lounge, waiting to board the plane for Lourdes, was a depressing experience. I was confronted by the terrible fragility of life—many of my fellow passengers were mentally or physically disabled. They were terminally ill, frail, in pain. And all were heading to this little town in the French Pyrenees looking for a miracle. What chance of that? How desperate can you get?

Maybe I should tell you a little bit about Lourdes.

The story began in 1858 when a poor fourteen-year-old French girl saw a ghostly woman dressed in white in a shallow cave at the rubbish dump, in the outskirts of town. Over a period of one month, Bernadette Soubirous saw the woman eighteen times. The woman said that she was the Virgin Mary, that she wanted a chapel built on the site and that people should come in procession. And she revealed a spring.

Right from the beginning, the spring water showed miraculous qualities. First a woman with a paralyzed hand was suddenly healed. More cures followed, and the crowds haven't stopped since. Five million pilgrims a year now visit Lourdes.

On first arrival, the place can seem shockingly tasteless. The narrow, windy streets leading to the grotto area are packed with gift shops full of religious curios—Virgin Mary water bottles, playing cards and even Mary flick knives. I found pictures of Christ being crucified with eyes that blinked and alarm clocks that played hymn tunes!

But near the grotto area, the commerce stops and the prayers begin. Pilgrims come to drink and bathe in the icy cold water and to gather in front of the cave where Bernadette saw the vision of Mary.

Tens of thousands of volunteers give up their holiday time to help those who are disabled and chronically ill as they struggle to complete their pilgrimage. Witnessing this potent mix of generosity, faith and courage is tremendously moving. There's a joy about the place—the coming together of all these ill people becomes not a reason to be depressed, but an excuse to celebrate the sheer power and wonder of the human spirit.

But the question still nagged at me: How do these people cope when they have to go home not cured? Officially the Catholic Church says there have been only sixty-five miracles at Lourdes since 1858. Hundreds of unrecognized, unexplained cures have happened here, too, but that must still mean millions go away disappointed.

And then I met Stephen. He has muscular dystrophy. It had already killed his brother and sister and now confines him to a wheelchair. This was his fourteenth visit.

"Why do you keep coming?" I asked.

"At the beginning, I came to Lourdes because I was actually looking to be healed," he replied, "but then as I grew older I got to understand that it isn't necessarily the physical problem which is being healed; it's actually coming to terms with your disability."

He looked around at some of the other visitors before continuing, "And when I come here now I recognize the same joy in the eyes of other pilgrims. They've come for the first time and gone away not being physically cured—throwing away their crutches or anything like that—but they have a better understanding of their disability and can cope with it. For me, that's the miracle of Lourdes."

In the days that followed, I thought quite a lot about Stephen's words and realized that although I'm not dying and I'm not disabled, I may also have experienced a miracle at Lourdes—somewhere near that grotto I lost a great big chunk of cynicism!

Martin Stott

One Hundred Million Prayers

I think that wherever your journey takes you, there are new gods waiting there, with divine patience—and laughter.

Susan Watkins

An old woman, with skin as red and creased as the mountains surrounding her, sits on a wooden bench and watches the daily bus from Leh Town wheeze to a halt. She gazes at me curiously as I disembark, a Westerner coming to spend the summer studying Buddhism in the monastery of her remote Himalayan village. One hand spins a portable brass prayer wheel. The other counts beads on a rosary while she mutters, *"Om mani padme hum."*

While a literal translation of the mantra might be "Blessed jewel in the heart of the lotus," the people of Ladakh believe it contains the essence of all Buddhist teachings: the jewel representing incisive wisdom, the lotus, unsullied compassion. Thus it is considered the ultimate prayer for the liberation from suffering of all sentient beings.

This prayer for universal peace is woven into the fabric of Ladakhi society. It fills the constantly rotating prayer wheels of the old men and women in the marketplace. Selling vegetables, they chant. Spinning wool, they chant. Puffing up the hills with a load of dung chips on their backs, they chant. Throughout the country, great walls have been built out of hundreds of thousands of stones, each one with the mantra hand-inscribed: not walls for defense or to divide nations, but walls of perpetual prayer.

Om mani padme hum flutters on the flags on every rooftop and is etched billboard-size on the sides of the mountains. The prayer permeates the air, soaks in through the skin, and comes back out through the lips with contagious ease.

During the short, warm summer before the harvest, the villagers take part in a Mani prayer. Its object: to recite *"Om mani padme hum"* one hundred million times. For about two weeks, hundreds of villagers leave their homes and fields to chant ten hours a day until the hundred million mark is reached. Each person's daily prayer count is tallied on their beads and the collective total added up at the end of each day.

I arrive while the festival is in full swing. Prayers are punctuated with sudden shouts and whistles from the crowd and cacophonous clatters from the musicians perhaps to frighten off demons or nosy tourists. Young red-robed novices race through the crowd with steaming kettles of butter tea to pour into the wooden drinking bowls of the congregation to keep their constantly praying lips and throats from getting dry.

With a flourish of clashing cymbals, another group of novices suddenly appear, each one carrying a basket filled with little balls of raw dough that they begin passing out to the villagers. The ritual seems suddenly familiar: the lamas are handing out the Ladakhi staple foods of butter tea and barley dough. It's the dietary equivalent of wine and bread, and this must be some sort of Buddhist Eucharist we are about to share. I feel a shiver of excitement. The similarity between the religious rites of East and West has never been more clear to me.

When a boy monk brings the basket near to me, I pluck out a dough ball and pop it reverently into my mouth.

"Eyah!" the boy shrieks, his eyes bulging, mouth open in horror. He shakes his head and waves his arms violently. The old men and women sitting near suck in their breath, aghast. Then they roar with laughter.

The lump of dough in my mouth tastes pasty, not at all like roast barley. I spit it out, noticing that the laughter has spread quickly through the crowd.

The little novice turns to me, face red and eyes serious, as if he must take me in hand like a very dumb child. He picks up another ball and rubs it over his hands, chest and arms until the dough is black with grime.

"Like this!" he demonstrates emphatically.

Like a boorish dinner guest drinking from the finger bowl, what I'd mistaken for the bread of life is, as I later learn, a ritual cleansing ball for removing evil spirits.

Tim Ward

Dancing with Isabel

If we are always arriving and departing it is also true that we are eternally anchored. One's destination is never a place but rather a new way of looking at things.

Henry Miller

Years ago, when I was working as an assistant cruise director, the male staff members had to dance with the elderly ladies who were traveling by themselves. Whenever we saw these passengers in one of the lounges, we were required to strike up a conversation and offer to dance with them.

It wasn't one of the more popular duties. Many times we would find ourselves tripping over our feet, struggling to dance a particular step. We affectionately nicknamed this routine "drag-a-bag."

On one particular Saturday night, the ship's program called for only fifteen minutes of music and dancing in the main lounge. We figured we'd have to dance with only a couple of women, which wouldn't be too bad.

I looked around and spotted a lady sitting off to the

side, her foot stomping away to the beat of a lively Glenn Miller tune. She looked like she was in her seventies, on the petite side, and was wearing a wig that was unevenly pulled to the side.

I walked up to her, introduced myself and asked her if she wanted to dance. She smiled at me and said, "No, thank you."

I mentioned that I had seen her tapping to the music and knew she was enjoying the Big Band sound. Reaching out my hand and gently placing it in hers, I said, "Come on, let's go have some fun."

She got up, and we made our way to the dance floor. To my surprise, Isabel was a very good dancer. Her eyes were all lit up, and she was smiling from ear to ear. She showed me all kinds of great swing-step moves, and I desperately tried to keep up with her. They were the kind of dance steps you'd see a professional swing dancer use. She was really phenomenal!

The music ended, and I walked Isabel back to her seat. As we sat down, I noticed the tears in her eyes. She reached down into her purse, pulled out a tissue and began to cry.

"Have I done something to upset you?" I asked. "Was it my poor dancing abilities? I'm sorry."

She looked up with her wet, shiny eyes and assured me that I had done nothing wrong. "I love to dance," she said. "My husband and I would go dancing every Saturday night. We never missed an opportunity."

Isabel tried to compose herself, but her face was overcome with emotion.

"Earl and I always dreamed of dancing at sea together. We talked about going on a cruise, and we saved up our money." She drew a deep breath and continued, "Then one Saturday evening, just as we were getting dressed to go out, he sat down on our bed and said he needed to rest for a few minutes. Well," she said gently, "he never woke up."

I could see her love for her husband in every wrinkle of her precious face.

"I haven't danced in twenty-eight years," she paused and looked at me with a smile, "until now."

Then she gave me a hug and whispered, "Thank you for being my partner tonight."

Some years later, I became a cruise director, but I never forgot that moment, especially on Big Band nights.

When the guys on my staff would offer up the same complaints I used to have, I had only to recount Isabel's story. No sooner would I finish than they were back on the dance floor again, perhaps with somebody's grandmother, or maybe with a lady who hadn't danced in far too many years.

Jim West

Gifts

He alone is great who turns the voice of the wind into a song made sweeter by his own loving.

Kahlil Gibran

I worked closely with Mother Teresa for over thirty years. One day, after my conversation had been filled with a litany of problems, some seemingly insoluble, Mother Teresa remarked, "Everything is a problem. Isn't there another word?"

I confessed that I knew no other word that carried the same weight.

"Why not use the word 'gift'?" she suggested.

With that I began a shift in vocabulary.

One of the first times that this new vocabulary came into use was on our return to New York City from a conference in Vancouver. She had tried without success to be excused from the conference and was extremely anxious to have time with the sisters in New York.

I was dismayed to learn that the trip had to be broken en route with a long delay. I was about to explain the "problem" when I caught myself and said, "Mother, I have to tell you about a gift. We have to wait four hours here, and you won't arrive at the convent until very late."

Mother Teresa agreed that it was indeed a great "gift." She settled down in the airport to read and ponder a favorite book of meditations.

From that time on, items that presented disappointments or difficulties would be introduced with, "We have a small gift here," or "Today we have an especially big gift." Now there were smiles at situations that earlier had been described by the dour word "problem."

Eileen Egan

A Visit with My Parents

Two of the greatest gifts we can give our children are roots and wings.

Hodding Carter

While I was serving as a Peace Corps volunteer in the Philippines, my parents came to visit me. They arrived three days before my birthday. We rested one day in the capital city of Manila before embarking on the twenty-four-hour boat ride to the small island of Sibuyan where I was assigned.

The heat was intense inside the ship's cabin. Rows of bunk beds with vinyl mats filled the small space, and every bed had at least one body. I had advised my parents to dress conservatively in below-the-knee attire to adhere to the cultural norms. Dad, who is claustrophobic by nature, sweated miserably in his pants and collared shirt; Mom fared little better in culottes and a T-shirt.

I lay on my bunk, accustomed to the discomfort and worried about how they would do once we actually arrived on the island. I lived in an eight-by-ten-foot hut by the ocean, without electricity, plumbing, beds or window screens.

Upon our arrival, we traveled to my host family's house in a 1970s vintage motorcycle with a creatively welded sidecar. There waiting for us were my host mother Nanay, father Tatay, two sisters Gina and Nene, and brother Bindel. Like the timid first meeting of spouses in a prearranged marriage, my two families stared inquisitively at each other as we sat together in the bamboo rest house.

Both had been anticipating this in-person assembly. After the initial introductions were complete, my mother with wavering voice tried to express in broken and simple English the gratitude she felt toward my Filipino hosts for taking care of me as one of their own. In her eyes and in her words, I could sense all of the worries that she had harbored for me in this place so far from home, so foreign. Nanay looked into my mother's eyes and smiled knowingly. She is the mother of six children.

We washed up at the river, then walked the half-mile through groves of mango and coconut trees, across the swamp outlet, and finally along the seashore to my hut. Mom and Nanay walked together.

As I watched them, I was struck with the awareness of my good fortune. These two amazing women are mine to learn from, to lean on, to love and to be loved by. Nanay possesses an enduring strength and peacefulness much like my own mother. It shows in the way she winnows rice in the wind until her arms won't raise up any more, in the tender way she holds her first grandchild, and in the way she spoke to me of love, family and the responsibilities of women.

Approaching my little hut, my parents grew quiet as they took in the seemingly impoverished human condition of island life—*my* life.

Dad stood on the bamboo platform under my roof and

cast his eyes seaward. His shoulders bespoke the sad and amazed bewilderment that his eyes would not show me. I had already been living on the island for over a year and was not prepared for how this lifestyle might appear to a "more comfortable" mind, especially my father's.

He was farm-raised on the ideal that hard work will get you somewhere. When we visited my host father at work, Dad stood solemnly watching as Tatay, clucking and grunting, trudged through the thick mud of his rice field. He guided a handmade plow with one hand, while wound around the other was a rope leading to the nose of the water buffalo straining against the plow. Tatay has toiled that way all of his sixty-seven years, and he will continue to do so until his body won't let him. Tatay and Nanay know hard work. Tatay and Nanay have lived hand-to-mouth every day of their lives.

While celebrating my birthday with coworkers from the Philippine Department of Environment and Natural Resources, we unwittingly ended up taking part in the confiscation and seizure of an illegal fisherman's boat. It was full of dynamite that the fisherman would have used to blast a school of fish, consequently destroying the already damaged corals.

There was some shooting and a boat chase, and the birthday party was over when our group was forced to flee—confiscated boat in tow—for fear of retaliation.

My parents were not comforted in the least by this display of my work environment. I tried to ease their fears and my own threadbare nerves by explaining repeatedly that this was not a normal day on the job.

At night, we retired to the comforts of my bamboo floor and the darkness, where Mom and Dad cringed in horror at the sounds of rats and mice scuttling, lizards chuckling, palm-sized spiders leaping, and carnivorous cockroaches gnawing just beyond the flimsy mesh barriers of their mosquito nets. While I slept soundly, my parents had an altogether different experience. In my mother's words, "It seemed as if dawn would never come."

When dawn did arrive, we were up at the crack of it. And I was the one, this time, cracking the whip. Chore time! Water needed to be fetched, food scavenged for, laundry soaked and scrubbed, and a fire started to heat the day's cooking and drinking water.

The day before my parents departed from the Philippines, we had lunch at a hotel overlooking the island's shore. As we finished eating, I glanced over at Dad and the look on his face stilled me. I saw tears where I hadn't seen them in years.

I asked him what was wrong. He shook his head and, looking deeply at my mother, he said, "We've seen so little of the world, other people, other customs, other ways of living." He paused before continuing, "Thank you, Leah, thank you for opening our eyes."

Leah Burgess

A Peace Corps Mama

I went to visit my daughter, Deidre, who spent two years with the Peace Corps in Cameroon from 1994 until 1996. I wrote this poem while I was waiting for the plane to take off from Africa and return home.

I taught my daughter to walk
And she showed me how to walk in the dark
I taught my daughter how to talk
And she spoke for me in French and Bamoun
I taught my daughter to eat with utensils
And she showed me how to eat with my fingers
I taught my daughter how to bathe
And she showed me how to take a bucket bath
I taught my daughter how to vacuum a carpet
And she showed me how to squeegee cement
I taught my daughter first-world greed
She showed me third-world need
I taught my daughter how to love her family
She showed me how to embrace the world.

Cheryl Reece Myers

Joe

A good holiday is one spent among people whose notions of time are vaguer than yours.

John Boyton Priestly

The remote Fijian island of Taveuni is one of those places on the planet that time has forgotten. Its people are so laid-back that visitors to the small island are often heard to say that on Taveuni, time not only stands still, it often lays down and takes a nap!

On one of my numerous visits to this special place, I met a man named Joe. Joe built *bures,* a traditional thatched house, and apparently was very good at it. While I suspected Joe was an old man, he was one of those fortunate few who appeared ageless. His thick, curly hair was graying at the temple, but the wrinkles etched in the dark skin around his eyes were better described as laugh lines.

The fact that he moved slowly was never to be mistaken for a sign of age on Taveuni, for there even spry youngsters moved slowly most of the time. The only thing that might have revealed Joe's maturity was his thoughtful approach to things. In Joe's life nothing happened quickly or without due deliberation.

I first met Joe while he was in the midst of building a *bure* for a mutual friend of ours. It was to be a rather large structure, as *bures* go, and Joe seemed determined to have this particular *bure* be the centerpiece of the three or four other buildings that stood nearby. Joe's trade was carried out with nothing more than a rusty cane machete knife, a homemade hammer and a handful of bent nails scavenged from bits of wood washed up on the beach. The lumber he used, if it can be called lumber, was cut as required from the surrounding forest using the large knife.

A big part of Joe's philosophy of building *bures* was that the job required a good deal of thought in order for it to be done correctly the first time. He told me that this thought process occurred while lying in the shade, and this he did with great regularity.

"Building a good *bure* takes a lot of resting," Joe said. I sat and watched Joe rest many times during the building of that *bure*. During those rest periods, Joe often asked me questions about other places, for he had never been off the island of his birth.

One hot afternoon, while resting and thinking under the shade of a mango tree, Joe noticed the daytime moon visible through the branches. He thought about this for a few moments before turning to me and saying, with some authority, "Did you know the Americans have been to the moon?"

In typical Taveuni fashion, I thought about that for a few moments before replying, "Yes, I did know that."

Joe thought a little longer while watching the moon chase the sun across the deep blue sky before adding, "The moon is a long way from here, isn't it? It must have taken them a long time to get there."

He was talking about it as if it happened quite recently.

At this point, I felt compelled to tell Joe that astronauts first landed on the moon in 1969, almost thirty years ago, and that they had been back several times since.

Joe turned to me and with little hesitation, but plenty of thought, said sincerely and with a smile, "Well, there couldn't have been much to see on the moon because I heard about it only last week."

Rob Bundy

Helen Keller at Niagara Falls

When the eyes see what they have never seen before, the heart feels what it has never felt.

Gracián

Born on June 27, 1880, in Tuscumbia, Alabama, Helen Keller was left deaf and blind by a prolonged high fever when she was only nineteen months old.

In 1887, the Keller family hired twenty-one-year-old Anne Sullivan as a live-in teacher for Helen. Anne was able to reach the little girl as no one else had and taught her how to cope with life in a dark and soundless world. Helen learned to read using the Braille system and to write using a special typewriter. She also learned to speak.

In March 1893, Helen and Anne, along with Alexander Graham Bell, who had become a good friend of Helen's, made a trip to upstate New York. Bell, while famous as the inventor of the telephone, was primarily a teacher of the deaf and wanted Helen to visit a school for the deaf in Rochester.

While there, Helen and Dr. Bell made travel arrangements to visit Niagara Falls, partly as a surprise treat for

Anne or "Teacher," as Helen usually called her.

To most visitors, it is a combination of the sight and sound of Niagara Falls that is so awe-inspiring and leaves such a lasting impression. Therefore, it's a wonder how Helen could understand or appreciate a visit to the world-famous site.

In fact, Helen had learned the concepts of distance and space and so was able to comprehend the size and even the appearance of the Falls after she had explored them in a variety of ways.

They stayed at a hotel in Niagara Falls, New York, that was located right beside the Niagara River so that she could feel the rush of the water simply by placing her hand on the window. Dr. Bell had also given her a down-filled pillow that she could hold against herself to increase the vibrations.

In a letter to her mother several weeks later, Helen wrote about the Falls:

> *I wish I could describe the cataract as it is, its beauty and awful grandeur, and the fearful and irresistible plunge of its waters over the brow of the precipice. One feels helpless and overwhelmed in the presence of such a vast force.*

Obviously, only someone who had been profoundly affected by Niagara's power and beauty could have written those words. In her mind, there was no doubt that Helen Keller saw and heard Niagara Falls.

Sherman Zavitz

My Brother

. . . A conversation with a foreigner whom you will probably never see again triggers no signal for caution.

Vikram Seth

The last time I was in Havana, I was approached, as I'd often been while there, by a young, strikingly articulate and well-informed character from the university who seemed (as almost everyone on that lonely island does) desperate for any contact with America.

His brother lived in California, he told me, in a place I'd never heard of called Tamal. He had a large house and a swimming pool, tennis courts and limousines. Please could I, on my return to the United States, take back a letter for his sibling in the hope that he might be able to do something—anything—to rescue his brother from the privations of Havana?

I did so—my suitcase always came back from Cuba crammed with such entreaties—although I knew, from five previous trips, that most of the letters would come back to me with "Addressee Unknown" stamped on them, or would arrive on the doorsteps of people who never wanted to think about Cuba again, if they were even alive.

In this case, however, an answer came back within a week, from Tamal, California.

Dear Pico Iyer, the brother in the large house wrote (and I paraphrase):

> *Thank you so much for sending me the letter from my brother in Havana: I think of him, I think of Cuba, all the time. I don't know if he knows my circumstances here, but I am in San Quentin Prison, for a long time. Is there anything he can do, do you think, to set me free and get me back to the safety of Havana? Please write me soon.*
>
> *Pico Iyer*

Peach Jam

The great affair is to move, to feel the needs and hitches of our life more nearly; to come down off this feather bed of civilization, and find the globe granite underfoot and strewn with cutting flints.

Robert Louis Stevenson

Backpacking through the African mountain kingdom of Lesotho, I carried a staple of food with me just in case I couldn't find something to eat. I always had a few cans of spaghetti, crackers, peanut butter and jam.

I was browsing through a local market one day when I chanced upon a jar of peach jam. I could find tins of apricot and strawberry in every corner store, but this was the first time I had seen peach. I grabbed it.

For the next few weeks, when I was feeling the need for a little treat, I would carefully remove the lid and spoon a bit on to a cracker along with some peanut butter. Mmm, delicious. I didn't share it with anybody. It sat safely in my pack, taken out only on special occasions.

One cold and cloudy afternoon, I was waiting for a local bus. As much as I tried to dismiss my shivering, I was miserable. It seemed that the bus would never arrive.

It started to rain, and very quickly the drizzle turned into a downpour. Everybody scattered for shelter. I took cover under a makeshift bamboo food stand with an old woman. I was drenched and quickly searched through my pack for some dry clothes.

In my desperate haste to avoid further discomfort, I forgot that the jar of peach jam was buried in my clothing. One forceful yank and my precious delicacy crashed to the concrete, smashing into pieces.

As often happens when traveling alone, the vultures of self-pity descended. I looked down at the raindrops, the mud and the morsels of peach and mourned my loss.

And then, from the corner of my eye, I noticed the old woman approaching. She looked up at me, down at the jam, and then back up at me. Without hesitating any further, she walked towards the fruity mess. Quickly, she bent down and retrieved the half of the jar that was still intact.

Still stooped over, she stuck two fingers in, scooped out the remaining jam and placed it into her toothless mouth. Carefully, like fish bones, she spit out the shards of glass and smeared her finger along the bottom to extract every last drop. She studied the shattered container until she was certain that there was nothing left.

The empty jar in hand, she turned to walk away. I reached into my pack and offered her my cans of spaghetti and crackers. She accepted. However, before I could give her the peanut butter, she scurried off and I watched as she guided her hungry grandchildren back into their humble hut.

My bus arrived shortly after, and as we drove off, I looked back and saw her grandson wiping the food from his mouth. I knew then that peach jam would never taste the same to me again.

Steve Zikman

A Life on the Road

*If you do not see what is around you every day,
what will you see when you go to Tangiers?*

Freeman Patterson

Once, looking for stories on the back roads of Ohio, we
were suffering a week-long dry spell. A colorful beekeeper
we'd been told about was away from home when we
called on him, visiting a niece in Colorado or someplace. A
promising old-time candy store had been sold and turned
into a pizza joint. A venerable amusement park where we
thought we might find a story had shut down for the season. We began to get a little discouraged.

We passed a farmhouse with a homemade banner
stretched between two oak trees in the front yard. The
banner said in huge letters: WELCOME HOME, ROGER!
We drove on for a mile or two. Somebody said, "Wonder
who Roger is?"

We turned around, went back there and knocked on the
door.

Roger was a soldier on his way home from the Vietnam
War. His family knew he was coming, but wasn't sure

what day he was going to arrive. Roger's mother was in the kitchen baking his favorite chocolate cake. Really— she was. His wife was there with a baby son Roger had never seen. We asked if they'd mind if we brought the camera into the house. Roger's mother said it would be all right if we'd give her a minute to fix her hair. I am sure we weren't there more than an hour, talking to those people who were all excited about Roger coming home. We never did see Roger, of course.

At my desk in the bus as we rolled on that afternoon, I wrote a simple story letting Roger represent all the GIs coming home to their families from Vietnam. We found an airport and skipped the film to New York, and Walter Cronkite put the story on the *Evening News* the next night.

Rarely has any of our stories caused such a reaction from viewers. It was just an account of waiting for Roger, that's all, but it resonated in the country. The CBS switchboard lighted up that night with dozens of calls from people moved by it in some way, and hundreds of letters came in, some of them asking that the story be repeated. There was so much interest nationwide that Cronkite felt compelled to report on the air a few nights later, "Oh, and by the way—Roger got home!"

That hour with Roger's family made it a good trip to Ohio, after all. I had done a fair amount of careful planning in preparation for the week's work, but careful planning got us nowhere. Then along came a banner stretched across a farmhouse yard.

Back at the office, people asked, "How do you *find* these stories?"

"Well," I said, "you do have to work at it."

All you really have to do is look out the window.

Charles Kuralt

8

THE KINDNESS
OF STRANGERS

*What place would you advise me to visit
now?" he asked. "The planet Earth,"
replied the geographer. "It has a good
reputation."*

Antoine de Saint Exupéry, The Little Prince

Looking for Abdelati

There is an emanation from the heart in genuine hospitality which cannot be described but is immediately felt, and puts the stranger at once at ease.

Washington Irving

The day began when Miguel and I descended from a cramped, cold bus at 7:00 A.M. and walked the stinking gray streets of Casablanca, looking for food. I had recently finished a volunteer project in Kenitra, an ugly industrial city on the Moroccan coast. This was my final day of travel before hopping a plane to sub-Saharan Africa and more volunteer work.

Miguel was one of five non-Moroccans on the project, a twenty-one-year-old vision of flowing brown curls and buffed golden physique. Although traveling with him took care of any problems I might have encountered with Moroccan men, he was inordinately devoted to his girlfriend, Eva, a wonderfully brassy, chain-smoking older woman of twenty-five, whom he couldn't go more than half an hour without mentioning.

Unfortunately, Eva had had to head back to Barcelona immediately after the work camp ended, and Miguel wanted to explore Morocco. Since I was the only other person there who spoke Spanish, and Miguel spoke no French or Arabic, his tight orbit shifted onto me, and we became travel companions.

This morning we were going to visit Abdelati, a sweet, gentle young man we'd worked with in Kenitra. He'd been expecting our arrival in Casablanca for a few days. Since he had no telephone, he'd written down his address and told us to just show up—his mother and sisters were always at home. After scoring some croissants at a road-side café, we set out to find his house.

Our poker-faced taxi driver had trouble deciphering Abdelati's scribbled address. When we got into the neighborhood, he started asking directions.

A policeman pointed us to a group of barefoot boys kicking a soccer ball in the park. A tiny boy informed us that Abdelati had moved, but he could take us to the new house. This seemed a bit odd, since Abdelati had given me the address only the week before. I chalked it up as another Moroccan mystery.

The boy came with us in the cab, full of his own importance, twisting to wave at other children as we inched down the narrow winding roads. Finally he pointed to a house, and our driver went to the door and inquired.

He came back with a teenage girl, who introduced herself as Abdelati's sister. She was visiting friends today, she explained. Her family's house was down the street.

When we arrived, we waited in the yard while the girl went inside. She returned accompanied by her mother, sisters and brother-in-law, all of whom greeted us with cautious warmth. I was surprised to see them dressed in Western clothes, since Abdelati was very religious. I'd assumed he came from a more traditional family.

Another surprise was skin color. Whereas Abdelati looked very African, this was a family of olive-skinned Arabs. Still, I'd seen plenty of unusual familial combinations in Morocco's complex racial mosaic, so I didn't give it much thought.

We were ushered into a pristine middle-class home, with an intricately carved doorway and swirling multicolored tiles lining the walls. The mother told us in broken French that Abdelati was out, but would be home soon. We sat on low-cushioned seats in the living room, drinking sweet, pungent mint tea and eating sugar cookies. Family members took turns sitting with us, making shy, polite conversation that frequently lapsed into uncomfortable silence. Every time anything was said, Miguel would say "What?" with extreme eagerness, and I would translate the mundane fragment into Spanish for him: "Nice weather today. Tomorrow perhaps rain."

"I wish Eva were here," he whispered, sinking back into the cushions in fidgety frustration.

After two hours had passed with no sign of Abdelati, the family insisted on serving us a meal of couscous and chicken.

"Soon," they replied when I inquired as to what time Abdelati might arrive.

"You come to the *hammam,* the bath," the teenage sister said after we'd finished lunch. "When we finish, he is back."

"The bath?" I asked, looking around the apartment.

"What?" said Miguel anxiously, sitting up.

The sister laughed. "The women's bath!" she said. "Haven't you been yet?" She pointed at Miguel. "He can go to the men's; it's right next door."

The women's bath consisted of three large connecting rooms, each hotter and steamier than the last. The rooms were filled with naked women of all ages and body types.

They toted buckets of water back and forth from the innermost room, then sat directly on the slippery tiles, talking and laughing as they washed each other with mitts of rough cloth. Tiny girls and babies sat directly in the plastic buckets—their own pint-sized tubs.

I looked around me with wonder. When I woke up this morning, sore and cranky, my head bouncing against the dirty glass window of the bus, could I possibly have imagined I'd find myself here?

"What was it like in there?" asked Miguel when we reconverged outside. He looked pink and damp as a newborn.

"I'd like to tell you all about it," I said eagerly, "but ..." I paused for emphasis, then leaned in and whispered, "I don't think Eva would approve."

When we got back to the house, the mother, older sister and uncle greeted us at the door.

"Please," said the mother, "Abdelati is here."

"Oh, good," I said, and for a moment, before I walked into the living room, his face danced in my mind—the warm brown eyes, the smile so shy and gentle and filled with radiant life.

We entered the tiled sitting room, and a handsome young Arab man in nicely pressed Western pants and shirt came forward to shake our hands.

"*Bonjour, mes amis,*" he said cautiously.

"*Bonjour,*" I smiled, slightly confused. "Abdelati—*est-ce qu'il est ici?*" Is Abdelati here?

"*Je suis Abdelati.*" I am Abdelati.

"But ... but ... ," I looked from him to the family and then began to giggle tremulously. "I-I'm sorry. I'm afraid we've made a bit of a mistake. I-I'm so embarrassed."

"What? What?" Miguel asked urgently. "I don't understand. Where is he?"

"We got the wrong Abdelati," I told him, then looked

around at the assembled family who'd spent the better part of a day entertaining us. "I'm afraid we don't actually know your son."

For a split second, no one said anything, and I wondered whether I might implode right then and there and blow away like a pile of ash.

Then the uncle exclaimed heartily, *"Ce n'est pas grave!"*

"Yes," the mother joined in. "It doesn't matter at all. Won't you stay for dinner, please?"

I was so overwhelmed by their kindness that tears rushed to my eyes. For all they knew we were con artists, thieves, anything.

Still, with my plane leaving the next morning, I felt the moments I could share with the first Abdelati and his family slipping farther and farther away.

"Thank you so much," I said fervently. "It's been a beautiful, beautiful day, but please . . . could you help me find this address?"

I took out the piece of paper Abdelati had given me in Kenitra. The new Abdelati, his uncle and his brother-in-law came forward to decipher it.

"This is Baalal Abdelati!" said the second Abdelati with surprise. "We went to school together! He lives less than a kilometer from here. I will bring you to his house."

And, after taking photos and exchanging addresses and hugs and promises to write, Miguel and I left our new-found family and arrived at the home of our friend Abdelati just as the last orange streak of sunset was fading into the indigo night.

There I threw myself into the arms of that dear and lovely young man, exclaiming, "I thought we'd never find you!"

After greetings had been offered all around, and the two Abdelatis had shared stories and laughter, we waved good-bye to our new friend Abdelati and entered a low, narrow hallway, lit by kerosene lamps. In the dim glow stood a tiny, stooped woman, covered from head to toe in black cloth.

"This is my mother," said Abdelati.

The woman moved toward me, arms outstretched in welcome. As she drew close, I saw her eyes. They were large and brown, like her son's, sparkling with tenderness. For the second time that day, I was overcome with emotion. *This is what I love about travel,* I thought. *Strangers get a chance to amaze you.*

And suddenly I found myself caught up in a crush of fabric and spice, gripped in the tight embrace of this fully veiled woman, who held me and cried over me and wouldn't let me go, just as though I were her own daughter and not a stranger at all.

Tanya Shaffer

Just a Little Scratch

The autumn after we graduated from college, my friend Marie and I took a trip to England. We planned every detail, determined to make this the vacation of a lifetime. Every penny we had went into our dream vacation. We decided that renting a car for the month would afford us the most freedom, and Marie's mother lent us her credit card for the rental.

By the time our flight arrived at Heathrow Airport, we were delirious with anticipation and lack of sleep. It was a crisp, bright morning, and we had four weeks ahead of us to explore a new country. We picked up our little blue rental car and were sent off with a map and a reminder to Marie to stay on the left side of the road. We drove away in high spirits, laughing as Marie tried to shift on the wrong side and smacked her arm on the door.

Within five minutes we were lost, but even that was exhilarating—our first time lost in a foreign country! We found ourselves driving down a narrow street in a small shopping district, and as I consulted our photocopied map, Marie gasped and there was a terrible scraping noise.

A car had cut us off and Marie, forgetting for an instant about the left side of the car, veered too far over and scraped a parked car. She pulled over. We sat there, frozen, staring at each other in horror. Then Marie burst into tears, sobbing brokenly, "Oh my God, what am I going to do? The insurance! My mother's credit card! They're going to sue me!"

"Maybe it isn't that bad," I said cautiously, getting out of the car to inspect the damage.

The car had a long white scrape on the driver's side and the wing mirror had been knocked loose, dangling at a drunken angle. Walking to the other vehicle, I saw a matching blue scar on the white paint. I heard a wail of anguish behind me as Marie surveyed.

I tried to reassure her.

"It's not so bad, Marie," I said. "Look, it's just scraped, not dented or anything. Maybe they'll let us just pay for a touch up or something."

But Marie was inconsolable. Weeping and trembling with fear, she cried out, "I've ruined our vacation! They'll sue me for all my money! My mother will never forgive me!"

She was certain that the repercussions would be awful. I had to admit I had no reason to think differently. When she had calmed down a bit, we decided to find the owner of the car she had hit and walked over to the shop closest to the scraped car. A bell tinkled over our heads as we opened the door and a middle-aged woman came out of the back room to greet us.

"Excuse me, but I was w-wondering if that wh-white car is yours, b-because I—" Marie faltered and started crying again.

The woman came forward in concern.

"Good heavens, are you all right, Dear?"

I explained what had happened. As I finished, a man came out of the back with raised eyebrows.

The woman guided Marie to a seat and said, "These poor girls have just come from the airport and gotten all muddled up and scraped a car. There dear, have a tissue."

As the woman fussed over Marie, I walked out with the man to survey the damage. After looking at both cars we went back into the shop and he said cheerfully, "Well, there's no harm done. It's just a little scratch, some polish will take care of that. Don't worry yourselves about it."

Still sniffling, Marie asked, "Is . . . Is it your car?"

"Oh, no, but we know the fellow who owns it. Don't worry, this happens all the time with people coming from Heathrow. We're quite used to it around here. It's just a shame that your holiday had to start out with such a scare." Marie and I looked at each other incredulously.

"Are you sure? I mean, won't your friend be mad? We should at least pay for—"

The woman wouldn't let Marie finish. "Don't be silly. It's just a scratch, and he knows the risk parking there. He'll be very sorry to hear you were so upset about such a little thing. Really, you mustn't let it spoil your holiday."

After repeatedly assuring us that the owner of the car would not be angry and offering us tea, the kindly couple waved us on our way with wishes for a wonderful vacation and a reminder to get some polish for the scratch on our rental.

Later that week we stayed with my uncle, who polished the scrape until it disappeared and popped the wing mirror back into place.

In the days that followed, Marie and I met many kind and generous people who helped make our dream vacation perfect. However, the most lasting impression was made in the first hour of our trip, by a couple who believed that a young woman's happiness was far more important than a blue scrape on some white paint.

Catherine Scott

Strangers in Our Home

And this is what the traveler discovers: In this great and endlessly fascinating world of ours, everywhere can be home.

Meredith Moraine

"Did they wreck anything?"

This is far and away the most frequent question people ask when my husband Fred and I tell them that we've traded homes with strangers from another country. The answer is a resounding "NO!"

We've exchanged our comfortable, old house in Canada twenty-five times with folks from thirteen different countries. We almost always return to a place that is cleaner than when we left it. Our neighbors tell us that the Belgians swept the driveway and even scrubbed the deck. A bottle of wine or a bouquet of flowers inevitably welcome us home.

However it was Wolf who taught us what it truly means to welcome strangers into our home.

Wolf lives in Bavaria. In 1985, we talked with him about exchanging homes, but he was unable to come to Canada.

Nonetheless, he invited us to look him up when we made it to Germany. We hesitated, but his letter had been so warm that we called him up and he insisted that we meet in Munich—at Oktoberfest.

It sounded impossible. Thousands of people would be milling around in a city with which we were totally unfamiliar. How were we supposed to find a man we'd never seen before? Simple: He told us to sit on the steps of a church just outside the fairgrounds at a given hour and he would find us.

In the end, there was no mistaking him!

Wolf was driving an old camper van with a Canadian flag on the hood. He drove it straight through the crowd right up to the base of the church stairs. Then he leapt out, a wiry man of around forty, with tiny Canadian flags affixed to both sides of his glasses. There wasn't a dull moment after that.

We expected a beer and a chat. A week later we were still with Wolf and his family. Sometimes we'd go cycling or kayaking. Other times we'd sit and talk for hours, eating warm plum strudel on the lawn of their modest village home.

Wolf was a renaissance man. He made most of the furniture in his home. His English was better than ours. And, while he was a good musician and an even better sportsman, flying was his passion.

One memorable day he took Fred gliding in the Alps. I was terrified as they silently floated near the rocky slopes but for Fred, it was a breathtaking and unforgettable experience.

We tried to tell Wolf many times that we should leave. His only reply was that his home was always open to friends and strangers alike. He believed in an unlocked door policy and fully expected people to fill his home whether he was there or not.

When we were finally too embarrassed to impose on his hospitality any longer, he persuaded us to borrow his camper van and go on a tour through Spain and Portugal. We protested but finally agreed to accept his generosity.

Since then we have lent our own van to family, friends and strangers. Often, they go away for weeks at a time on some journey to Florida or Canada's East coast.

Like Wolf, we've opened our doors to hundreds of strangers, many of whom have stayed at our house even though we never laid eyes on the Italian doctor, or the writer from Scotland, or the endearing pair from Holland who write us every Christmas.

Not one person has damaged our home, and all of them have enriched our lives. But, of course, we had a great teacher.

Thank you, Wolf.

Eleanor McMullin

A Christmas Dinner

If you are wise and know the art of travel, let yourself go on the stream of the unknown and accept whatever comes in the spirit in which the gods may offer it.

Freya Stark

My work calls for me to venture to the farthest reaches of the world, but one of my most memorable encounters occurred while traveling close to home.

A few years ago, a group of my far-flung friends decided to gather in Connecticut to celebrate Christmas.

I was to buy all the soft drinks, champagne and wine, and a doctor friend would get the turkey and trimmings.

On our way from New York City to Connecticut, my friend and I stopped in for a Christmas Eve party in upstate New York. As we left, I ran into the doctor and casually asked him what size bird he had bought. His eyes widened with surprise—he had bought all the drinks.

So here we were on a snowy Christmas Eve with sufficient drinks to serve a cruise ship but not one piece of food for twelve hungry people! We searched around, but every supermarket was closed. Finally, just before midnight, we found ourselves at a gas station quick-food shop.

The manager was willing to sell us cold sandwiches. Other than potato chips, cheese and crackers, he didn't have much else. I was very agitated and disappointed. It was going to be a rather miserable Christmas dinner. The only bright spot was that he did have two cans of cranberry jelly!

In the midst of my panic, an elderly lady stepped from behind one of the aisles.

"I couldn't help overhearing your dilemma," she said, "If you follow me home, I would happily give you our dinner. We have plenty of turkey, potatoes, yams, pumpkins and vegetables."

"Oh no, we couldn't do that!" I replied.

"But you see, we no longer need it," she explained, "Earlier today we managed to get a flight to Jamaica—to see our family down there, for the holidays."

We couldn't say no to such kindness. We thanked her and followed her car. The journey seemed endless as we meandered through back roads and dimly lit streets. Eventually, we reached this kind woman's house.

We followed her in and, sure enough, she removed a turkey and all the trimmings from the fridge. Despite our attempt to reimburse her for her generosity, she refused our money.

"This is just meant to be," she said, "I don't need it anymore—and you do."

So we accepted her gift, asked her for her name and address, and went on our way.

The next day we impressed and surprised our friends by presenting them with a complete feast and telling them our amazing about the old lady's help. Despite the last-minute scramble, Christmas dinner turned out to be a great success.

Before we left Connecticut, we went to a department store, picked out a gift and drove to the lady's home to leave our small token of appreciation.

We searched and searched but we couldn't find her place. We couldn't find the street address on any maps. The name she had given us wasn't listed anywhere. Baffled, we questioned several local store owners, yet no one knew of the elderly lady. Even the gas station manager told us that he had never seen her before. Every effort we made to locate our Christmas angel failed.

As I returned home, I pondered our bizarre encounter with this beneficent woman. Who was this lady who had appeared just in time to help out two desperate strangers, only to disappear with the night?

Years later, when I look back upon that particular holiday season, I recall the joy of gathering with friends from across the world and an amazing little old lady whose generosity embodied the very meaning of the Christmas spirit.

Robin Leach

The Nomads of Sabalon

I was once asked if I would like to meet the president of a certain country. I said, "No. But I'd love to meet some sheepherders." The sheepherders and taxi drivers are often the most fascinating people.

James A. Michener

When I was a young soldier stationed in the British Sector of West Berlin, I took part in an eight-man overland expedition to Iran with the purpose of climbing a mountain. Our destination was Khu-e-Sabalon, which, at 15,788 feet, is the second highest peak in Iran.

To reach the foothills of Mount Sabalon, it took us two weeks of driving over some of the roughest and harshest landscape I have ever encountered. As we passed from west to east, we drove our two Land Rovers through ancient cities, mud-hut villages and three days of desert terrain.

The long journey behind us, we established base camp on a small plateau eight thousand feet up on the northern slopes of the mountain. Then, at three o'clock in the morning, we began our cold and moonlit ascent.

Unfortunately, I was one of two members of the climbing party who failed to reach the summit. Altitude sickness hit me hard at 13,700 feet and dashed my hopes of standing on the snow-capped peak even as it lay within sight. After all the preparation and hardship in getting there—failure! My disappointment was as intense as the terrible headache, nausea and dizziness I was experiencing. The two of us were forced to descend.

On our way down, both of us became quite disoriented and found ourselves stumbling into the lower foothills of Sabalon, on the wrong side of the mountain. We were lost, we were hungry and we had little energy to continue.

As desperation set in, our salvation suddenly materialized before us, in the form of a nomadic shepherd named Reza. While none of our expedition members were aware of their presence, these nomads apparently knew of our presence on the mountain. This man knew exactly where our camp lay. Luckily for us, he had a donkey with him, and Willy and I took welcome turns riding it as Reza escorted us on the three-hour trek back to the comforting embrace of our little orange tents and the sound of a kettle whistling on the campfire.

Two days later, with the other climbers safely back and rested after successfully conquering the summit, we were invited to visit the nomads' camp. Reza returned to guide us. Arriving at a grassy plateau, we discovered a large grouping of dark circular tents, with some thirty nomads waiting to greet us.

We were welcomed immediately into the chief's large tent, where we sat around the tall samovar, cross-legged, upon hand-woven carpets, embroidered quilts and thick cushions. As we attempted to communicate, using signs and sand drawings, we sampled strong tea, unleavened bread and goat's milk yogurt. Occasionally, we were afforded glimpses of the chief's six wives who whispered and giggled softly to each other in the shadows, their dark eyes flashing in the flickering lamp light.

Once we had dined, we were able to mingle with the other nomads who were waiting outside. They were intrigued by the seemingly unproductive clicking of our camera. With my Polaroid, I was able to convince them otherwise. One press and a sweep of the arm, and I had an instant portrait to present to the awestruck onlookers!

It was obvious that I could easily and quickly use up my Polaroid film as everyone clamored for a personal picture. So I persuaded people to form family groups, the head of each family being left to jealously guard his prized photo. Only two men received individual portraits that day: the chief, naturally, and Reza, the man who had rescued me and Willy.

With the chief acting as guide, we watched sheets of tent felt being made. Teased and dampened wool was wrapped around a pole and then pummeled along the ground by a line of people dancing and kicking the pole as it rolled along. We joined in this ritual dance, arms linked and trying hard not to trip over our own feet as laughing children cavorted around us.

We caused an uproar of laughter when we tried, unsuccessfully, to master the art of riding their camels. I took many photographs, and before we knew it, our incredible day came to an end.

My visit to Sabalon remains one of the highlights of my life, and the defeat I suffered at my failure to reach the summit of the mountain was softened by the two days I spent in the company of those wandering shepherds.

Since then, I have harbored a heartfelt desire to return to Sabalon. Of course, I would love to finish what I had set out to accomplish on that expedition—the conquering of that 15,788-foot peak. But more so, I wish to enter the nomads' tents once more and find, illuminated by the wavering lamp light, a crumpled and faded Polaroid photo wedged behind the willow frame—a twenty-five-year-old photo of a smiling nomad named Reza and his faithful donkey.

Steve Foreman

CLOSE TO HOME   JOHN McPHERSON

"What do you mean you forgot to buy film?!"

Japanese Good-Bye

A thousand words will not have so deep an impression as one deed.

Henrik Ibsen

I looked up at the signs, trying to decipher which train I needed to take to Narita Airport. After ten months back-packing through Africa and Asia, using every form of transport from donkey to rickshaw, I was on the final leg of my journey, the flight that would take me home to Canada.

I was feeling the weight of my huge pack. Knowing that I would soon be shedding the burden on my back, I finally allowed myself to purchase gifts for my family. The Japanese language was a complete mystery to me, and I stared up at the board, searching for any symbol that appeared familiar. Anything at all.

Everywhere salary men were rushing to catch their crowded trains. Everybody, everything was moving fast. No Zen here.

And then, out of the masses, a woman stopped and asked, in English, which way I wanted to go. She took me to the station master. She spoke to him in Japanese, found out the platform number, the price of a ticket and the time of departure. I had half an hour.

I thanked her and bid her farewell, but she said she had ten minutes and insisted I join her for a quick tea.

She told me she had been born in Japan, but had spent a year backpacking in New York and knew what it was like to be a woman traveling solo. We excitedly traded stories, but soon our brief chat was over. Her train was leaving. She hurriedly paid for both our drinks.

"Save your money," she said and wished me luck. And then she was gone.

I stood up to go, pulling the load once more onto my back. Suddenly, she reappeared, out of breath, with a square box wrapped in white and red paper.

"You aren't vegetarian are you?" she asked.

"Uh, no . . ." and she pushed the box into my hands. It was warm.

"For the train. Good-bye." And she was gone, again.

I had seen these specially prepared boxed meals for sale in the stations. They looked delicious, but they were beyond my budget.

As I waited on the platform, my pack didn't feel as heavy. Even though I had been given one more gift to carry, I felt lighter—blessed with the taste of warm food, the dreams of my homecoming and the generosity of a Japanese woman I would know only this once. And I never even caught her name.

Julie Booker

Roasted Chestnuts

At its most pure, travel is an effort to explain life, not just from the familiar perspective, but from every perspective. To understand it fully, you must look to its extremes and taste them side by side.

Andrew Bill

Ever since I became a runner, traveling has taken on a whole new dimension. My sneakers take me places that no tour bus can maneuver and no typical traveler would bother to go.

Two and one-half years ago, my husband Larry accepted an eighteen-month assignment to help with economic recovery in Sarajevo after the signing of the Dayton Peace Accord. The agreement ended the cruel war that raged for over five years and resulted in the final breakup of Yugoslavia, leaving hundreds of thousands of people homeless, orphaned and maimed.

Runners were an unusual sight on these city streets; when we ran, we ran alone. Our routes would take us along narrow sidewalks crowded with Bosnians waiting for the bright new yellow buses to take them to work. We ran by markets where people earned a living by selling cabbage, peppers, oranges and whatever else cropped up at that time of year. We darted through groups of kids walking to school and giving us odd quizzical looks, shouting "Welcome to Sarajevo" and then laughing.

Despite the miles we logged through this town, we were separate, running through people's lives, observing as outsiders. The line between "expatriate" and "local" was well-defined.

On less-traveled mountain roads, our running would subtly disturb the quiet patterns of the goats and their herders. At the edge of town, the library that once majestically contained millions of books had been turned to ashes along with its contents. Just past it was a peaceful paved road that followed the flow of the river, winding its way up the hillside like a goat path. The view from the top was spectacular. Sarajevo stretched out before you. Nestled in the mountains were homes, red roofs ablaze with the sun's reflection.

This natural beauty lay in stark contrast to the gross physical destruction. Upon closer examination, many of the houses were simply shells. The roofs were damaged, the windows were gone, as were the contents and the tenants. Burned-out cars inhabited the river, washed there by the spring's heavy rains. Tanks drove by on the highway overpass. Helicopters flew overhead. The possibility of land mines in the shrubs along the side of the road was very real.

One rainy morning, during an exceptionally long run up the goat path, the clouds had been moving in and out of the city. Two storms came and went, and the third was a deluge. The roads were flooded, and cars showered us with water as they passed. By the time we reached the edge of town and the goat path, we were drenched.

We jogged steadily up the hill, keeping our heads down to avoid the sheets of rain. Suddenly, inside one of the few garages that still had a roof, we noticed a family huddled around a trash can, seeking shelter from the downpour. This structure had probably been their home before the war. Many people returned to visit the sites that were once their homes, to assess the damage, clean, salvage or just grieve.

"*Dobar dan*," we said, wishing the family good day in Bosnian as we ran past. They returned the greeting.

About an hour later, we ran back down the road, again passing this row of shattered houses. When the family saw us for a second time, the mother began to yell and run towards us, holding a big box. We stopped to see what she wanted.

She shoved the box at us. "Take some," she said in Bosnian.

We looked inside to find freshly roasted chestnuts.

Hesitating, Larry and I each took one and said, "*Hvala*." Thank you. And we headed back toward the path.

But one wasn't enough.

"*Jedan, dva, tri, cetri, pet* . . . one, two, three, four, five . . ." The woman couldn't speak English, except to count to five. This was her way of telling us to take more.

"*Jedan, dva, tri* . . ." Take more, she insisted while her husband and three children nodded and smiled eagerly behind her.

This family and others lost nearly everything they had during the war: homes, clothes, heirlooms, loved ones. Yet on this cold rainy morning, in the shattered hills surrounding Sarajevo, they cared only about sharing what they had with two strangers jogging through what remained of their town.

For the first time, I felt welcome in Sarajevo.

Karen Woodrow

The Heart of Paris

*One of the great things about travel is you find
out how many good, kind people there are.*

                                                    Edith Wharton

My friend Peggy and I had both been to Paris before,
but always as chaperones for youth groups or part of adult
groups, seeing all the usual tourist sites and hearing the
same tour guide recitations. This would be the first time
on our own—without responsibilities and free to go anywhere and try anything.

On previous trips, we had seen all the famous monuments and "tourist sights." The guidebooks claimed that
locals were rude and indifferent to visitors, but there had
to be more to the people of Paris than that. This time we
wanted to find the real Parisians.

We spent some time exploring small shops and lesser-
known museums and churches. We walked along canals
and down narrow lanes, seeing a different Paris, but still
not making any real contact with the people of this
magnificent city.

One evening, with the help of the night clerk at our

quaint hotel, we found a tiny café known only to locals. Nestled inside a dark passage, its unlit sign read, Chez Maurice. We peeked in the small window on the door to see a small room with half a dozen tables, each with enough chairs for eight patrons. We opened the heavy door and went inside.

We were greeted by a burly proprietor, whose smile faded when he discovered we were foreigners with a limited command of the French language. He turned his back and retreated to the kitchen, muttering under his breath and slowly shaking his head from side to side. Not a good start.

A moment passed and a young woman led us to our seats at the other end of a table already occupied by an elderly couple. She gave us two menus.

For a few minutes, we struggled to recall a few French words, but discovered that the descriptions of each dish were too much for us.

Our table-mates noticed our dilemma. The old man leaned over and began explaining each dish, one at a time. Since he spoke very little English, his translations took the form of elaborate gestures and animal sounds. A fish entree was depicted as a fish swimming upstream, jumping and splashing in the water. For the beef dish, he pretended that his hands were horns on the side of his head, accompanied by a "mooing" sound.

When the young waitress returned, we placed our order and our new friends gave her explicit instructions on how to prepare the food and what side dishes we should have.

Despite our limited ability to speak the other's language, we continued our lively conversation throughout the meal. We discovered that they were in their seventies and had been sweethearts for about ten years. She lived nearby in Paris, while he lived in the country. They met here once a week to share a pleasant dinner. Frankly, I have no idea how we understood each other, but we talked about the beauty of Paris, our lives and families and, of course, our other travels.

Near the end of the evening, a flower vendor made her way through the café. We watched as the old gentleman purchased a bouquet. Artfully, he plucked two flowers from the bunch, presented the bouquet to his lady and gave her a kiss. Then, bowing smartly in our direction, he held out a rose, one for each of us.

We had found our Paris.

Betty Corbin

2

WISDOM ALONG THE WAY

How long the road is. But, for all the time the journey has already taken, how you have needed every second of it in order to learn what the road passes by.

Dag Hammarskjöld

Excess Baggage

I found I like to travel, because it got me out of my routines and my familiar patterns. The more traveling I did, the more organized I became. I kept adding things I liked to have with me on my trips. Naturally I took books to read. Then I'd take my Walkman and the tapes I liked to listen to. Pretty soon I'd also take notebooks and colored pens for drawing. Then a portable computer for writing. Then magazines for the airplane trip. And a sweater in case it got cold on the airplane. And hand cream for dry skin.

Before long traveling became a lot less fun, because now I was staggering onto airplanes, loaded down with all this stuff that I felt I had to take with me. I had made a new routine instead of escaping the old one. I wasn't getting away from the office anymore; I was just carrying most of the contents of my desk on my shoulders.

So one day I decided I would get on the plane and carry nothing at all. Nothing to entertain me, nothing to save me from boredom. I stepped on the plane in a state of panic—none of my familiar stuff. What was I going to do?

It turned out I had a fine time. I read the magazines that

were on the plane. I talked to people. I stared out the window. I thought about things.

It turned out I didn't need any of that stuff I thought I needed. In fact, I felt a lot more alive without it.

I've come to take a rather simple-minded view of all this. There's a natural human resistance to change. We all fall into patterns and habits that eventually constrict our lives, but which we have difficulty breaking anyway. Rilke described the problem in this simple way:

> *Whoever you are: some evening take a step*
> *out of your house, which you know so well.*
> *Enormous space is near . . .*

Michael Crichton

The Talker

We don't receive wisdom; we must discover it for ourselves.

Marcel Proust

It had been a long, long day, and I was tired, cranky and in desperate need of sleep. As the flight attendant showed me my row, I swore silently to myself. Looking up at me brightly from the seat next to mine was a small, dapper man, a dusty, green plaid suit hanging on his thin, wiry frame.

A talker, I thought grimly. *Just what I need on this flight.* I was in Johannesburg, South Africa, on my way to London—one of the longest aviation routes on Earth. And I was seated next to someone I just knew would talk my head off the whole way.

His eyes were eager, and he grinned as I squeezed past him in the tight space. I avoided eye contact and pulled out a paperback novel. He was undeterred.

"I'm eighty-five years old," he said proudly, his English accent distinct and crisp. I looked at him and nodded, a little surprised. He looked a good decade younger than that. "When I'm one hundred, the queen's going to send me a birthday card!"

He seemed awfully certain he was going to enjoy that birthday. "The queen sends birthday cards?" I asked.

"Yes. But she's going to have to send it to me in South Africa. I'm moving, going to live with my grandchildren."

He went on to tell me about the beautiful little seaside English town he would be leaving, about the farm in South Africa where he would live. He mentioned his family's marriages and divorces, the great-grandchildren's school successes, and his wonderment at how his savings in England would buy three times as much in South Africa, thanks to the favorable exchange rate.

I nodded politely, and turned away from him to dig through my carry-on bag. *Where are those ear plugs?* I wondered. It was getting late into the evening, and I was so tired I thought I might resort to rudeness, or even violence, for a bit of peace. Then, just as I was about to clamp on my headphones to drown him out, his voice changed, from eager to somber.

"My wife . . . she died last year," he said. He sounded like he was trying the words on for size, attempting to make sense of their enormity, and of his loss.

"I'm sorry to hear that," I said.

He nodded. "We were married fifty-six years." He reached into his jacket and pulled out a brown envelope. His thin fingers shook as he fingered the flap. He grasped the edges of a British military service record and three photographs.

The service record showed he was a radio operator. "I first saw the world in World War II," he said. "They sent me all over Europe and into Africa, too."

He pointed to the first photograph. "That's me," he said, laughing. "See, I still have all my hair." The black-and-white photo was hand-touched with color, in the 1940s style, like my own parents' wedding photos. He was in uniform, posed rakishly in mid-lean, his arm slung casually across one knee. A full head of reddish-brown hair topped his slim, handsome face. He was smirking mischievously, both in the photo and now, a few inches from my face. "My wife took one look at me, and that was it!" he said.

He handed me the next photo, a full-length posed black-and-white photograph of a raven-haired woman in a cotton dress. Her eyes were pretty, but her smile was tentative, her face tense. "Isabel," he said slowly. "That photo was taken before we met."

"And here she is, a few years ago." He handed me a color snapshot. I had to hold the two photos next to each other to see any resemblance. This silver-haired woman was laughing, her gentle face open and warm. Her pretty eyes sparkled, and her only prominent wrinkles were crinkles at the edge of her eyes and the strong laugh lines around her mouth.

"She looks well-loved," I said.

He nodded. "She was. She was an angel. I know people talk about their husbands and wives, and say how there are all these problems. We weren't perfect, but we just enjoyed spending time with each other. She was a wonderful woman." He smiled at the snapshot and shook his head slightly. "I miss her so much."

My eyes began to well with tears. My own mother died suddenly fifteen years ago, and sometimes that day feels as close as yesterday. My father had been in shock afterwards, his pain so deep and untouchable that in some ways, emotionally, he didn't survive the loss. For years, he was lost, aimless, as if his rudder and compass and wind had all left him at once.

I looked at the stylish little gentleman beside me and wondered if my dad had talked to strangers, or if he had ever carried around photos of my mom. I hoped no one had turned away from him, if he had ever tried to discuss it.

I told him about my mom and my dad, subjects I rarely ventured into beyond the phrase, "My mom died." It had taken me years to be able to say those three words without forming fat tears and a heavy lump in my throat.

Suddenly, somewhere over the Atlantic, a wind buffeted us, jolting the plane with a prolonged, rattling shudder. I shivered and looked out at the blackness beyond. "I hate it when it does that," I said nervously. Despite my fatigue, I was now wide awake and anxious.

"Oh, I don't mind flying," he said softly, his smile returning to his face. "I feel like I'm closer to Isabel, somehow, when I'm up here in the clouds. I'm able to spend a little time with her again."

I smiled back at him. "I've never thought of it that way." His words comforted me. The cabin lights began to dim, and the flight attendants passed out blankets. I tucked mine around me snugly. "I'm exhausted, but I can never fall asleep on airplanes."

"Maybe it will be different tonight," he said gently.

I looked out into the void outside my little round window. My mind drifted off to the people I have loved and lost—my mother, my grandparents, an old fiancé and several dear friends—all people who were a part of my life, all of whom I still miss terribly. I remembered their faces and eyes, their voices and the sound of their laughs, and I wondered if this little man was right, if I really was somehow closer to them, up here in the clouds.

At some point, my eyes closed, and I fell fast asleep. But it was not the tortured, forced, half-awake naps I've had on past flights. This was a deep, profound sleep, restful and nourishing, the kind of sleep only angels can give.

JoBeth McDaniel

Three Men and a . . .

As much trouble as I've had on this little journey, I'm sure one day I'm going to look back and laugh.

Steve Martin

There are four skills that any true traveler must master: patience, tolerance and respect—all of which honor the people we encounter—but it's the last, a sense of humor, that is a gift to ourselves.

Traveling in India is the ultimate test for most Westerners. Every sense works overtime, and out of necessity, there is a countrywide spirit of entrepreneurship that is relentless. Visit the Taj Mahal and someone will badger you to show you the best photography angle (for a small fee). Arrive at a rail station and a swarm of rickshaw drivers converge, each fighting to get you to go to a hotel of their choosing (which also throws some rupees their way).

I was in Bhubaneshwar, in the eastern state of Orissa, and had just spent the afternoon scrambling around the ruins of Konark, a thirteenth-century Surya temple. It was hot and dusty, and my car thumped along rutted roads for the forty-mile ride back to my hotel. All I wanted to do was get my hands on a sealed, safe, bottle of cold water.

We pulled into the hotel grounds, and I stumbled my way up to the front desk. The hotel had little cottages, and mine was a lengthy walk away, but I knew that the kitchen was just behind the desk, so I asked for a bottle of cold water.

"Please to go to your room, Ma'am. It will be delivered," the clerk replied.

But I didn't want to walk all the way to my room. I just wanted to buy a bottle of cold water. I pleaded with the man.

"Yes, Ma'am, it will be delivered shortly," he responded with a smile.

I could see what was going on. I wasn't going to get that bottle of water unless I walked to the other end of hotel grounds, just so someone from room service could earn an additional fee for carrying it to me!

Exasperated, I slumped off to my room, called in the order and stewed for twenty minutes until there was a knock at my door. I opened it.

And there before me stood three men balancing a refrigerator, inside of which was one bottle of ice-cold water—as I had requested.

Lucy Izon

Frying Onions

A traveler's most interesting meals tend to happen by surprise.

David Dale

One time, while traveling through northern Australia, I was sitting in a small café located on the grounds of an Aboriginal reservation. The restaurant was just outside the local high school and catered to the few children and many teachers who could afford lunch. While chomping away on a sandwich, I witnessed an interaction that seemed, at first, quite inconsequential.

The manager had his back to us, frying heaps of onions. The cashier, an Aboriginal girl, was chatting with an older man who was huddled with her to the side. While they were thus engaged, a line of customers began to form, patiently waiting to be served. The girl continued her conversation oblivious to the line of people that was growing longer by the minute.

The manager then turned to her and curtly asked her to finish the conversation another time. *Seems reasonable to me,* I thought.

But the old man, who turned out to be her father, was greatly offended by this interruption, "How dare you talk to her like that!"

To my surprise, the manager quickly backed down, apologizing with the lame excuse he was only doing his job. The father was not to be pacified. He abruptly turned and walked out of the store. The girl then began serving the waiting customers.

What was that all about, I wondered? Obviously, some sort of cultural misunderstanding. *What else could the poor guy have done,* I asked myself? *Was he supposed to let the restaurant fill up with impatient customers while the cashier chatted with her father?* Through my eyes as a cultural observer, I could have seen no other alternative. It seemed to me that the daughter was irresponsible and that the father overreacted.

I decided to check things out with a group of Aboriginal teachers I had been sitting with. They, after all, witnessed the same interaction and noticed my curiosity about the scene.

Their impression turned out to be quite different from mine. They figured the manager should have kept frying his onions and left the girl alone.

"But what about all the impatient people waiting in line?" I pointed out incredulously.

"Were they really impatient?" they asked me in return. "To us, they looked quite content to wait as long as it took for the girl to finish her conversation. That man showed disrespect to the father, who was right to be angry about it."

Again I queried, "But what about the customers?"

"Look," they explained carefully. "If it bothered them very much then they might have asked the father's permission to have the daughter's attention. For the manager to interrupt was wrong. If it bothered him so much that customers were waiting, then he should have helped them. After all, he was only frying onions whereas she was talking to her father."

Jeffrey Kottler

"This must be a good place."

Miss You, Love You

I have a compulsion to wander and a compulsion to return—a homing instinct like a mother bird.

Bruce Chatwin

Staring at the arrival screen, my eyes searched anxiously for the airline flight number. The flight was expected on schedule. There was still plenty of time since I had allowed myself sufficient leeway to cover any unexpected situation. Now all I had left to do was amuse myself and pass the next long hour. I grabbed a coffee at a nearby kiosk, found a bench facing the arrival lounge doors and made myself comfortable for the wait. As I sipped the steaming liquid and tried to relax, my mind wandered back over the last couple of months.

Had it really been only eight weeks? It seemed like an eternity since I had tearfully kissed my son good-bye and watched him disappear as the departure doors swallowed him up whole. From the time my children had been quite young, we had traveled together regularly. I was a strong advocate of travel as an important educational tool. Logic told me that he was a young adult with a good head on his shoulders and he would be fine, but at that particular moment he seemed like a small child, and my fears could not be assuaged by common sense.

Ryan had set his heart on exploring Europe after high school. We had visited many countries together, and he was familiar with what to expect, but this time he wanted to do it alone.

While I had put on a brave front and encouraged him to realize his dream, inside I was a wreck. I felt myself becoming overprotective and uncharacteristically paranoid. I worried nonstop. Was he eating enough? Would he find a place to sleep? Would he be safe? Would he call?

Ryan had never been one to talk on the phone, but I had given him a long-distance calling card hoping that he would keep me up to date. I didn't have to wait long to find out. Shortly after landing in Scotland, he called to assure me that everything was fine. His voice was filled with the excitement and enthusiasm of youth.

The days and weeks slipped by and my son's calls came with increasing frequency. Soon, he was calling every second or third day. When I was out he talked at length to the answering machine as though it were an old friend.

I knew what he saw, what he ate, where he was staying and whom he had met. We laughed together, discussed art and culture, and thoroughly enjoyed each other's company long distance. Every call ended with, "I miss you" and "I love you." By the end of two months, my phone bill was well over two thousand dollars. It was worth every penny.

As Ryan made his way through Holland, Belgium, France and Italy, I could sense that something was troubling him. He insisted that he was fine in spite of the constant rain, which seemed to follow him from country to country. But there was a curious tone in his voice that made me wonder.

Needless to say, I was happy and not entirely surprised when out of the blue he told me that he had decided to come home. And now here I was again at the same airport waiting impatiently.

Sitting on the hard, molded airport seat, I contemplated the crowd of people. They were a mélange of ages and nationalities, each waiting just as I was, each with his or her own personal reason for being there: to welcome home a relative, greet friends or meet a business associate. The arrival screen was our common link as we passed the time, together yet alone.

I'm not certain who noticed it first. His flight began flashing on the screen, and we knew that the flight had touched down. An infectious buzz spread through our rapidly expanding group. My stomach began to churn with anticipation. The milling flock congregated along the rope barriers, blocking my view.

Tense minutes dragged by until finally, in singles and pairs, passengers started to filter through the blank, windowless exit doors. They were met by a sea of hopeful faces. Excited waving and squeals of happiness broke out here and there as friends and families were reunited. I moved closer for a better vantage point.

The door slid open yet again to release a new corps of passengers. My heart jolted. Recognition. There he was. Back home, safe and sound.

Ryan tried to look nonchalant as his eyes scanned the throng for a familiar face. He reached the end of the barriers just as I pushed my way through the wall of bodies, into the opening and flung my arms around him. I couldn't remember when I had felt so happy. Tears of joy streamed uncontrollably down my cheeks. As we embraced, the world stood still. All the airport noise stopped. Silence.

Ryan was the first to speak.

"Mom," he said, looking straight into my eyes, "I have learned so much about myself and what's important. I know that no matter where you go in the world and what you see, you need someone to share it with in order to make it special."

A warm smile spread across my tear-sodden face. And then I felt new, fresh tears—the tears of pride. I may have said good-bye to a child, but a mature young man had come home, and he was my son.

Penny Fedorczenko

Land Without Mirrors

No matter where you go—there you are.

Earl MacRauch

A clay pot sits alone on top of my bookshelf. It measures about eight inches tall and is rounded in form, the two sides flaring out like the bellies of two pregnant women standing back-to-back. The shelf is reserved for this single piece of pottery.

I am constantly clearing away books, papers and other things that accumulate there. People visiting my apartment often comment on the pot, perhaps because they're attracted to the simplicity of its design or maybe because it seems odd that I've given such an ordinary vessel a shelf of its own in an otherwise cluttered space. But that doesn't bother me or the pot. It stands there steadfast and proud. I look at it every day.

Sometimes I run my hands over the smooth surface, proof that the women mastered the polishing technique I taught them. Other days I turn the pot over to look at the base, where the artist's name, Pilar, is chiseled in childlike letters.

My work in developing a rural pottery project in Nicaragua led me up the steep, rocky trail to Los Chaguites, a brittle, sun-baked settlement. It is usually labeled "inaccessible." I was searching for communities where the women had a tradition of working with clay.

It was on my first trip, poking around this isolated gathering of mud and stick homes four hours by foot from the nearest road, that I met Doña Pilar and her family. They offered me a stool in the shade and answered some of my questions about their town. When I pulled out my camera to photograph several pieces of pottery they had brought out of their home, they insisted that the photo would be much nicer with people in it. I willingly obliged their request for a family portrait.

A few weeks later, I returned to conduct a pottery workshop. As I climbed over the fence to the dirt patio surrounding Doña Pilar's house, she came running out to greet me with a generous hug. *"Y la foto?"* she asked hopefully. I pulled the photograph from my backpack. The family, nine people in all, looked very handsome indeed, with a clear resemblance to one another.

Doña Pilar studied the image carefully. After a long lapse of silence, she pointed to a short, gray-haired, grandmotherly woman in a faded blue dress held together precariously by safety pins and asked timidly, "Is this me?"

I realized at that moment that Doña Pilar clearly had no idea what she looked like.

I asked if she had ever owned a mirror. Yes, she said, there used to be one in the house, but it had broken. Occasionally, she says, if the sun is right, she sees her reflection in a jug of water. This is rare as, whatever water there is, she must scoop out from an underground spring, cup by cup, using a long stick with a tin can tied to the end.

I asked her what it was like not to see herself regularly.

"I know who I am inside," she replied, "and that's what I see every day."

When I returned to the United States and began to set up a household, I thought of Doña Pilar. After a day or so of repeatedly turning to see my reflection and finding a blank wall, I hustled off to the hardware store to buy a mirror. Something I considered a necessity, this woman had probably lived a quarter of a century without.

Was this perceived need inspired by habit, or by unpardonable vanity? How old would I feel if I didn't daily view my aging mask? I wonder how differently we would act in a world without mirrors?

Several years have passed, and my clay pot overflows with memories from my journey to the land without mirrors. The pot sits confidently on my shelf, solid red clay with no showy exterior, no fashionable sheen nor trendy shape. The pot's plain surface offers me no reassuring reflection, only a simple challenge to grow old in the spirit of Doña Pilar.

Jane E. Hall

Digging Dirt, Digging Deep

There's no such word as can't.

Constance Clayton

The village where I was assigned in the grassland region of central Zaire was a simple collection of mud huts and barefoot people. The twentieth century has paid little attention to this part of central Africa.

The men carry spears, and many villagers still use flint and steel to light fires. My job was to improve the local diet, which was woefully lacking in protein. I was a fish culture extension agent for the Zairean Department of Agriculture.

A few weeks after I arrived I got my first customer, Ilunga Mbumba. He was a thin, serious-faced village man with three young sons counting on him to keep them healthy.

"I want to raise fish," he told me.

"Great," I said, "but first you have to dig a pond." I handed him a shovel. No bulldozers here. This was the developing world.

There is no easy way to dig a fish pond with a shovel.

You just have to do it. You have to place the tip to the ground, push the shovel in with your foot, pull up a load of dirt and then throw the load twenty or thirty feet to the pond's edge. Then you have to do it again: Tip to the ground, push it in, pull it up, throw the dirt. After you do this about fifty thousand times, you have an average-sized pond. Indeed, long and hard is the road out of African poverty.

For me, it was painful visiting Ilunga each week. I'd come to check on the pond's progress and find him grunting and shoveling, chipping away at the fifty-thousand-stroke total. I winced each time his bare foot drove the thin shovel blade into the ground. I groaned inwardly at the sight of his clothes, ragged, full of yawning holes that revealed a glistening, overworked body. Guilt gnawed at me. Ilunga wanted to improve his life, but the digging was too much. I was killing him with work.

One week I couldn't stand it any longer.

"Give me the shovel," I told him.

"Oh no, Michael," replied Ilunga. "This work is too much for you."

"Give it to me," I insisted. "Take a rest."

He shrugged and handed me the shovel. I began digging. *Okay,* I thought, *tip to the ground, push it in, pull it up, throw the dirt.* I did it again. It wasn't nearly as hard as I had thought. I kept going. But after about twenty minutes, it got hot. The African sky fixed me with an unblinking blue stare and the sun pelted me with rays. I paused to take off my shirt.

Ilunga, thinking I was quitting, jumped from a nearby dike and reached for the shovel.

"No, no," I said. "I'm still digging. Sit down."

He shrugged again and left to go check on his nearby corn field.

Shirtless and alone, I continued. Tip to the ground, push

it in, pull it up, throw the dirt. An hour passed. Tip to the ground, push it in, pull it up ... throw ... throw ... darn it, throw the dirt. My arms were signaling that they didn't like tossing dirt over such a long distance. But I couldn't stop. How could I ask villagers to do work I was incapable of doing myself?

I kept going. Twenty minutes passed and things got ugly. My back and shoulders joined my arms in screaming for an end to hostilities. I was no longer able to throw the dirt. Instead, I carried each load twenty feet and ignobly spooned it onto the dike. And was it hot—the hottest day I could ever remember. Even occasional breezes murmuring through the surrounding savannah grass didn't help. And then I looked at my hands. Both palms were blistered.

Fifteen minutes later, my hands wouldn't grip the shovel. It fell to the ground. After just two hours of digging, I couldn't do any more. My contribution to the pond was wholly inconsequential. I collapsed on a dike next to Ilunga, who had just returned.

"I think I'll stop now," I managed.

Ilunga grabbed the shovel and began working steadily. Tip to the ground, push it in, pull it up, throw the dirt. Lying on my side, exhausted, I watched him. His determination was mystifying.

Day after day, for three months, he kept going. He worked like a bull and never complained. Not once. Not when he hit a patch of gravel-size rocks. Not when, at the pond's center, he had to throw each shovel-load twice to reach the dikes. And not when he became ill.

His hand was on fire one morning when I arrived and shook it.

"You're sick," I said.

"I know," he said and resumed digging.

"Then quit working and get some rest."

"I can't," came the reply. "I've got a pond to dig."

A few weeks later, it was finished. Ilunga drove his shovel into the earth one last time and there it was: a forty-five-by-sixty-foot pond, gloriously finished. We filled it with water and stocked it with fish, and then I turned to Ilunga and shook his hand over and over again.

We ran around the banks hooting and hollering, laughing like children, slapping each other on the back and marveling at the pond, its surface now sparkling with a wondrous poetry of reflected light. Six months later, the first harvest produced ninety-seven pounds of fish, enough to feed Ilunga's family and bring in cash for clothes and supplies.

Oh, sweet joy, Ilunga had done it. He had taken my instruction and accomplished a considerable thing. And on that day when we finally stocked his pond, I knew that no man would ever command more respect from me than one who, to better feed his children, lifts and throws fifty thousand shovel-loads of dirt.

I had a hero.

Mike Tidwell

Daju

*It is only with the heart that one can see rightly;
what is essential is invisible to the eye.*

Antoine de Saint-Exupéry

It was almost winter, and nearing the end of my stay in Katmandu, much of my time was occupied with saying good-bye. I had gotten to know many new people on this particular visit, but those persons whom I most actively sought out were those whom I had gotten to know the least.

They were waiters, merchants, black-market money changers; they were little children and old women who sold single cigarettes and matches along damp, narrow streets. I certainly did not know these people as one knows a friend or even an acquaintance for that matter, but for the past several months they had been my landmarks along countless streets and in innumerable restaurants, and they were by now as familiar to me as any back home. It was this collection of little faces, brief greetings and equally brief conversations that always endeared Nepal to me.

Upon finding one of these persons prior to my departure, I rarely would actually say good-bye. Instead, I found that all I really wanted to do was just look at them once more; to memorize them in their world, perhaps foolishly thinking that the moment could later be recalled with the same life and clarity as the original.

Sometimes, in my marginal Nepali, I would say that I am returning to my own country. Most often the reply was simply a smile, accompanied by the characteristic little sideways nod of the head which in Nepal means understanding. And that was all.

One person with whom I did speak was an old man I used to see almost every day. He seemed to spend most of his time just sitting in the sun on a small, raised wooden platform. Next to him was an outdoor marketplace where aggressive women with clumps of wrinkled and faded rupees in their fists deftly negotiated the cacophonous buying and selling of fruit and vegetables.

The first time I saw him he smiled at me. He said nothing, nor did I stop to speak with him. I recall giving him a rather cursory smile in return, and then continued on my way without another thought.

A few days later I saw him again, still seated in the same place. As I passed him he smiled at me again just as he had before. I was taken by how sincere this man's expression was, and also how peaceful he seemed to be. I smiled back and offered the traditional *"namaste,"* which he returned. I could not quite explain why, but it was that genuine smile of his that many times made me detour just to see him and say hello.

Eventually I found that he spoke a few words of English, and sometimes we would have a cigarette together and exchange pleasantries. Sometimes, after dinner, I would walk through the silent streets that were now only sporadically lit by the incidence of weak light insinuating itself through greasy restaurant windows. Then I would come upon him, still seated in the same place. He would be sitting quietly, smoking, and sometimes drinking tea out of the ubiquitous glass tumbler that someone had probably bought for him.

One evening, on the way back to my room after dinner, I saw him in his usual spot, and I stopped to say hello. For the first time since I had known him, I glimpsed his feet protruding from under the rough woolen blanket that always covered him. They were severely misshapen and deeply ulcerated, and the toes were unusually short and seemed strangely small for his feet. I remembered having seen similar symptoms during a brief stint of clinical work I had done several years earlier. No doubt it was very difficult for this man to walk, and it was now apparent why so much of his time was spent sitting. He had leprosy.

Some time after this I again stopped to say hello to him. He smiled as he returned my greeting and appeared glad to see me. We spoke easily now; he in his broken English, and I in my fractured Nepali. Out of respect I now called him *daju* or "older brother," as was the custom. The first time that I did this his expression did not change, but from then on he called me *bhai*, or "younger brother," as though he had been doing so for years.

I cannot explain the feeling, but there has always been something exquisitely heartwarming about being referred to as *bhai* or *daju* by the Nepalese. Perhaps these words were intended to convey nothing more than simple courtesy to a foreigner, but countless times I have been struck by the intimacy these words implied, and the genuine affection with which they were spoken.

We talked for a few more minutes, and when I left, I gave him a couple of cigarettes wrapped in a five-rupee note. He accepted this graciously and with dignity. I said good-bye, but resolved to continue to see him until I had to leave.

This I did, and in the course of my last few days in Katmandu we would talk frequently. I would do as much as I could manage in Nepali, but we usually relied considerably more on English. We sometimes had a glass of tea together in the pale afternoon sun, limiting our conversation to superficial things, but enjoying it nevertheless.

It gets cold at night in November, and prior to leaving I wanted to bring the old man a pair of heavy woolen socks that I had brought for use in the mountains. On my last night in Nepal, I found him sitting in his usual place. Tonight it was very cold. I approached him and said that tomorrow I was leaving. I then said that I wished to give him my socks. He said nothing. I felt awkward, and as gently as I could I lifted the blanket that covered his legs. I put the socks on what remained of his feet and tried to explain that I would be pleased if he would keep them.

For a long moment he did not speak. I feared that I might have made him uncomfortable, but then he looked at me with marvelous compassion in his eyes and said, "God bless you, *bhai*. No one has touched me in a very long time."

Robert J. Matthews

Cutting Across Cultures

Travel is fatal to prejudice, bigotry and narrow-mindedness.

Mark Twain

Against a worn strip of water buffalo leather, the Vietnamese barber slapped his straight razor back and forth. He paused to tilt my head back, leaving my Adam's apple fully exposed to the blade. Looking up now, I saw the flowers of a flaming mimosa tree, its branches forming the delicate ceiling of this one-man outdoor barber shop. I smelled the incense of a nine-hundred-year-old Confucian temple a hundred feet away. I heard the bright bells of bicycles gliding down the wide Hanoi boulevard.

Yet we'd gotten off to a bad start, this barber and I. I figured he was trying to fleece me when, after I asked how much he charged, he demurred. But he was just being polite in Vietnamese fashion, saying I would pay afterward, as much as I wanted, only if I was happy. When I pressed the issue, he just waved me into his wooden chair. I got in, huffing, our cultures colliding as we attempted to communicate.

"How many fallen yellow leaves do you have?" the barber asked me, still whacking his long, gleaming razor against the leather strap. He was asking my age.

"Thirty-three," I answered.

He asked what country I was from. "America," I said.

"I killed many Americans during the war," he said softly. "Many Americans." Moments later, I felt the razor on my throat.

Only when the barber had finished shaving my face and was putting away his razor did it seem safe to raise the issue of price again. Years of travel had led me to anticipate this tactic: The merchant insists on an enormous, unmovable price after the service is rendered. But I hesitated bringing up the subject again. The barber seemed to read my mind nevertheless.

"We Vietnamese people are not so direct as you. We are easier in our ways," he said. "For us, it is not so hard to trust."

He pulled out his scissors now.

"So will I like this haircut?" I asked with a conspicuous hint of sarcasm.

The barber gave me a bright, scolding laugh, his dark eyes narrowing above wrinkles that suggest he had at least sixty fallen yellow leaves himself.

"I, young friend, am a sculptor. Under my hands, rough stone is turned into a beautiful, delicate statue."

"So it's an art form, hair-cutting?" I asked.

He responded sharply, leaving me temporarily confused. "No, it is not an art form. Few people can really cut hair. It is a *high* art form."

At this he lapsed into ebullient laughter again—and so did I, my suspicions gradually receding.

He began cutting my hair without once asking what I wanted, a common occurrence in my travels in the developing world. Nor did I try to direct him except to ask that he not cut it too short.

"Why do you cut hair outdoors?" I asked. "Is it too expensive to rent a shop?"

He feigned huge offense. "Not at all," he said, now working the scissors across my bangs. "I have many, many clients. I have plenty of money for a shop. But why be a prisoner of walls? I prefer to be outdoors. I feel the wind and sun every day when I work. I smell the flowers of this tree." He then quoted a line from Ho Chi Minh: "There's nothing as good as freedom and independence. Nothing."

Since his adolescence, the barber told me, all he'd wanted to do was cut hair. It was his one true passion. Even during the war he cut hair for his platoon. "I was working on someone's hair once when your country sent rockets into our camp. Rockets everywhere. I jumped into a foxhole still holding my scissors and comb."

Now that the war was over, the barber wanted nothing more to do with it. "It was a bad time. I fought to make my country free. Now I just want to do good, to make people beautiful."

As a matter of principle, he said, he never bought any of the tools in Vietnam still widely recycled from old war material. "When I need new scissors, I ask: Was this made from a tank? From a cannon? If so, I don't buy."

My haircut was nearly over now, and the barber suddenly made an announcement. The snipping stopped. "You're the first American whose hair I've cut," he said, swinging around till our eyes met. "I shot at many Americans, but never this. You're my first."

As he finished up, the barber told me he cut fifteen to twenty heads a day, every day, and he never missed work because of illness. *Quite a record for a man his age,* I thought. *What was the secret?*

"Never sleep late," he said. "Eat when you're hungry.

And always help people. Always love people." Then he added, "I pray, too. I go to the pagoda twice a month and light incense and pray for the peace and happiness of all the people in the world. I never leave anyone out. I've prayed for you all your life."

Shortly thereafter, he pulled his barber's sheet off of me as if from a masterpiece. If not totally a new man, I felt like I was refurbished.

"What do I pay you if I'm very, very happy?" I asked, now quite won over by the original gentleman's arrangement.

"Nothing," he said with unbreachable finality. "That you are happy is big enough payment for me."

I protested effusively, of course, even tried leaving the money tucked in the mimosa tree. But it was no good.

"You owe me nothing," he said.

We parted company with a handshake. As I walked away, it struck me that cutting a traveler's hair must be nearly as interesting for the barber as for the traveler. Perhaps I had given him a minor amusement, a new, small way of thinking about himself. He, meanwhile, had given me something much more than a haircut.

For my haircut not only changed the way I look—but also the way I see.

Mike Tidwell

Never Take It for Granted

The aim of life is to live, and to live means to be aware—joyously, drunkenly, serenely, divinely, aware.

Henry Miller

When I awaken on morning sixty-four of my One Hundred-Day Trip Around the World, my train is half an hour from Mombassa. The sun has just risen over a hilly green plain dotted with small round huts that look like beer barrels hidden under hula skirts. The air is cool and smells of ocean and palm trees.

Africa!

The aging shed that served as Mombassa's railroad depot lies at the western edge of town, across from a small overgrown park. Several people have spent the night in the park, and now they are sitting up in the tall, littered weeds—yawning, stretching, looking around as though surprised and perhaps a bit disappointed to still be here.

I walk down Haile Selassie Road, past seedy hotels and old dry goods stores whose wooden awnings reach out to shade the sidewalks. Mombassa strikes me as lazy, sleepy, messy—a seductive, peeling version of Key West in the late 1960s. And I am enchanted by its name, now ringing in my head like a mantra. Mom-BAH-sa. Mom-BAH-sa. Mom-BAH-sa.

On Jomo Kenyatta Road I take a two-dollar and fifty-cent hotel room with insect screens on the windows and a ceiling fan so lethargic I fear each rotation might be its last—and I begin unpacking.

Toward the middle of every trip, I am nagged by the dawning awareness that sometime in the all-too-foreseeable future—tomorrow, next week, two months from yesterday—I will be going home. The sand in the hourglass, so full and trickling so slowly at the trip's beginning, is suddenly seen to be slipping away like water down an unplugged sink.

I acknowledge with a catch in my heart that I am on the downside of this trip's halfway hump. As each passing hour and spent dollar brings me closer to the end, I am developing a wistful, unsettled feeling. The road has become my home again, and the thought of returning to America and gearing back up to rat race speed is distinctly unattractive.

Old fishing boats are docked in the Mombassa harbor. Muscular black men sit atop wooden barrels along the wharf, beer bottles in hand, gossiping, reliving the morning's sail. Others bend over the catch of the day—silver fishes, four feet long—gutting them and tossing them into waiting carts.

Fort Jesus, built by the Portuguese in 1593, still guards the harbor mouth. Stubby black cannons poke through the portals of the crumbling walls, aiming impotently at two anchored trawlers. The tide is out, and boys walk barefoot along the harbor's exposed bottom, searching for shells or things to salvage.

Several small *dhows*, their triangular sails lashed to their masts, are keeled over in the mud, awaiting the tide's return and a spot of wind. Stretching from the harbor's mouth to the distant, curved horizon, is the Indian Ocean—becalmed this morning, and so gray and shiny it looks like a planet-sized ball bearing.

Beside the fort, boys kick a soccer ball back and forth. I sit in the shade of a mango tree, my back against a wall, feeling a heat-induced listlessness. A warm breeze blows the hair up off my forehead. I think of America.

In a month plus change I will land in New York, where it might be ten degrees below freezing. There will be things to do, people to see. Thank God I still had five weeks of the road's unpredictability remaining.

Each morning I rise to a day of mystery—see new landscapes, eat new foods, meet only strangers and rarely know where I might lay my sleeping bag that night. But a month at home and this adventure will surely fade.

Days will pass where I will speak only to the same two or three familiar people, and months where I will eat in the same two or three predictable restaurants. I might even forget which closet my sleeping bag was stored in. I will gradually come to fear the uncertainty and unsettling freedom of the road. I will be able to cite a hundred different reasons why I can't go traveling this year. Next year, maybe.

Now I close my eyes, listen to the ocean's hum, the boys' yelps, the shrill complaints of the harbor birds and the rustle of palms. A two-fifty room. Fresh fish dinners. Fifty cent beers. *Remember all this,* I think. Enjoy it.

Never take it for granted.

Brad Newsham

The Art of Traveling

When you pack your bags to explore the beauties of your own country or to travel around the world, consider these keys to a happy journey:

Travel lightly. You are not traveling for people to see you!

Travel slowly. Jet planes are for getting places not seeing places; take time to absorb the beauty and inspiration of a mountain or cathedral.

Travel expectantly. Every place you visit is like a surprise package to be opened. Untie the strings with an expectation of high adventure.

Travel hopefully. "To travel hopefully," wrote Robert Louis Stevenson, "is better than to arrive."

Travel humbly. Visit people and places with reverence and respect for their traditions and ways of life.

Travel courteously. Consideration for your fellow travelers and your hosts will smooth the way through the most difficult days.

Travel gratefully. Show appreciation for the many things that are being done by others for your enjoyment and comfort.

Travel with an open mind. Leave your prejudices at home.

Travel with curiosity. It is not how far you go, but how deeply you go that mines the gold of experience. Thoreau wrote a big book about tiny Walden Pond.

Travel with imagination. As the old Spanish proverb puts it, "He who would bring home the wealth of the Indies must carry the wealth of the Indies with him."

Travel fearlessly. Banish worry and timidity; the world and its people belong to you just as you belong to the world.

Travel relaxed. Make up your mind to have a good time. Let go.

Travel patiently. It takes time to understand others, especially when there are barriers of language and custom; keep flexible and adaptable to all situations.

Travel with the spirit of a world citizen. You'll discover that people are basically much the same the world around. Be an ambassador of goodwill to all people.

Wilferd A. Peterson
Submitted by Rebecca Esparza

"I see you taking a trip."

More Chicken Soup?

Many of the stories and poems you have read in this book were submitted by readers like you who had read earlier *Chicken Soup for the Soul* books. We publish at least five or six *Chicken Soup for the Soul* books every year. We invite you to contribute a story to one of these future volumes.

Stories may be up to twelve hundred words and must uplift or inspire. You may submit an original piece, something you have read or a favorite quotation from your refrigerator door.

To obtain a copy of our submission guidelines and a listing of upcoming *Chicken Soup* books, please write, fax or check our Web site.

Please send your submissions to:

Chicken Soup for the (Specify Which Edition) Soul
P.O. Box 30880
Santa Barbara, CA 93130
fax: 805-563-2945
Web site: *www.chickensoup.com*

Just send a copy of your stories and other pieces to the above address.

We will be sure that both you and the author are credited for your submission.

For information about speaking engagements, other books, audiotapes, workshops and training programs, please contact any of our authors directly.

Travel with a Different Set of Eyes

A portion of the proceeds from *Chicken Soup for the Traveler's Soul* will be donated to the following organizations:

National Federation of the Blind

The National Federation of the Blind is the largest organization of blind people in America. Interested sighted people also join.

NFB members believe that with healthy attitudes and good training blind people can live satisfying lives, and they live and teach this philosophy wherever and whenever they can. For further information, please go to: *www.nfb.org.*

One World Sight Project

One World Sight Project, Inc. (OWSP) is a California-based non-profit organization which works toward providing sight to the world's 25 million people who are needlessly blind from bilateral cataracts and who could be permanently cured by a simple operation that can often be performed in less than 20 minutes at a cost of $30–$50.

For further information, please go to: *www.owsp.org.*

International Institute for Peace through Tourism

The International Institute for Peace through Tourism (IIPT) was founded in 1986 with a vision of "Tourism as the world's first global peace industry"—an industry that promotes and supports the belief that "Every traveler is potentially an Ambassador for Peace."

The Institute and it partners also promote the IIPT Credo of the Peaceful Traveler:

Grateful for the opportunity to travel and experience the world and because peace begins with the individual, I affirm my personal responsibility and commitment to:

- *Journey with an open mind and gentle heart*
- *Accept with grace and gratitude the diversity I encounter*
- *Revere and protect the natural environment which sustains all life*
- *Appreciate all cultures I discover*
- *Respect and thank my hosts for their welcome*
- *Offer my hand in friendship to everyone I meet*
- *Support travel services that share theses views and act upon them and,*
- *By my spirit, words and actions, encourage others to travel the world in peace.*

Persons interested in more information and/or becoming members of the IIPT are invited to visit the IIPT Web site: *www.iipt.org.*

Peace Corps Writers

PeaceCorpsWriters.org and its precursor newsletter, *RPCV Writers & Readers* (founded in 1989), are at the heart of the third goal of the Peace Corps—to "bring the world back home." The novels, short stories, essays and poetry of Returned Peace Corps Volunteers (RPCVs) are a positive way of educating Americans about the world. For further information, please head to: *www.PeaceCorpsWriters.org.*

* * *

We also highly recommend that you check out the following organizations that were very supportive of our efforts on this book and exemplify the very essence of the traveler's spirit:

World T.E.A.M. Sports

World T.E.A.M. (The Exceptional Athlete Matters) Sports brings individuals with and without disabilities together to undertake unique athletic events throughout the world to encourage, promote and develop opportunities in sports for all people. For more information visit their Web site at *www.worldteamsports.org*.

Earthwatch Institute

Since 1971, Earthwatch Institute, an international nonprofit volunteer organization, has placed travelers on leading research and conservation projects around the world. Explore *www.earthwatch.org* or call 800-776-0188 for more information.

Who Is Jack Canfield?

Jack Canfield is a bestselling author and one of America's leading experts in the development of human potential. He is both a dynamic and entertaining speaker and a highly sought-after trainer with a wonderful ability to inform and inspire audiences to open their hearts, love more openly and boldly pursue their dreams.

An ardent traveler, Jack has visited many places across the United States, Canada and around the world, including Italy, France, Scandinavia, Morocco, Turkey, Thailand, India, Australia and a three-month journey with his then six-month-old son through Mexico and Guatemala. Despite his far-flung adventures, he still cherishes his annual trips to Hawaii and spending time at home with his family in Santa Barbara, California. He believes that "more than anything, travel offers us the chance to connect with people from different cultures in a meaningful way, demonstrating how similar we really are."

After graduating college, Jack taught high school in the inner city of Chicago and in Iowa. In recent years, Jack has expanded this to include adults in both educational and corporate settings.

He is the author and narrator of several bestselling audio- and videocassette programs. He is a regularly consulted expert for radio and television broadcasts, and has published more than fifty books—all bestsellers within their categories—including more than forty *Chicken Soup for the Soul* books, *The Aladdin Factor, Heart at Work, 100 Ways to Build Self-Concept in the Classroom, Dare to Win* and *The Power of Focus.*

Jack addresses over one hundred groups each year. His clients include professional associations, school districts, government agencies, churches and corporations in ten countries.

Jack also conducts an annual eight-day Training of Trainers program in the areas of building self-esteem and achieving peak performance.

For further information about Jack's books, tapes and trainings, or to schedule him for a presentation, please contact:

The Canfield Training Group
P.O. Box 30880 • Santa Barbara, CA 93130
phone: 800-237-8336 • fax: 805-563-2945
e-mail: *speaking@canfieldgroup.com*
Web site: *www.chickensoup.com*

Who Is Mark Victor Hansen?

Mark Victor Hansen is a professional speaker who, in the last twenty years, has made over four thousand presentations to more than two million people in thirty-three countries. His presentations cover sales excellence and strategies; personal empowerment and development; and how to triple your income and double your time off.

Mark has traveled all over the United States, Canada and the world, including Ireland, Italy, India, Mexico, Australia, the Philippines and Hong Kong. He and his family also savor the beauty and wonders of Hawaii, which has become their second home. "Wherever I have traveled," he says, "I have discovered that underlying everything, there really is a universal kindness of the human heart."

Mark has spent a lifetime dedicated to his mission of making a profound and positive difference in people's lives. Throughout his career, he has inspired hundreds of thousands of people to create a more powerful and purposeful future for themselves while stimulating the sale of billions of dollars worth of goods and services.

Mark is a prolific writer and has authored *Future Diary, How to Achieve Total Prosperity* and *The Miracle of Tithing*. He is the coauthor of the *Chicken Soup for the Soul* series, *Dare to Win* and *The Aladdin Factor* (all with Jack Canfield) and *The Master Motivator* (with Joe Batten).

Mark has also produced a complete library of personal empowerment audio- and videocassette programs that have enabled his listeners to recognize and better use their innate abilities in their business and personal lives. His message has made him a popular television and radio personality with appearances on ABC, NBC, CBS, HBO, PBS, QVC and CNN.

He has also appeared on the cover of numerous magazines, including *Success, Entrepreneur* and *Changes*.

Mark is a big man with a heart and a spirit to match—an inspiration to all who seek to better themselves.

For further information about Mark, please contact:

Mark Victor Hansen & Associates
P.O. Box 7665
Newport Beach, CA 92658
phone: 949-759-9304 or 800-433-2314
fax: 949-722-6912
Web site: *www.chickensoup.com*

Who Is Steve Zikman?

The *Washington Post* called him "the man who wrote the book on wanderlust." Born and raised in Canada, Steve Zikman has ventured through over fifty countries on six continents. In fact, this former attorney left behind a successful law practice in Toronto to set out on a three-year, around-the-world journey.

Combining writing with his passion for the road, Steve is the author of the highly acclaimed book, *The Power of Travel: A Passport to Adventure, Discovery and Growth* and coauthor of the forthcoming *Chicken Soup for the Outdoor Soul, Chicken Soup for the Everyday Hero's Soul* and *Chicken Soup for the Soul: A Celebration of Home.*

Steve is the founder of GOscape, providing powerful tools to enrich, enhance and expand the appreciation of travel, the outdoors and the adventure of life.

His syndicated column, "The Soulful Traveler," appears on leading Web sites including the National Business Travel Association. Steve is a contributor to a variety of multimedia publications including: *Interline Adventures, SoulfulLiving.com, Rudy Maxa's Savvy Traveler, Porthole Cruise* and *Personal Journaling.* He has also appeared on numerous radio programs including National Public Radio's *The Savvy Traveler.*

A dynamic speaker, in-house seminar leader and certified workshop facilitator, Steve shows audiences how to get the very most out of our travels . . . and life! Using seasoned and successful practices to minimize travel's anxieties and maximize its countless benefits, Steve demonstrates how travel can help us shift our perspective, conquer our fears and embrace life's challenges.

When he's not speaking, writing or reviewing the many stories sent in from all over the world, Steve heads out again—to riverbeds teeming with wildlife in the Kalahari Desert, a golden-hued farmhouse in Italy, or the majestic mountains near his home in Los Angeles.

To submit your own inspiring travel stories, or for further information on Steve's speaking programs, consulting services or other writings, please visit his Web site at *www.GOscape.com* or contact:

GOscape.com
P.O. Box 292581
Los Angeles, CA 90029
phone: 323-644-9064
e-mail: *explore@GOscape.com*
www.GOscape.com

Contributors

Several stories were taken from previously published sources, such as books, magazines, newspapers and on-line publications. Most of the other pieces were sent in from readers of previous *Chicken Soup for the Soul* books and others who responded to our requests for submissions. To learn more about our contributors please refer to the information provided below.

Sandra Andrews is a retired elementary school principal. She enjoys reading mystery novels, being involved with her local Little Theatre, both on and off the stage, and traveling with her husband, Bob. She can be reached at *bsandrews@yahoo.com.*

John Balzar is a roving correspondent for the *Los Angeles Times* and author of *Yukon Alone* (Henry Holt Co., 2000). He writes about travel, adventure and the outdoors.

Donna Barstow feels blessed to be a cartoonist. Her humorous drawings have appeared in over 180 publications, including *The New Yorker, The Los Angeles Times, Reader's Digest, NatureMedicine, InfoWorld, Harvard Business Review* and *The Salt Lake Tribune.* Donna's work has been featured in six gallery shows and many books, including other *Chicken Soup* books. Her favorite topics are relationships, relationships with computers, pets and mayhem. You can see more of her work at *www.reuben.org/dbarstow.*

Michael Bell is a graduate of the University of Maryland and former member of the U.S. Air Force. He is currently an engineer in the software computer industry, who recently relocated from Silicon Valley in California to northern Virginia. Michael enjoys traveling, basketball, softball and spending time with his dog, Dakota. Please reach him at *mbell1970@hotmail.com*

Caryl Bergeron has bachelor's and master of science degrees in aerospace engineering. After fifteen years working in the engineering profession, she and her husband left their careers to travel. Since 1995 they have journeyed worldwide, spending six months bicycle touring and six months in a camper. Join them at *www.geocities.com/wriedy.*

Cindy Bertram holds an MBA from Loyola University Chicago (1985) as well as a B.A. from Indiana University. She has worked in the travel industry for over thirteen years and also does freelance writing. She has contributed guest columns and business commentaries to travel industry trade publications, including *Travel Weekly, ASTA Agency Management* and *Leisure Group Travel*. A special thank you to Richard Sasso "for building a front porch." Please reach her at *cindybertram@hotmail.com*.

Mick Bird is on a solo rowing voyage around the world aboard his vessel *Reach*. Through his satellite communication equipment and his Classroom at Sea Program, he is linked with over 32,000 schools throughout the world. You can follow his voyage at *www.naau.com* or contact him directly at *mikbird@mediaone.net*.

Nancy Blakey lives on an island in Puget Sound with her husband and four children. She is the author of the Mudpies activity book series: *Recipes for Invention, 101 Alternatives to Television, Lotions, Potions and Slime,* and *Boredom Busters*.

Marybeth Bond *(www.marybethbond.com)*, a featured guest on the *Oprah Winfrey Show*, is the travel expert for CBS's *Evening Magazine* and an award-winning author/editor of five books in the "Traveler's Tales" series. She is an international lecturer and has given travel advice on over 250 television and radio shows. Her bestselling book, *Gutsy Women*, was featured on the *Today Show*.

Julie Booker is a poet, filmmaker and teacher who lives in Toronto, Canada. Much of her prose and poetry is based on her year of travel through Asia and Africa. Her work has been published in *Cottage Life Magazine* and various journals and anthologies.

Retired from scientific sales, **Ed Boyle** now operates a business that provides historical musical performances in Philadelphia. When a visitor hears fife and drum music anywhere in town, it is usually Ed and his Philadelphia Fife & Drum. He also teaches others to play in person, or at *www.beafifer.com*.

Rob Bundy is an avid traveler and writer. In addition to having traveled the world on numerous occasions, he is also the author of seven full-length plays and one book. Rob lives with his wife and two daughters near Goderich, Ontario, and can be reached at *rbundy@odyssey.on.ca*.

Leah Burgess has lived and worked throughout the Rocky Mountain west as a river ranger, horsepacker, raft guide, and a research and writing assistant. As a Peace Corps volunteer, she worked on a small island in the Philippines where she assisted the local community in protecting the island's natural heritage. She currently works for a nonprofit farmland conservation organization in Colorado. You may reach her at *leahburgess@hotmail.com*.

Adele Carney is retired from a career in retailing and is pursuing her interests in volunteer work, studying Spanish and writing. She continues to travel in the enthusiastic spirit of her late husband, Larry.

Robin Chapuis is owner and president of A Higher Path, Inc. As a "heart activist," Robin conducts adventure-based leadership and team building workshops to help people, families, teens and organizations realize their highest potential. Robin can be reached at 303-984-0930.

Betty Corbin, recently retired from both a career in financing and almost twenty years of volunteer work with Girl Scouts, now operates Grand River Inn, a bakery/café near Grand Lake, Colorado. She may be reached at Grand River Inn, 10658 Hwy 34, Grand Lake, CO 80447 or *grandriverinn@rkymtnhi.com.*

George Crenshaw is an old pro with a long track record of success. He is an ex-Walt Disney animator, a magazine cartoonist with top sales to top slicks for three decades, the creator of NUBBIN by King Features, creator of GUMDROP by United Features, creator of the MUFFINS by Columbia Features, creator of BELVEDERE by Post Dispatch Features and the President of Post Dispatch Features, Masters Agency, Inc.

Arthur Dawson is a freelance writer and poet/teacher with California Poets in the Schools. His *Stories Behind Sonoma Valley Place Names*, from Kulupi Press, is a local bestseller. "A Passport from the Elements" in this volume is an excerpt from a to-be-published book of the same name.

Jeff Degner is a graduate of St. Norbert College and a senior customer service agent with Delta Air Lines at Chicago's O'Hare International Airport. He lives with his wife, Marcie, and their dog, Charm, in Barrington, Illinois, and can be reached via e-mail at *DEG821@aol.com.*

Eileen Egan (1911–2000) was born in Ireland, raised in Wales, and went to live in the United States in 1926 at the age of fourteen. She was a cofounder of Catholic Relief Services and was active in relief efforts around the world. She met Mother Teresa in 1955 and began a lifelong friendship and collaboration, aiding her order's growth to its present membership. She has written four books on Mother Teresa. During this time Eileen served as editor of the *Catholic Worker,* became founder of Pax Christi USA with Dorothy Day. Her last book *Peace Be with You* revived the Catholic Peace Tradition.

Heidi Ehrenreich has been working since 1971 as a speech/language pathologist, dance/movement psychotherapist, workshop leader and instructor. Her creative spirit, love of multicultural dance and music, and genuine interest and skill in participating in meaningful interactions with people of all abilities and backgrounds makes her a true "communication artist." Her book *Moving Stories* is in process. Please reach her at *hydeco@massed.net.*

Jane Winslow Eliot lived for years in Spain, Italy, Greece, England, Japan and Canada, with a journey around the world and many a side trip. She is published in *Atlantic Monthly, Travel and Leisure* and *Newsday.* Her last book was *Let's Talk, Let's Play.* She has also constructed tape guides to Venice, Italy, but lives happily in Venice, California.

Mark I. Farber holds a Ph.D. in marine science and applied statistics. After working for the government in marine fisheries for twenty-three years, Dr.

Farber recently began a consulting practice and is a professor of statistics at the University of Miami. Please reach him at *HYPERLINKarkfarber@adelphia.net.*

Penny Fedorczenko lives in Oshawa, Ontario, Canada. She has a bachelor of arts in sociology and teaches public school. She is the mother of two adult children. Penny enjoys traveling, music, theatre, sports and writing. She can be reached at *pfed@infinity.net.*

James Feldman, CITE, MIP, SP, (a.k.a. Doctor Travel) is a certified facilitator and internationally recognized professional motivator, trainer, speaker and author. As president of Incentive Travelers Cheque International, Inc., he has been responsible for providing individual and group incentive travel awards for many Fortune 1,000 clients. Please visit his Web site at *www.DrTravel.com.*

Paul Fell had to learn Nebraskaspeak when he came to the Cornhusker State from Massachusetts to attend Peru State College. He married a Nebraska farm girl and has been here ever since. He can't remember when drawing wasn't his favorite activity and his career has reflected this: He has been a high-school art teacher and coach, a college art professor and an award-winning newspaper editorial cartoonist. Fell now operates his own cartoon and humorous illustration studio in Lincoln. In addition, he draws three editorial cartoons a week for the Lincoln *Journal Star* and teaches classes in graphic design at the University of Nebraska-Kearney. He is also in demand as a speaker and draws caricatures at receptions, trade shows and conventions. He continues to be amazed that he gets paid for doing the same thing that used to get him into trouble as a kid.

Steve Foreman is the senior tour leader and training manager at A Tent with a View Safaris Ltd., of P.O. Box 40525 Dar es Salaam, Tanzania (*www.saadani.com*). He was licensed as a professional guide by the Botswana Wildlife Department, and is a fellow of the Royal Geographical Society. Please contact him for services and information by e-mail *tentview@intafrica.com* or *www.saadani.com.*

Robert Fung has been drawing since he was six years old. Born in England, he studied animation and received his B.A. in art from UCLA. He loves traveling, sketching, photography and Rollerblading at the beach. He can be reached at *robertfung1@hotmail.com.*

Steve Gardiner teaches high-school English and journalism in Billings, Montana. He has a bachelor's degree from Chadron State College and a master's degree from Montana State University, Billings. He has traveled throughout the world, including mountain-climbing expeditions to Alaska, Peru, Bolivia, Switzerland, Italy, Greenland and Mount Everest.

Gloria Goldreich writes on a wide range of Jewish and women's themes. In 1979 she won the National Book Award for fiction with her first book, *Leah's Journey*—a national bestseller. Most recently she is the author of *Year of Dreams*, a novel that examines the friendship between four women. Her stories and essays have appeared in *Commentary, Hadassah, McCall's, Redbook, Mademoiselle*,

Ms. and other publications. She is also the editor of the prize-winning anthology *A Treasure of Jewish Literature*. Goldreich is married, and is the mother of two daughters and a son. They live in Westchester County, New York.

Reg Green is the father of Nicholas Green, a seven-year-old boy who was shot in Italy by highway robbers. The Greens' decision to donate his organs to seven Italians focused the world's attention on the shortage of donors everywhere. Green's book *The Nicholas Effect* (*www.nicholaseffect.com*) tells the complete story.

Jane E. Hall and her husband Scott have been traveling the world together since meeting in a lost luggage line in Luxembourg in 1977. In addition to extensive personal travel, Ms. Hall's experience includes fifteen years leading corporate travel programs and eight years as co-owner of a bicycle touring company. From 1994 to 1996, she served as a Peace Corps Volunteer in Jinotega, Nicaragua, where her work included organizing a pottery cooperative for rural women. Ms. Hall currently teaches English as a Second Language in Saint Paul, Minnesota.

Pico Iyer is the author, most recently, of *The Global Soul: Jet Lag, Shopping Malls, and the Search for Home*. Among his earlier books are *Video Night in Kathmandu, The Lady and the Monk* and *Cuba and the Night*. He lives in suburban Japan.

Lucy Izon, youth/budget travel columnist for the *Toronto Star, Los Angeles Times* and *Chicago Tribune,* has served as Canadian chapter chairman and vice president of the Society of American Travel Writers (*www.izon.com*). She's the author of *Izon's Backpacker Journal* (Ten Speed Press), and creator of Canada Cool, a Canadian travel writing and photography competition (*www.canadacool.com*).

Daniel Jensen is currently a freelance commercial photographer and a full-time student at Augustana College in Sioux Falls, South Dakota. He is pursuing a degree in exercise physiology and prosthetics. He is an endurance athlete and musician. *Djensen49@hotmail.com* or (605) 335-8736.

Hungarian-born **Eva Kende** has lived in Canada since 1956. She is the author of two cookbooks: *Eva's Hungarian Kitchen* and *Eva's Kitchen Confidence*. Lately, Eva started writing about her reminiscences and experiences to be published in a future book. She can be reached at *ekende@telusplanet.net* and *www.telusplanet.net/public/ekende*.

Jeffrey R. Knight graduated from Central Washington University in 1995 with a degree in building construction management. In 1998, Jeff founded The Quarry, a young adult ten-month intern program designed to passionately develop young Christian leaders throughout the United States and Mexico. In February of 2000, Jeff became senior pastor/leader of The Rock Church, known as Total Velocity Ministries, with his wife Melinda, and recently completed a music CD entitled *URY (You Are Why)*. In addition to being a host on TBN television, Jeff has traveled throughout the United States presenting the word of God with passion and excitement.

Jeffrey Kottler, Ph.D., is the author of over forty books in education and psychology about transformative change including: *Travel That Can Change Your Life, On Being a Therapist, Doing Good* and *Beyond Blame.* He is chair of the counseling department at California State University, Fullerton.

Pat Hanna Kuehl took early retirement from the *Rocky Mountain News* in Denver to become a freelance travel and food writer in 1987. She travels the world in search of stories that appear in major newspapers and magazines. Her e-mail address is *PatKuehl@juno.com.*

Charles Kuralt's job for twenty-eight years was to drive the back roads of America in a CBS camper. More than six hundred episodes of *On the Road with Charles Kuralt* were filed from every state in America. Audiences will long remember the rich, slow, mahogany tones of his voice on *Sunday Morning with Charles Kuralt.* He leaves us seven bestselling books, so many stories and so many memories.

Robin Leach, world authority on the good life and host of *Lifestyles of the Rich and Famous,* was instrumental in launching the TV Food Network. He has produced and hosted over three hundred hours of award-winning special programs and twelve television series. His latest project is the BidBash TV series on the new ShopNBC network.

Timothy Leland is a former managing editor and vice president of the *Boston Globe.* Retired, he now spends his spare time playing golf, tutoring prisoners, learning to fly, bicycling in Europe, consulting for the *Globe* and writing articles for the *Globe* whenever he travels, which is often. He can be reached at *leland@globe.com.*

Jason Lewis discovered a passion for being on the road in 1990, having driven an old car purchased in New York as far as Montana (where it blew up in a snowstorm) and hitchhiked the rest of the way around the United States. He can be reached at *jason_x360@yahoo.com* or 1-800-943-0114 (USA).

Joy Schaleban Lewis is a freelance journalist based in Milwaukee, Wisconsin. She is a member of the Society of American Travel Writers, winner of two Lowell Thomas Awards for Excellence in Travel Journalism, and was twice named Mark Twain Travel Writer of the Year by Midwest Travel Writers Association. You may reach her at *gioiandro@hotmail.com.*

April MacNeil manages a school bus company in Lakeville, Connecticut. She likes camping, reading and anything to do with cows. This story was made possible thanks to all the wonderful people at Starlight Children's Foundation who made Kevin's wish to see a volcano come true.

William P. Magee, Jr., a leading plastic and craniofacial surgeon, devotes half of his professional life as a volunteer to the organization, Operation Smile, that he and his wife, Kathy, founded in 1982. Dr. Magee joins Operation Smile's volunteer teams on numerous overseas missions each year to perform reconstructive surgery on impoverished children. In private practice, he serves as president of Magee-Denk Plastic Surgery, Inc., in Norfolk, where he has practiced medicine since 1978. He may be contacted at Operation Smile, Inc., 6435 Tidewater Drive, Norfolk, VA, 23509, or at *bmagee@operationsmile.orp* or *www.operationsmile.org.*

Robert Matthews' passion for mountains and photography first brought him to Nepal, but it was the wonderfully ingenuous Nepalese people who compelled his subsequent visits. Robert writes and teaches mathematics and literature in San Francisco where he indulges in pasta, flying radical kites, and coffee and sunsets from the back of his '91 Trooper.

JoBeth McDaniel is a journalist and author living in Georgia. More of her writing can be viewed at *www.jobeth.com.*

Paula McDonald has sold over a million copies of her books and gone on to win numerous awards worldwide as a columnist, feature writer and photojournalist. When not writing, she is an adventure traveler who roams the world but always comes home to her wide, sandy beach in Rosarito, Mexico. Paula can be contacted in the United States by writing PMB 724, 416 W. San Ysidro Blvd., Ste. L, San Ysidro, CA 92173-2443, or by e-mailing *eieiho@compuserve.com.*

Marilyn McFarlane is the author of several travel books about the Pacific Northwest and California. She has written a weekly newspaper column and contributed to numerous travel guides and journals. Her most recent book is *Sacred Myths: Stories of World Religions.* She writes poetry, essays and stories of sacred sites of the world, and she's active in environmental causes. Write to her at *mmcf@easystreet.com.*

Kristie McLean has traveled extensively through Europe, Asia, Africa and the South Pacific and most recently completed a year-long, solo backpacking voyage around the world. She has been previously published in *Jeopardy Magazine* and the *Bellingham Review* and welcomes your comments and suggestions for travel writing opportunities at *travelpoet@hotmail.com.*

Eleanor McMullin and her husband Fred exchange homes three months of the year. Much of the rest of their time is devoted to organizing future trips or extolling the virtues of house exchange. You may contact the McMullins at *mcmullf@netcom.ca* or check out *www.homelink.org.*

James A. Michener, one of the world's best-loved writers, was known for his trademark epics exploring major themes and cultures, beginning with *Tales of the South Pacific,* which won a Pulitzer Prize in 1947. He devoted much of his life to public service and in 1977 was awarded the Medal of Freedom.

Matthew L. Miller has worked as a professional writer since his graduation from Pennsylvania State University in 1992. He regularly publishes stories on the outdoors, business and higher education. His travels have taken him to Africa, Australia, Europe and Central America. Please reach him at *miller_outdoors@hotmail.com*.

Nancy Mills is a native of Los Angeles, but considers her home to be wherever she is in the world. Formerly the editor/publisher/founder of *Travelin' Woman* newsletter, she also led the popular TW seminars, a self-empowerment series for women travelers. Nancy is writing her first inspirational book. Please reach her at *nmtravwom@aol.com*.

Roy Mingo is manager of Premium Customer Services with American Airlines at LaGuardia Airport in New York. He has been with American for thirty-one years in various management positions at LaGuardia and Kennedy International and as general manager of American Airlines on a Caribbean island in St. Maarten.

Kelly Mustian has worked as a tour leader in Greece, Israel, Egypt and Turkey. She has written numerous short stories, essays and articles published in literary journals and commercial publications and has recently completed a novel.

Cheryl Reece Myers, A.S.I.D., is a professor at the University of Central Oklahoma in Edmond, Oklahoma. She is the director of the interior design program, conducts educational and motivational seminars for industry, and writes articles for design journals and travel magazines. She is a wife and mother of two grown children. While she makes her home in the rural countryside of Oklahoma, she frequently finds her bags packed, ready to explore a new destination or to revisit a familiar locale that inspires her traveler's soul. She can be contacted at *cmyers@ou.edu*.

If your San Francisco cab driver is **Brad Newsham,** mention his book *Take Me with You: A Round-the-World Journey to Invite a Stranger Home* (Travelers' Tales, 2000), and he says your ride will be free—"unless it's over five bucks, in which case we flip double-or-nothing." See *www.bradnewsham.com*.

Terry Paulson, Ph.D., C.S.P., C.P.A.E, of Agoura Hills, California, is the author of *They Shoot Managers Don't They?* and *50 Tips for Speaking Like a Pro.* As a speaker who travels the globe, he helps leaders and teams make change work. Contact him at *www.terrypaulson.com*, 818-991-5110, or *terry@terrypaulson.com*.

Craig and **Kelly Perkins** are internationally recognized crusaders for organ donor awareness. In addition to appearing on multiple television programs, magazines and newspapers, they are sought-after speakers by private and public organizations. Craig and Kelly are also the founders of SecondWind, Inc., where through their experience as outdoor enthusiast, they have developed and patented a new hydration-ensuring device for athletes, patients and health-conscious consumers. In an effort to continue to share the positive aspects of living with a second chance, Craig and Kelly are currently working on a new nonfiction book detailing the inspirational comeback of their challenging journey. On October 21, 2001, Kelly became the first heart transplant recipient to summit the 19,340-foot Mt. Kilimanjaro in Africa. For further information, please write to P.O. Box 51701, Irvine, CA 92619, or visit their Web site at *www.secondwindinc.net*.

Wilferd A. Peterson (1901–1995) authored a series of bestselling inspirational books in the 1960s: *The Art of Living Books, The Art of Living Treasure Chest* (Simon & Schuster, 1977) and *The Art of Creative Thinking* (Hay House, 1990, still available: ISBN-4670-004-5). He is survived by his daughter, Lilian Thorpe, of Pinehurst, NC.

Peace Pilgrim, at age forty-four, began a twenty-eight year pilgrimage of walking as a penniless pilgrim to awaken others to the urgent need for peace. She spoke to individuals, reporters, church groups and college groups, on radio and TV. After her death in 1981, her message in books and tapes has gone around the world. For more information, visit *www.peoplepilgrim.com*.

Dawn Rambin is a certified personal computer and network technician for Continental Airlines. In the past two years, she has traveled to Ireland, Italy, Singapore and Hawaii. She graduated from Portland Community College with a degree in general studies and a certification in management. She is currently studying to be a Microsoft certified systems engineer at Southern Methodist University.

Sheila Reid lives with her husband on a homestead on the prairies in the heart of Canada. They both write plays—Sheila in English and her husband in Low German. Sheila's portfolio also includes children's books, biographies of Canadian heroes and CBC Radio commentaries. When they aren't writing, they enjoy creating farm vacations for their grandchildren.

April Riggs is currently with a charitable community foundation in Amarillo, Texas. She works with at-risk, first-generation, college-bound students. Previously, she was the director of a child advocacy organization in Dalhart, Texas. April can be reached at *riggsapril@hotmail.com*.

Rose Marie Sand is a freelance writer who is inspired by the love and support of her family and friends. E-mail her at *rosesand@bellsouth.net*. Look for her latest publications and other interests at her Web site at *www.sandenterprises.com*. She dedicates "The River of Life" to her daughter, Gina, her husband of thirty-two years, Milton, and her son, Clint.

Dante Jericho Schmoeker is a writer, healer and mystic who enjoys studying and writing works of a spiritual and inspirational nature. She has written *Sacred Changes, Sacred Choices* and *Meditations from the Ichive*. She is a part-time emergency dispatcher in northen Alabama and can be reached at *djeriho@juno.com*.

Beth Schrank was a Peace Corps volunteer in Niger, West Africa, from 1988 to 1990. She holds an M.F.A. in fiction from the Iowa Writers' Workshop and an Ed.M from Harvard University. She currently teaches creative writing at the

Charlottesville Writing Center in Charlottesville, Virginia, and is working on her first novel, also set in Niger.

Harley Schwadron has been a full-time, freelance cartoonist since 1984, and lives and works in Ann Arbor, Michigan. His cartoons appear in such publications as *Harvard Business Review, Barron's, Reader's Digest, Wall Street Journal* and *Medical Economics*. A former newspaper reporter and university public relations writer and editor, he always aspired to be a cartoonist. He worked at cartooning on evenings and weekends while holding a full-time job, but after building up a clientele, he made the plunge into full-time cartooning. He can be reached at P.O. Box 1347, Ann Arbor, Michigan 48106, phone/fax (734) 426-8433.

Catherine Scott received her A.A. in acting from the American Academy of Dramatic Arts in Pasadena, California, in 1995. In addition to acting and writing fiction, Catherine enjoys cooking, reading and horseback riding. Recently married, she currently resides in central Washington and looks forward to a creative life filled with adventure.

Tanya Shaffer is a San Francisco-based writer, actress and nationally acclaimed solo performer. Her stories have appeared on *Salon.com* and in travel-writing anthologies. She is currently completing *Girl in the World*, a collection of stories set in West Africa. Visit her online at *www.TanyaShaffer.com*.

Monica Sheehan is a freelance artist living on the Jersey Shore. She has illustrated twelve books including cowriting *50 Reasons Not to Go Home for the Holidays*, and creating *The Breakup Book*. Ms. Sheehan's latest effort is *Girlfriends (from Campfires to Crow's Feet)*, published by Andrews McMeel, which she wrote, illustrated and designed. She presently has a monthly feature in *Real Simple* magazine. Monica Sheehan can be reached at *monicaink@earthlink.net*.

Cheryl Slowey graduated from the University of South Dakota. She has been a career nurse for thirty years at Avera Sacred Heart Hospital in Yankton, South Dakota. Her husband Tom is the Fire Chief in Yankton, daughter Rae Slowey and daughter and son-in-law Erin and Justin Munson live in Elko, Nevada. She is also president of the South Dakota State Firefighters Auxillary.

Alice Steinbach's most recent nonfiction book is *Without Reservations: The Travels of an Independent Woman*, published by Random House. Steinbach, whose work at the *Baltimore Sun* was awarded the 1985 Pulitzer Prize for feature writing, will have a new book entitled *Universal Lessons: The Further Travels of an Independent Woman* published by Random House in 2003.

Mike Tidwell grew up in Marietta, Georgia, and graduated from the University of Georgia in 1984. He is the author of five books, including his prize-winning Peace Corps memoir, *The Ponds of Kalambayi*. His newest book is *Bayou Farewell: The Rich Life and Tragic Death of Louisiana's Cajun Coast*. You can reach him at *mwtidwell@aol.com*.

Mona and **Art Vanek** are avid RV travelers, having visited every state. Mona offers free writing courses via e-mail, is a Montana Arts Pro writing consultant, videographer and local historian. Her award-winning books, *Behind These Mountains* vols. 1, 2, and 3 are available at *www.Amazon.com*. Reach her at *nox2368@blackfoot.com*.

Nancy Vineski has been married to her husband, Tom, for twenty-two years. They have two grown children, Bill and Cathy. Nancy has always been a loose chicken, although until she encountered the loose chickens, she didn't know it. Both Nancy and Tom are full-time RVers and members of Escapees RV Club (*www.Escapees.com*). Their piece originally appeared in the club's book of RV stories entitled "Rocking Chair Rebels" in support of CARE, a nonprofit organization providing a home for Escapees whose travels are temporarily limited or permanently stopped because of age or disabilities. She can be reached at: *TNVineski@aol.com*.

Joyce Vullo is an avid reader, freelance writer, mother, wife, teacher and aspiring at-home entrepreneur. She fills her remaining free time with traveling, youth ministry and volunteer work. She believes in the power of the human spirit to guide her through the daily affirmations of God's existence in her life and she believes strongly in the Son even when it rains.

Judy Wade is a freelance travel writer and the author of *The Arizona Guide*, one of the state's bestselling guidebooks, available at bookstores nationwide. She contributes to a number of national publications, frequently sharing bylines with her husband/photographer Bill Baker. The couple packs and unpacks in Phoenix.

Tim Ward, a native, Canadian is the author of *What the Buddha Never Taught, The Great Dragon's Fleas* and *Arousing the Goddess*. He writes and teaches in Maryland.

Betty Ann Webster is a retired psychiatric social worker, writer, confirmed Berkeleyite and addicted traveler who lived in India thirty-five years ago and has returned there at least nine times since. She has three children, four grandchildren and two great-grandchildren and would be delighted to hear from you at *bettyann@lanminds.com*.

Erik Weihenmayer is a speaker, writer and adventurer. He has scaled four continental summits plus El Capitan, the famed thirty-three-hundred-foot rock face in Yosemite, and Polar Circus, a three thousand-foot ice waterfall in the Canadian Rockies. Erik has never let his blindness interfere with his passion for an exciting life. On May 25, 2001, Erik became the first blind person to summit Mt. Everest, an expedition sponsored by the National Federation of the Blind. "Someone once told me that I would need to realize my limitations, but I've always thought it more exciting to realize my potential." To learn more about Erik's adventures, read his new autobiography *Touch the Top of the World*, published by Dutton, and visit his Web site at *www.touchthetop.com*.

Matt Weinstein is the nation's foremost authority on the use of fun and humor in team building. Matt is the founder and emperor of Playfair, Inc., an international team-building organization based in Berkeley, California, and the author of *Managing to Have Fun* and *Work Like Your Dog.* Contact him at *Matt@Playfair.com.*

Richard Weiss, M.D., is a clinical professor at the University of California at Irvine and has practiced in Newport Beach since 1985, where his practice is limited to cataract surgery, laser vision correction and ophthalmic plastic surgery. Dr. Weiss is founder and president of One World Sight Project, an international fund-raising project to cure blindness around the world. For more information contact *www.owsp.org* or *www.drweiss.com.*

Jim West is the author of the bestseller *The Essential Little Cruise Book* and one of the foremost authorities on cruise travel. As a former cruise director, he's logged over 724 cruises. Today, Jim personally plans cruises for individuals groups and large corporations. Contact him at 800-708-0880 or *www.travelwest.com.*

JoAnne Stewart Wetzel lives in the San Francisco Bay area. An award-winning writer of works for both adults and children, she teaches a popular class, How to Write Children's Picture Books, at local colleges. For information on the class or her latest books, e-mail *joanne.wetzal@stanfordalumni.org.*

Bob White resides in Willis, Texas, with his wife of twenty-five years. He is employed by a major international airline. He enjoys traveling, sailing, fly-fishing and indulging his two wonderful grandchildren. "A Christmas Gift" is his first published work. Bob can be contacted at *bwsail@msn.com.*

Felix Winkelaar is an adult education teacher in Lindsay, Ontario. In his spare time he rides motorcycles, plays guitar and hangs out with his wife and teenaged kids. Their dream is to travel the world in a totally accessible motorhome. Felix has written other articles and stories and has created an interesting series of doodlings and cartoons. He can be reached at *skinny_billy@hotmail.com.*

Karen Woodrow is adjusting to life back in the United States and writing about her adventures overseas. Her daily runs now take her through the wilds of Washington, D.C., where the smell of roasted chestnuts reminds her of her three years living and working in Sarajevo. Please reach her at *KWandLM@Bellatlantic.net.*

Peggy Andy Wyatt's work has appeared in numerous national publications and countries worldwide. She was editorial cartoonist for the Scripps Howard newspaper in Destin, Florida, winning several Florida Press Association awards. She studied at Boston University, the Arts League in New York City, with a B.A. degree at the University of Miami, Florida. Her work can be viewed at the Gallery East in Ocala, Florida.

Sherman Zavitz, a retired teacher, is the official historian for the city of Niagara Falls, Canada. The author of several books, he also writes a weekly newspaper column, conducts bus and walking tours around Niagara Falls and speaks to groups about the area's heritage. Please reach him at *snmzav@vaxxine.com* or fax 1-905-356-7053.

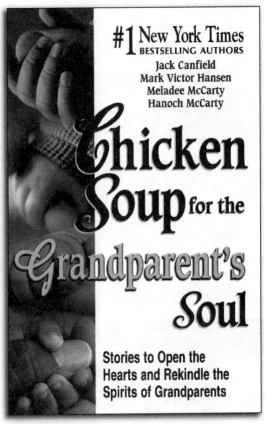

#1 New York Times
BESTSELLING AUTHORS
Jack Canfield
Mark Victor Hansen
Meladee McCarty
Hanoch McCarty

Chicken Soup for the

Grandparent's Soul

Stories to Open the
Hearts and Rekindle the
Spirits of Grandparents

Code #9748 • Paperback • $12.95

The perfect gift to show grandparents
how much they are loved.

#1 New York Times
BESTSELLING AUTHORS
Jack Canfield
Mark Victor Hansen

Chicken Soup for the
TEACHER'S Soul

Stories to Open the
Hearts and Rekindle
the Spirits of Educators

Code #9780 • Paperback • $12.95

Chicken Soup for the Teacher's Soul is required reading
for every teacher, student and former student.

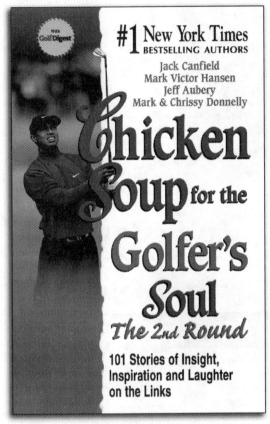

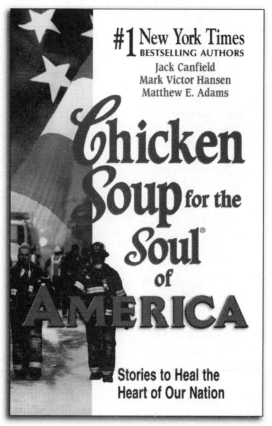

Also Available

Chicken Soup for the Baseball Fan's Soul
Chicken Soup for the Cat & Dog Lover's Soul
Chicken Soup for the Christian Family Soul
Chicken Soup for the Christian Soul
Chicken Soup for the College Soul
Chicken Soup for the Country Soul
Chicken Soup for the Couple's Soul
Chicken Soup for the Expectant Mother's Soul
Chicken Soup for the Father's Soul
Chicken Soup for the Gardener's Soul
Chicken Soup for the Golden Soul
Chicken Soup for the Golfer's Soul, Vol. I, II
Chicken Soup for the Grandparent's Soul
Chicken Soup for the Jewish Soul
Chicken Soup for the Kid's Soul
Chicken Soup for the Little Souls
Chicken Soup for the Mother's Soul, Vol. I, II
Chicken Soup for the Nurse's Soul
Chicken Soup for the Parent's Soul
Chicken Soup for the Pet Lover's Soul
Chicken Soup for the Preteen Soul
Chicken Soup for the Prisoner's Soul
Chicken Soup for the Single's Soul
Chicken Soup for the Soul, Vol. I–VI
Chicken Soup for the Soul of America
Chicken Soup for the Soul at Work
Chicken Soup for the Soul Cookbook
Chicken Soup for the Soul Christmas Treasury
Chicken Soup for the Soul Personal Journal
Chicken Soup for the Sports Fan's Soul
Chicken Soup for the Surviving Soul
Chicken Soup for the Teacher's Soul
Chicken Soup for the Teenage Soul, Vol. I, II, III
Chicken Soup for the Teenage Soul Journal
Chicken Soup for the Teenage Soul Letters
Chicken Soup for the Teenage Soul on Tough Stuff
Chicken Soup for the Traveler's Soul
Chicken Soup for the Unsinkable Soul
Chicken Soup for the Veteran's Soul
Chicken Soup for the Woman's Soul, Vol. I, II
Chicken Soup for the Writer's Soul
Condensed Chicken Soup for the Soul
Cup of Chicken Soup for the Soul
Sopa de Pollo para el Alma, Vol. I, II, III
Sopa de Pollo para el Alma de la Madre
Sopa de Pollo para el Alma de la Mujer
Sopa de Pollo para el Alma del Adolescente
Sopa de Pollo para el Alma del Trabajador
Sopa de Pollo para el Alma del Cristiano